Microsoft® SQL Server™ 2000 Reporting Services Step by Step

Hitachi Consulting
Stacia Misner

PUBLISHED BY
Microsoft Press
A Division of Microsoft Corporation
One Microsoft Way
Redmond, Washington 98052-6399

Library of Congress Cataloging-in-Publication Data
Misner, Stacia.
  Microsoft SQL Server 2000 Reporting Services Step by Step / Hitachi Consulting, Stacia Misner.
      p. cm.
  Includes index.
  ISBN 0-7356-2106-3
  1. SQL server.   2. Client/server computing.   I. Hitachi Consulting.   II. Title.

  QA76.9.C55M57   2004
  005.75'85--dc22   2004054268

Printed and bound in the United States of America.

1 2 3 4 5 6 7 8 9   QWT   9 8 7 6 5 4

Distributed in Canada by H.B. Fenn and Company Ltd.

A CIP catalogue record for this book is available from the British Library.

Microsoft Press books are available through booksellers and distributors worldwide. For further information about international editions, contact your local Microsoft Corporation office or contact Microsoft Press International directly at fax (425) 936-7329. Visit our Web site at www.microsoft.com/learning/. Send comments to *mspinput@microsoft.com*.

Microsoft, Microsoft Press, MSDN, PivotTable, SharePoint, Visual Basic, Visual C#, Visual Studio, Windows, Windows NT, and Windows Server are either registered trademarks or trademarks of Microsoft Corporation in the United States and/or other countries. Other product and company names mentioned herein may be the trademarks of their respective owners.

The example companies, organizations, products, domain names, e-mail addresses, logos, people, places, and events depicted herein are fictitious. No association with any real company, organization, product, domain name, e-mail address, logo, person, place, or event is intended or should be inferred.

This book expresses the author's views and opinions. The information contained in this book is provided without any express, statutory, or implied warranties. Neither the authors, Microsoft Corporation, nor its resellers or distributors will be held liable for any damages caused or alleged to be caused either directly or indirectly by this book.

Acquisitions Editor: Hilary Long
Project Editor: Karen Szall
Technical Editor: Carl Rabeler
Copy Editor: Vicky Thulman
Indexer: Ginny Bess

Body Part No. X10-81700

Table of Contents

Part 3   Managing the Report Server

Chapter 8   Managing Content 223

Part 4   Delivering Reports

Acknowledgments

Everyone that helped bring this book to completion deserves my deepest thanks. The team put together by Microsoft Press worked hard to keep the project on track under challenging deadlines. Thanks to Hilary Long and Maureen Zimmerman for kicking off the project, Karen Szall for keeping the project rolling smoothly, Vicky Thulman for thoughtfully improving my words, and Carl Rabeler for meticulously reviewing the technical details of this book. Thanks also to Jason Carlson and Brian Welcker of Microsoft for introducing me to Reporting Services early in the development cycle of the product, and for answering my questions to help me better understand the product.

I owe many thanks to the team at Hitachi Consulting who made significant contributions to the content of this book. Much of the thinking about teaching others how to use Reporting Services was developed with my coauthors of the *Fast Track to Reporting Services* course: Elizabeth Vitt, Reed Jacobson, Scot Reagin, Susan O'Connell, and Dave DuVarney. Special thanks to Reed Jacobson for helping me expand upon the ideas from that course through many hours of brainstorming together, for undertaking experiments with me to test our understanding of Reporting Services, and for sharing his advice as an author of Step by Step books. Thanks to Dave DuVarney, Steve Muise, and Mark Dreesen for providing invaluable insights and useful code samples. Elizabeth Vitt deserves my thanks not only for sharing her technical knowledge about Reporting Services, but also for her moral support at any hour of day or night. Thanks also to Hilary Feier and the management of Hitachi Consulting for giving me the opportunity and time to work on this book.

Introduction

Microsoft Reporting Services is the newest component of Microsoft SQL Server 2000 that adds a server-based reporting solution to the Microsoft business intelligence framework. The goal of this book is to guide you through the installation of Reporting Services and through each stage of the reporting life cycle so that you can easily create, manage, and share reports in your organization. In support of this goal, step-by-step exercises are included to give you the opportunity to explore Reporting Services with confidence. When you complete these exercises, you'll be ready to tackle real-world reporting challenges!

To help you learn the many features of Reporting Services, this book is organized into five parts. Part 1, "Getting Started with Reporting Services," explains how the components of Reporting Services fully support the reporting life cycle, shows you how to install these components, and provides you with a hands-on introduction to the reporting life cycle. Part 2, "Authoring Reports," starts by showing you to build simple reports, and then gradually introduces advanced techniques to teach you how to use Reporting Services features to satisfy a variety of reporting requirements. Part 3, "Managing the Report Server," covers all of the activities that you need to perform when managing the reporting environment. Part 4, "Delivering Reports," describes the many ways that you can use Reporting Services to provide reports to the user community. The companion CD-ROM contains bonus chapters in Part 5, "Programming Reporting Services." These chapters introduce how to use Reporting Services as a development platform for custom applications that author, manage, or deliver reports.

Finding Your Best Starting Point

Although the range of topics addressed in this book is comprehensive, this book also caters to readers with varying skills who are involved in one or more stages of the reporting life cycle. Accordingly, you can choose to read only the chapters that apply to the stages of the reporting cycle for which you are responsible and skip the remaining chapters. To find the best place to start, use the following table.

If you are	Follow these steps
An information worker or analyst who develops reports	**1** Install the sample files as described in "Installing and Using the Sample Files." **2** Work through Part 1 to get an overview of Reporting Services and to install the product on your computer. **3** Complete Part 2 to develop the necessary skills to author reports. **4** Review the chapters that interest you in Part 4 to understand how reports are accessed by users.
An administrator who maintains server resources	**1** Install the sample files as described in "Installing and Using the Sample Files." **2** Complete Part 1 to understand the technologies used by Reporting Services and to install the product on your computer. **3** Complete Part 3 to learn how to manage and secure content on the server and how to configure and manage server components.
An information consumer who uses reports to make decisions	**1** Install the sample files as described in "Installing and Using the Sample Files." **2** Complete Chapter 2 to install the product on your computer. **3** Work through Part 4 to discover how to retrieve and save reports as well as how to subscribe to reports.

If you are	Follow these steps
A programmer who develops applications with reporting functionality	**1** Install the sample files as described in "Installing and Using the Sample Files."
	2 Work through Part 1 to get an overview of Reporting Services and install the product on your computer.
	3 Skim Parts 2–4 to understand the functionality that is included in Reporting Services.
	4 Work through one or more chapters that interest you in Part 5 to explore specific areas of customization. These bonus chapters can be found on the companion CD.

About the Companion CD-ROM

The CD that accompanies this book contains the sample files that you need to follow the step-by-step exercises throughout the book. For example, in Chapter 3, "Building Your First Report," you use a sample file that contains a SQL query so you don't have to type in the query yourself. In other chapters, you use Visual Studio solution files that have reports or programs created for you as starting points in preparation for adding other features to the reports or programs. These sample files allow you to build on what you've learned rather than spend time setting up the prerequisites for an exercise.

In addition, you will find three bonus chapters and an electronic version (eBook) of this book.

System Requirements

To install Reporting Services, your computer will need to meet the following minimum system requirements:

- *Processor*: Intel Pentium II or compatible 500-MHz or higher processor
- *Operating system*: Microsoft Windows 2000, Windows XP Professional, or Windows Server 2003 with the latest service pack applied
- *Database*: Microsoft SQL Server 2000, Standard or Enterprise Edition, with SP3a applied using Windows or Mixed Mode authentication

- *Memory*: 256 MB of RAM; 512 MB or more is recommended (additional memory may be required based on your operating system requirements)
- *Hard disk*:
    - 50 MB for Report Server
    - 100 MB for Microsoft .NET Framework 1.1
    - 30 MB for Report Designer
    - 145 MB for Reporting Services samples and Books Online
- *CD*: CD-ROM drive
- *Monitor*: VGA or higher resolution monitor
- *Input device*: Microsoft Mouse or compatible device

To use the samples provided on the companion CD and perform the exercises in the book, your computer configuration will need to include the following additional requirements:

- Microsoft Internet Explorer 6.0 or later (*http://www.microsoft.com /windows/ie/evaluation/sysreqs/default.mspx*)
- Microsoft Internet Information Services (IIS) 5.0 or later
- Microsoft Visual Studio .NET 2003, any edition (*http: //msdn.microsoft.com/vstudio/productinfo/sysreqs/default.aspx*)

The step-by-step exercises in this book and the accompanying sample files were tested using Windows XP Professional, Visual Studio .NET 2003 Enterprise Architect, and Reporting Services Developer Edition. If you're using another version of the operating system or a different edition of either application, you might notice some slight differences.

▶ **Important**   Reporting Services Service Pack 1 was released as this book was entering publication. Because the step-by-step exercises detailed in this book have not been tested with this service pack, you might experience different results if you choose to apply the service pack before working through this book.

Installing and Using the Sample Files

The sample files require approximately 140 MB of disk space on your computer. To install and prepare the sample files for use with the exercises in this book, follow these steps:

1   Remove the CD-ROM from its package at the back of this book, and insert it into your CD-ROM drive.

▶ **Note**   If the presence of the CD-ROM is automatically detected and a start window is displayed, you can skip to Step 4.

2   Click the Start button, click Run, and then type **d:\startcd** in the Open text box, replacing the drive letter with the correct letter for your CD-ROM drive if necessary.

3   Click Install Sample Files to launch the Setup program, and then follow the directions on the screen.

The Setup program will copy the sample files from the CD-ROM to your local hard drive and clear the read-only flag on the files. The default installation folder is C:\rs2000sbs. You can change this installation folder to a different location, and reference the new location when working through the exercises. For each chapter that uses sample files, you will find a corresponding folder in C:\rs2000sbs. You will be instructed where to find the appropriate sample files when an exercise requires the use of an existing file.

▶ **Tip**   In the C:\rs2000sbs\Answers folder, you will find a separate folder for each chapter. Each folder contains the completed sample files; these files are copies of the sample files you will complete in each chapter. You can refer to these files if you want to preview the results of the exercises in a chapter.

4   Remove the CD-ROM from the drive when installation is complete.

Using the Sample Files

Now that you've completed installation of the sample files, you need to follow some additional steps to prepare your computer to use these files. You start by setting up fictional user accounts and groups.

1   Click the Start button, right-click My Computer, and then click Manage.

▶ **Important**   Do *not* create these accounts on a production server. It is recommended that you work through the exercises in this book on a test or development server. If you don't plan to perform the exercises in Chapter 9, "Managing Security," or Chapter 13, "Managing Subscriptions," you can skip to Step 15.

2   Expand Local Users and Groups, right-click the Users folder, and then click New User.

3   Type **EuropeDirector** in the User Name, Password, and Confirm Password boxes to create a new account, and then click the Create button.

4 Repeat the previous step to create the following accounts: **PacificDirector**, **NADirector**, and **SalesAnalyst**.

5 Click the Close button.

6 Right-click the Groups folder, and then click New Group.

7 Type **AWSalesDirector** in the Group Name box, and then click the Add button.

8 In the text box, type **EuropeDirector;PacificDirector;NADirector**.

9 Click the OK button to close all dialog boxes.

10 Right-click the Groups folder, and then click New Group.

11 Type **AWSalesAnalyst** in the Group Name box, and then click the Add button.

12 In the text box, type **SalesAnalyst**.

13 Click the OK button to close all dialog boxes.

14 Click the Start button, click Run, and then type **C:\rs2000sbs\Setup\Restore\restore_databases.cmd** in the Open box.

This step attaches the SQL Server databases that are the data sources for the reports that you will create and use throughout this book. It also creates the user logins and user tables that are used for demonstrating security and subscriptions.

15 Open Analysis Manager, right-click the server, and then click Restore Database to restore the rs2000sbs.CAB file found in the C:\rs2000sbs\Setup\Database folder.

This step restores the database that is used to demonstrate how to use an Analysis Services database as a data source for a report.

You're now ready to get started!

Conventions and Features in This Book

To use your time effectively, be sure that you understand the stylistic conventions that are used throughout this book. The following list explains these conventions:

- Hands-on exercises for you to follow are presented as lists of numbered steps (1, 2, and so on).
- Text that you are to type appears in **boldface** type.
- Properties that you need to set in Visual Studio or in Report Manager are sometimes displayed in a table as you work through steps.

- Pressing two keys at the same time is indicated by a plus sign between the two key names, such as Alt+Tab when you need to hold down the Alt key while pressing the Tab key.
- A note that is labeled as **Note** is used to give you more information about a specific topic.
- A note that is labeled as **Important** is used to point out information that can help you avoid a problem.
- A note that is labeled as **Tip** is used to convey advice that you might find useful when using Reporting Services.

Corrections, Comments, and Help

Every effort has been made to ensure the accuracy of this book and the contents of the companion CD-ROM. If you run into a problem, Microsoft Press provides corrections for its books through the following Web site:

http://www.microsoft.com/learning/support/

If you have problems, comments, or ideas regarding this book or the companion CD-ROM, please send them to Microsoft Press.

Send e-mail to *mspinput@microsoft.com.*

Send postal mail to:

Microsoft Press
Attn: *Microsoft SQL Server 2000 Reporting Services Step by Step Editor*
One Microsoft Way
Redmond, WA 98052-6399

Please note that support for the software product itself is not offered through the preceding addresses. For product support, go to *http://support.microsoft.com.*

To connect directly to the Microsoft Knowledge Base and enter a query regarding a question or issue that you have, go to *http://support.microsoft.com.*

Part

1

Getting Started with Reporting Services

Understanding Enterprise Reporting

In this chapter, you will learn how to:

- The purpose of enterprise reporting.
- The characteristics of a reporting platform.
- The constituents of enterprise reporting user communities.
- The stages of the reporting life cycle.
- The features and components of Reporting Services.

The chapters in Part 1 provide a broad introduction to Microsoft SQL Server 2000 Reporting Services (Reporting Services). This chapter explains what enterprise reporting is and how Reporting Services supports this function. Chapter 2, "Installing Reporting Services," shows you how to install the components and explains the implication of decisions that you must make as you create your enterprise reporting environment. In Chapter 3, "Building Your First Report," you get your first hands-on experience with the reporting life cycle in preparation for examining Reporting Services components in greater detail throughout the remainder of this book.

In this chapter, you see what enterprise reporting is all about and how it differs from other types of reporting. You also review how different groups within your organization need to use or support enterprise reporting and how they participate in the reporting life cycle. With this foundation, you'll better understand how the various components of Reporting Services fully support the enterprise reporting needs of your organization.

Reporting Scenarios

Because you're reading this book, chances are good that you work for a company that needs to be able to share information. Whether your company is small or large, can you imagine what would happen if no one had access to the information needed to do his job? The quality of the decisions that each individual employee makes during the course of his daily tasks has a profound impact on the operations of the business and relies on easy and regular access to information.

One way that a company regularly shares information is through enterprise reports. For the purposes of this book, an *enterprise report* is considered to be the presentation of information that is formally distributed to some or all individuals across an enterprise, or even to individuals external to the enterprise. This information can be presented in a variety of formats, for example, as a Microsoft Excel spreadsheet or a text document. It can also be delivered as a printed report or sent to a list of recipients as an e-mail attachment. Information can also be made available in a central location, such as on an HTML page on a corporate intranet or embedded in a portal where users can access reports when needed.

Not all reports that you might work with can be considered enterprise reports as defined in this chapter. If your job is to analyze information, you likely already have some type of query tool that allows you to retrieve data from a relational database management system. To answer a one-time specific business question, you can manipulate the data you retrieve by computing ratios or combining it with data from other sources using an Excel workbook, which you can then share with your manager. Although the workbook you create in this scenario can be considered a report, it doesn't fit the definition of an enterprise report. First, you're not sharing the information across a workgroup or throughout the company on a regular basis. Second, because the information is intended for one-time usage, you're using ad hoc techniques to build a report rather than creating a standard predefined structure and format.

So what exactly does fit the definition of enterprise reporting? The diverse types of organizations that use enterprise reporting and the differences in their information needs make it difficult to compile a comprehensive list. However, you can look at who is using the shared information to develop the following generalizations about reporting scenarios:

- Internal reporting is probably the most common enterprise reporting. This category of reporting involves the sharing of information within an organization across all levels of employees and usually involves standard departmental reports. For example, employees in the product warehouse might regularly receive printed order detail reports every morning. Elsewhere in the company, management might get a financial statement in an Excel workbook delivered as an e-mail attachment after the books are closed each month.

- External reporting can take many different forms but is defined as the exchange of information to people outside of an organization. This information might be printed and mailed, such as shareholder reports. Increasingly, companies are publishing annual reports as PDF files for interested parties. External reporting can even include the exchange of information between business systems, such as invoicing information sent electronically to a customer's receivables system.

You can also consider how the information is being accessed to develop the following additional generalizations:

- *Standard reporting* relies on a central storage location that can display a list of contents or catalog of the available reports so that users can find the reports that they need. Usually, security is applied to report storage to control the reports that individual users can see. Reports might be organized in a proprietary reporting platform repository or some other type of document management system.

- *Embedded reporting* is the integration of reports into portals and in-house or third-party applications. For example, many companies are migrating to Web-based line-of-business applications for accounting and payroll functions. Instead of building reporting processes into these applications, these companies can leverage an extensible enterprise reporting platform to allow users to access information as part of using these applications.

These enterprise reporting scenarios have the following two characteristics in common:

- **Central storage**   Reports are accessed from a central location or delivered directly to users. Many people need access to the same information, possibly in different formats. Often, information needs to be secured with access limited to those with a need to know.

- **Standardization**   Information is provided in a report that is updated on a regular basis. The report conforms to a standard design with a consistent layout.

In addition, the proliferation of information that can (or should) be available to the average worker has led to increasingly more sophisticated requirements for an enterprise reporting solution. For example, users need to be able to do the following:

- Navigate easily within a large report.
- Move from one report to another while maintaining context.

- ‏Access previous versions of a report to compare information at different points of time.
- View data consolidated from multiple sources into a single report.

An enterprise reporting solution also needs to satisfy administrative requirements. A reporting platform should have the following characteristics:

- Flexibility to store a single report from which multiple versions are generated based on changeable parameters or user profiles.
- Ability to support a push-pull paradigm, in which users can seek out the information they need online or subscribe to information that is sent to them on a periodic basis.
- Capability to manage reports using a Web interface so that administrators can perform tasks without being tied to their desks.

Reporting User Communities

Many people within an organization are usually involved in some aspect of enterprise reporting. Typically, users are members of one or more of the following communities: information consumers, information explorers, and analysts.

Most users—typically 65–80 percent of the total user population—are information consumers. Information consumers usually view static and predefined reports. If they use printed reports, they might get them the old-fashioned way—someone does a batch print, then sends it out or delivers it to each recipient's in-box. A more technical environment might make a document repository available, providing the electronic equivalent of a file cabinet that information consumers can access at will. In some cases, information consumers need to receive information on a recurring basis, such as a weekly update on key performance measurements.

One of the many strengths of Reporting Services is its ability to provide easy access to a wide array of predefined reports, making information consumers a key audience served by Reporting Services. Although many people might prefer to view information online, they can still get printed reports or they can have reports delivered by way of e-mail. In either case, reports can be processed on demand (where information is as current as the data in the source system) or on a scheduled basis (where information represents a specific point in time). For maximum flexibility, an information consumer can choose from a variety of formats that can be delivered to a range of devices.

Information explorers typically constitute 15–25 percent of the user population. Like information consumers, they use predefined reports, but they also interact with reports. A common type of interaction is the use of filters to isolate segments of data. Information explorers might also interact with reports by starting with summary information and then moving to more granular levels of detail, whether through drilldown to view details in the same report or through drill across to view related information in a separate report.

Interactive reports suitable for information explorers require more work to develop than static reports, but Reporting Services has a wide array of features to support the development of these reports. Parameters can be designed into a report to support filtering data at the source or in the report. An information explorer can change parameter values on demand, or an administrator can predefine specific parameters for different groups of information explorers. Reports can also include dynamic visibility to support drilldown or actions to support drill across.

The smallest user community, typically representing 5–10 percent of users, includes analysts. This group possesses the skills to develop free-form reports that facilitate complex data analysis. Such reports are often in spreadsheet form, containing data that analysts can enhance with sophisticated calculations like linear regressions and allocations. These reports can eventually be shared with information consumers and information explorers.

Out of the box, Reporting Services supports analytical needs by providing the ability to export a report to Excel. Conversely, an Excel workbook created by an analyst can be uploaded to Reporting Services as a resource to be shared with the rest of the user community. Also, because Reporting Services is an extensible architecture, a custom application or third-party plug-in could give analysts complete flexibility to develop free-form reports within the Reporting Services environment.

The Enterprise Reporting Life Cycle

The *enterprise reporting life cycle* is a process that breaks down into three stages, through which a report progresses linearly from authoring to management to delivery. A reporting platform must not only serve the needs of each reporting community, but must also fully support each stage of the reporting life cycle. It should also provide the architecture, functionality, and utilities to support the activities of authoring, managing, and delivering reports. In other words, everything you need from beginning to end of the reporting process should be in one integrated product set. Reporting Services provides just that.

Authoring

The primary activities of the authoring stage include the definition of the data to be presented in a report, the organization of the data into a structured layout, and the application of formatting to enhance the report appearance. For example, when executive management needs to monitor sales performance across product lines, a report author creates a report to present sales data in a table layout. To facilitate analysis, the report author applies conditional formatting to highlight products for which performance exceeds defined performance goals or fails to meet these goals.

To support authoring, Reporting Services provides a broad set of features to present data in structures such as tables and charts, to group data within these structures, to allow calculations, and to add conditional formatting. This reporting platform also facilitates access to a variety of organizational data sources, such as online transactional processing (OLTP) systems, or data warehouses that store relational or online analytical processing (OLAP) data (or both). Reporting Services allows a report author to easily combine data from multiple sources into a single report. All types of structured data are supported—relational, hierarchical, and multidimensional data. To access data sources not explicitly supported by Reporting Services, custom data processing extensions can be added, which means the possibilities are limitless.

In addition, Reporting Services allows the report author to design a report with consideration for its purpose. A rich feature set enables the development of both static and interactive reports to meet the information needs of all user communities. For example, static reports, such as print-ready invoices for mailing, or interactive online reports can be quickly and easily developed. Interactive reports can also be designed that factor in how users need to explore and analyze data. Parameters, dynamic visibility, and actions can be used individually or in combination to affect both the information visible in a report and the information's appearance.

Management

The management stage begins when a report is published to a server. This stage continues with the organization of the report with other content on the server and the performance of other administrative tasks, such as setting report properties, managing report execution, and applying security. Either a report author or an administrator is responsible for publishing a report to a centrally managed server. After the report is on the server, a report execution schedule can be established to update the report regularly, such as every Monday morning. In addition, security is applied to the report so that only certain users, perhaps executive management, can view the report.

Reporting Services provides mechanisms to publish reports to a central server through the authoring tool or through management tools. After a report is online, security can be implemented to control access to reports or to restrict visibility of data within a report as needed. Further, the execution of reports is configurable so that reports can be produced on demand or on a scheduled basis. Reporting Services includes all this functionality using a server infrastructure that can exist on a single server or be distributed across many servers or incorporated into a Web farm.

Access and Delivery

The access and delivery stage includes all activities related to the distribution of reports, such as accessing reports online, rendering reports to various formats, saving and printing reports, and subscribing to reports. Some users, for instance, might choose to have reports e-mailed directly as soon as these reports are executed each week, or they might choose to receive a notification that a report is ready for viewing online. Other users, by contrast, might prefer to view the reports online using the company intranet only as the need for information arises.

To support delivery, Reporting Services can produce reports using a variety of output formats, which are referred to as *rendering formats*. A report can be made available through the intranet using a Web browser, or it can be sent embedded in an e-mail message or as an e-mail attachment in one of many formats, such as PDF or Excel. Reporting Services also provides flexible delivery mechanisms to support both push and pull distribution methods for internal and external users. Because Reporting Services is an extensible system, you can add rendering formats, different security frameworks, or alternative delivery options. In addition, the access or delivery of reports can be integrated into corporate applications.

Reporting Services Components

The requirements of a solid enterprise reporting solution are formidable, but Reporting Services meets this challenge with a set of integrated, multi-tiered components. Because Reporting Services is a .NET-based platform that can use both a Web service and an application programming interface (API), it can be customized to fit within existing technical infrastructures. Furthermore, by separating components into discrete functional units, the Reporting Services architecture can be scaled to accommodate even the largest organization by distributing components across several servers. (You learn how to install these components in Chapter 2.) Together, these components support the authoring, management, and access and delivery requirements of a reporting platform.

The Reporting Services architecture consists of three layers. The application layer includes a client component used to author reports and a server component called Report Manager, which is installed on a Web server and used for report access and for some server management tasks. The server layer is Report Server where all the processing and management of the reporting platform occurs. The data layer includes data providers to access data sources used in reports as well as a pair of databases for the storage of reports and information used by Report Server. These components can be installed on a single server or distributed across several servers. The Reporting Services components are illustrated in the following figure:

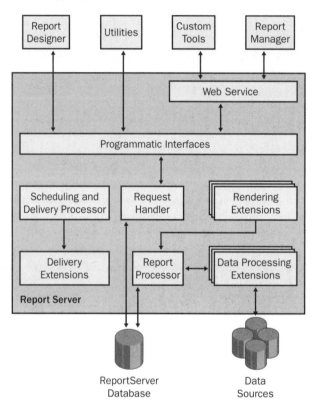

Authoring Components

When Reporting Services is installed, a client component called Report Designer is added as a set of templates to the Microsoft Visual Studio .NET development environment. The easiest way to build reports is to use these templates. If you're a report author, you don't need to have programming skills to effectively use this tool. However, if you're already an experienced programmer, you can also take advantage of the programmatic interfaces to build a custom authoring tool.

Report Designer

As a report author, you can use a graphical interface to build feature-rich reports by using drag-and-drop techniques to create a query to retrieve data and to define the layout and appearance of data in the report. You can use ADO.NET data providers to access OLE DB and ODBC data sources. If you need access to other data sources, you can build your own data providers. After defining a query to retrieve data from a selected data source, you use Report Designer to place data into one or more structures. You also use Report Designer to apply calculations to the data as well as access a complete set of features that support presentation options such as formatting and visibility. The result is a report definition in the form of an XML document using a non-proprietary schema known as Report Definition Language. You learn about Report Designer and Report Definition Language in Chapter 4, "Developing Basic Reports."

Report Designer also includes a preview version of the functionality used by the server to produce reports, so you can test a report before putting it on the server. That way, you can get an idea of how the users will see the report while you're still developing it. When you're ready to publish the report to the server, you use the Visual Studio build and deploy processes.

Programmatic Interface for Authoring

Using the Reporting Services API, application developers can build custom applications to create reports or add functionality to reports. In Chapter 14, "Report Authoring with Custom Development," you can learn how to use custom code to extend the authoring capabilities of Reporting Services and how to generate Report Definition Language files programmatically. Chapter 14 can be found on the companion CD.

Management Components

Report Manager is installed on a Web server and used both for management and for access and delivery tasks. Additionally, Reporting Services provides command-line utilities for specific server management tasks. You also have the option to build your own Windows or Web-based management tools by using the Reporting Services API.

Report Manager

Report Manager is a Web-based content management tool included with Reporting Services. Reporting Services separates administrative tasks into two main groups: content management and system management. If you're an administrator responsible for content management, you can use Report Manager to manage how reports are organized on the Report Server and how users interact with those reports. Content management using Report Manager is covered in more detail in Chapter 8, "Managing Content." As an administrator responsible for server resources and performance, you can use Report Manager to configure execution options (described in Chapter 8), to set security (described in Chapter 9, "Managing Security"), and to manage subscription and delivery options (described in Chapter 13, "Managing Subscriptions").

Command-Line Utilities

Reporting Services includes command-line utilities that allow you to manage a Report Server locally or from a remote location. The following command-line utilities are provided by Reporting Services for server administrators:

- **rsconfig**   A connection management utility used to change the connection used by Report Server to connect to the ReportServer database.
- **rs**   A script host that you can use to execute Microsoft Visual Basic .NET scripts for management tasks, such as publishing reports or copying data between ReportServer databases.
- **rskeymgmt**   An encryption key management tool that you can use to back up encryption keys for future recovery of a database or to change encrypted data used by a Report Server.
- **rsactivate**   A tool that you can use to activate a report server instance when you add a Report Server to a Web farm, migrate the ReportServer database to a new server, or rebuild the computer hosting the server.

You learn more about these utilities in Chapter 10, "Managing Server Components," except for the rs utility, which is discussed in Chapter 15, "Programming Report Server Management." Chapter 15 can be found on the companion CD.

Programmatic Interface for Management

You can also use the Reporting Services API to perform server management activities, such as publishing or deleting reports. You can build your own application, or you can build Visual Basic .NET scripts to use in conjunction with the rs utility to perform administrative tasks on Report Server. You learn how to use the Reporting Services API for server management in Chapter 15.

Access and Delivery Components

The components of Reporting Services that are involved in the access and delivery of reports break down into two groups: client components and server components. You can choose to use the supplied client components or build your own client applications. However, you must use the core server components of Reporting Services, although you can use custom or third-party applications to extend the capabilities of the server components.

Report Manager

Report Manager is not just a management tool. The user community also uses Report Manager to access reports and subscribe to reports. You learn about general report access using Report Manager in Chapter 11, "Accessing Reports."

Processor Components

Report Server is the heart of Reporting Services. Although administrators interact with Report Server using the management components, the bulk of activity that occurs on Report Server is related to supporting the access and delivery of reports. Report Server runs as a Web service, allowing Report Manager, your own custom programs, and third-party applications to access server processes.

Report Server uses Microsoft Internet Information Services (IIS) to receive requests, and then activates the applicable subcomponents in response to the requests. There are two processor subcomponents of Report Server that act as command central to manage these requests and the corresponding output returned by the other subcomponents. The core processor, Report Processor, handles all requests related to the execution of reports and the production of the final output. To complete these requests, the Report Processor calls other subcomponents, referred to as *extensions*, to handle data processing, rendering, and security. The Scheduling and Delivery Processor responds to scheduled events and delivers reports. This processor uses delivery extensions to send reports to their destinations.

Report Processor   The Report Processor is responsible for retrieving the report layout from the report definition and merging it with data returned from the query included in the report definition. At this point, the report is in an *intermediate format*. What happens next depends on the report request. If a user wants to see the report online, the intermediate format is passed to the appropriate rendering extension so that the proper output format can be created, such as an HTML page.

On the other hand, if the request is to generate a *report snapshot* (which is a report at a specific point in time), the intermediate format is stored in the ReportServer database. When a user requests the snapshot, the Report Processor retrieves the intermediate format, calls the rendering extension, and then sends the final format of the report to the user.

By separating the presentation processing from data retrieval and rendering, multiple users can view the same report at the same time, and each can change the viewing format. You learn more about execution options in Chapter 8.

Scheduling and Delivery Processor   As its name implies, the Scheduling and Delivery Processor is responsible for running scheduled reports and for delivering reports to a location or a device on a scheduled basis. It uses SQL Server Agent to process schedules. When the applicable time arrives, SQL Server Agent sends instructions related to the schedule to the Scheduling and Delivery Processor. The report is rendered and passed to the delivery extension to send the report to specified recipients or a target location on a file share.

A report snapshot is an example of a scheduled report. The schedule information is specified by a user or administrator using Report Manager and stored in the ReportServer database. When the Scheduling and Delivery Processor finishes processing the snapshot, the intermediate format is stored in the ReportServer database. When a user wants to view the report, Report Server takes over by retrieving the intermediate format of the snapshot and calling the specified rendering extension to finalize the output. In Chapter 8, you learn about scheduling reports.

When users subscribe to reports, the desired delivery extension is selected and the time of delivery is specified. When the time comes to deliver a report, the Scheduling and Delivery Processor gets a rendered report and then passes the report to the applicable delivery extension. Delivery options for subscriptions are described in Chapter 13, "Managing Subscriptions."

Server Extensions

Server extensions are used to perform specific functions. Reporting Services uses four different types of server extensions: security, data processing, rendering, and delivery. Over time, you can expect to see more extensions available for Reporting Services, whether developed by Microsoft or by other commercial software developers.

Security Extensions   Security extensions are used to define the authorization model used by Reporting Services. Only one security extension is supplied, which supports Windows and SQL Server security. You can, of course, create your own security extension to integrate Reporting Services with another security architecture.

Data Processing Extensions   Data processing extensions are responsible for processing the query requests received from the Report Processor. The query request includes a data source, a query, and possibly query parameters. The applicable data processing extension then opens a connection to the data source, returns a list of field names from the query, executes the query, and retrieves the query results, which are then returned to the Report Processor.

Reporting Services comes with four data processing extensions: SQL Server, Oracle, OLE DB, and ODBC. However, you can also use any ADO.NET data provider or build your own data processing extensions. You learn how to create a custom data processing extension in Chapter 14, which can be found on the companion CD.

Rendering Extensions   Rendering extensions are called by the Report Processor to take the data that was received from the data processing extension and merge that data with the report definition. The result is a finished report in a format specific to the device that will receive the report.

At the time of this writing, Reporting Services has the following rendering extensions: HTML, HTML with Office Web Components, MHTML, Excel, Acrobat PDF, CSV, and TIFF. As with other extension types, you can develop your own rendering extension to produce other output formats.

Delivery Extensions   Reporting Services currently includes the following three delivery extensions:

- The e-mail delivery extension allows Reporting Services to embed a report in an e-mail message or send the report as an attachment. Alternatively, an e-mail notification can be sent that includes a link to the report. If the delivery is an e-mail notification, it can also be sent without the link to a pager, cellular phone, or any device that can receive a simple message.

- The file share delivery extension can be used to store reports in a centrally accessible location independent of the ReportServer database or as part of a report archive strategy.

- A null delivery provider is available for data-driven subscriptions to periodically load reports into the cache in advance of user viewing. This option is useful for reports that take a long time to execute.

You can also develop your own delivery extension to expand the delivery functionality of Reporting Services.

Report Server Databases

Reporting Services centralizes report storage in two SQL Server databases. The ReportServer database stores information used to manage reports and resources, in addition to the reports themselves. In addition, this database is the storage location for security settings, encrypted data, data related to schedules and delivery, and information about extensions. The ReportServerTempDB database stores temporary data used for caching purposes. More information about these databases can be found in Chapter 10.

Programmatic Interface for Access and Delivery

You can use the Reporting Services API to create assemblies when you need to accommodate specialized security, data processing, rendering, or delivery scenarios. In Chapter 14, you learn how to build a custom data processing extension. The Reporting Services API also enables you to develop your own applications to allow users to view reports or to produce reports using different formats. You learn more about custom reporting in Chapter 16, "Building Custom Reporting Tools." Chapters 14 and 16 can be found on the companion CD.

Chapter 1 Quick Reference

This term	Means this
Report	Information that is structured and formatted for print or online viewing.
Enterprise reporting	Sharing of information on a regular basis across a wide audience.
Enterprise reporting life cycle	The process of authoring, managing, and accessing reports.
Extensions	Subcomponents of Report Server used to provide specific functionality, such as data processing, rendering, security, and delivery.
Intermediate format	The result of merging data from a query with layout information from a report definition. The intermediate format is sent to a rendering extension to produce the final output, such as an HTML page or an Excel file.
Report snapshot	A report that preserves a record of data at a point in time. A report snapshot is stored in the Report-Server database in its intermediate format and rendered only when a user requests the report.

Installing Reporting Services

In this chapter, you will learn how to:

- Select an edition and configuration of Reporting Services appropriate to your site.
- Prepare your technical environment for a successful installation.
- Install Reporting Services.

In Chapter 1, "Understanding Enterprise Reporting," you learned how the various components of Reporting Services combine to fully support enterprise reporting requirements. By understanding how each component functions and interacts with other components, you can better decide how to deploy Reporting Services in your organization. This chapter explains the available deployment options, reviews the prerequisites for installation, and walks you through an installation of Reporting Services.

Considering Deployment Options

To use Reporting Services to support the authoring, management, and delivery of reports, you need to install its components somewhere. But which components should you install where? Before you can start installing, you need to understand how features compare across the four Reporting Services editions and how one or more servers can be configured to support Reporting Services. You also need to consider whether the existing naming conventions of your Web applications will influence the names that you assign to the virtual directories used by Report Server and Report Manager.

Choosing a Reporting Services Edition

Reporting Services is bundled with Microsoft SQL Server 2000, which is available in four separate editions. You can choose to implement either of the two corresponding Reporting Services editions for production—Standard Edition or Enterprise Edition. For development purposes, you can implement Developer Edition. If you're still evaluating Reporting Services, use the Evaluation Edition. You should understand the differences in features supported by each edition to make the proper selection. You can select from the following editions:

- **Standard Edition**   Supports a single server configuration only. This edition does not support subscriptions that use a database query to set delivery options, known as *data-driven subscriptions*. Use Standard Edition when you have a limited number of users.

- **Enterprise Edition**   Supports a Web farm configuration that scales to satisfy high-volume reporting requirements and a large user population. Additionally, Enterprise Edition supports data-driven subscriptions. This edition is required for deploying a large-scale reporting platform.

- **Developer Edition**   Supports all features of Enterprise Edition, but is licensed only for use in a development and test environment. If you are a developer who is building custom applications for Reporting Services, or if you need a separate environment for authoring reports or for viewing your reports on a test Report Server, use this edition.

- **Evaluation Edition**   Supports all features of the Enterprise Edition, but expires after 120 days. You can use Evaluation Edition to explore all the features of Reporting Services before making a purchasing decision.

▶ **Note**   When you decide to upgrade, you can simply install the Standard or Enterprise Edition on the same server. You don't need to uninstall the Evaluation Edition first. During the installation process, you are prompted for the name of the Report Server database. Just use the same database name that was created for use with the Evaluation Edition, and you're all set!

Planning a Site Configuration

If you're using Standard Edition, you must use the single server configuration for your Reporting Services deployment. You can use any of the other editions to deploy Reporting Services in a multiple server configuration. If you choose the multiple server configuration, remember that the Enterprise Edition is the only edition licensed for production usage.

A single server deployment of Reporting Services requires only that you install Report Server and Report Manager on the same server. You have the option to install the Reporting Services databases on a local or remote SQL Server instance. However, the instance that you use must be either in the same domain or in a trusted domain. During the installation, when you select the SQL Server instance, you will also have an opportunity to supply a name for the main Reporting Services database. By default, the main database is named Report-Server, and its companion database is named ReportServerTempDB. If you change the name of the main database, that name will be appended with TempDB to create a name for the companion database.

If you need a reporting platform that supports high availability or high volume, deploy Reporting Services in a multiple server configuration. In this configuration, multiple Report Servers run as a single virtual server with one set of Reporting Services databases supporting all Report Servers. These Reporting Services databases can also be part of a SQL Server failover cluster, even if you don't cluster the Report Servers.

▶ **Note** Reporting Services does not include tools to manage a Web farm, so you'll need to use Microsoft Application Center or third-party software to set one up and manage it. However, during installation of Reporting Services, you can add a Report Server to an existing Web farm.

Deciding Naming Conventions

In preparation for installation, you will need to consider the naming conventions that you will use for the Report Server and Report Manager virtual directories on the Web server. Users and administrators will access these virtual directories when using a browser to connect to Reporting Services. You can accept the default virtual directory names suggested during installation, or you can supply a different name at that time if you prefer. However, if you decide to replace the default virtual directory names, keep the virtual directory name length to 50 characters or fewer.

By default, the Report Server virtual directory is /ReportServer unless you're installing Report Server on a named instance, in which case the default virtual director is /ReportServer$NamedInstance. For Report Manager, the default virtual directory is /Reports.

Preparing for Installation

Reporting Services has several prerequisites for installation. More specifically, each component of Reporting Services has certain software requirements that must be met for that component to be successfully installed. You need to understand how the operating system affects your installation options, what software must be installed prior to a Reporting Services installation, and how your technical environment needs to be configured.

Reviewing Operating System Requirements

The server and client components can be installed on any of the following operating systems: Microsoft Windows 2000, Windows XP Professional, or Windows Server 2003. Of course, the latest service pack should be applied.

If you're using Windows Server 2003, you must configure the server as an Application Server for Microsoft Internet Information Services (IIS) and ASP.NET. To do this using Add/Remove Programs in Control Panel, select the Application Server check box and then click the Details button. Make sure that both the IIS and ASP.NET components are selected in the Application Server dialog box, click OK to close the dialog box, and then click Next to contine the update to the server configuration.

Reviewing Software Requirements

Regardless of whether you're using a single or multiple server configuration, you must install the server components, Report Server and Report Manager, on a Web server that is already running IIS 5.0 or later. It's possible to install these components on separate Web servers when using Enterprise Edition.

Each Web server on which you install Report Server or Report Manager must be configured to use the Microsoft .NET Framework version 1.1 or later. The Reporting Services installation process will automatically install and register ASP.NET in IIS if the .NET Framework is missing. You must also already have MDAC 2.6 or later, but only on the server on which you're installing Report Server.

Reporting Services also requires a pre-existing installation of SQL Server 2000. You must ensure that the latest service pack—which is SP3a at the time of this writing—has been applied. The Reporting Services installation requires access to a SQL Server instance to create a ReportServer database that is used as a central repository for Reporting Services.

> ▶ **Note**   If you decide to install the server components on separate Web servers, you will need to first install the ReportServer database independently to a SQL Server instance. You also need to install the ReportServer database first if you're using the Standard Edition and separating the server components from the database components. After the ReportServer database is in place, you can install any of the other components in any order. You will then need to specify the SQL Server instance hosting the ReportServer database during installation of the server components.

Report Designer, as a client component of Reporting Services, can be installed on the same server as Report Server or on a separate computer. Either way, any edition of Microsoft Visual Studio .NET 2003 must be installed prior to beginning the installation of Reporting Services. You will also need to have MDAC 2.6 or later installed on the same computer as Report Designer.

Reviewing Configuration Prerequisites

The Reporting Services Setup program uses the Microsoft Distributed Transaction Coordinator (MS DTC) service. You need to make sure that the DTC service is running before you start installation, or Setup will fail.

Additionally, the Setup process uses the IWAM_*computername* account to configure services on IIS. This account is enabled by default when IIS is installed, but it is often disabled for security reasons. You will need to make sure this account is enabled before starting the Reporting Services installation. You can disable the account again after the installation is complete.

During installation, virtual directories will be added in IIS to the Default Web Site. For the Reporting Services installation to successfully complete this task, the IP address of the Default Web Site must be the default value—(All Unassigned). In fact, the installation will fail if you have disabled the default site.

▶ **Note** For installation of Reporting Services, you must enable the Default Web Site. If you really don't want to use this site, it is still possible to move the virtual directories following the installation. For more information about relocating these virtual directories, refer to *http://www.sqljunkies.com/HowTo/525B575A-7F61-483A-AC8F-FEC700C34674.scuk*.

You can use Secure Sockets Layer (SSL) to secure your data if you're distributing confidential data in reports or passing passwords as part of a URL. To use SSL, you need to install an SSL certificate on the Web server on which you will install Report Server prior to installing Reporting Services. You also need to associate the certificate with the default Web site on the IIS server. During installation, you can configure the Reporting Services virtual directories to use SSL connections.

▶ **Note** Installation of Reporting Services will fail if you select the option to use SSL connections before the Web server is correctly configured for SSL. If necessary, you can bypass this step during installation and set up SSL on the Web server later. Then you will need to set the *SecureConnectionLevel* value to 3 in the RSReportServer configuration file. Editing configuration files is discussed in Chapter 10, "Managing Server Components."

If you plan to use e-mail delivery for subscriptions, one option is to install Simple Mail Transport Protocol (SMTP) on the Web server and have the service running when you install Reporting Services. Another option is to use an SMTP or POP3 server that is already running on your network. The Setup routine for Reporting Services will prompt you for the name of the e-mail server and a valid account to use for generating e-mail messages. However, you can edit the Report Server configuration file after installation to change e-mail delivery settings at a later time.

> ▶ **Note**   Refer to Reporting Services Books Online for more information about e-mail settings in the RSReportServer configuration file. Reporting Services Books Online will be installed if you follow the instructions later in this chapter. Alternatively, you can view the same material in the MSDN Library at *http: //msdn.microsoft.com/library/default.asp?url=/library/en-us/RSPORTAL/HTM /rs_gts_portal_3vqd.asp*.

Creating Reporting Services Credentials

To install and run Reporting Services, you will need to have available one or more user accounts to perform the following functions:

- **Log on to a SQL Server instance and install the Reporting Services databases**   When you install Reporting Services, your account must be a member of the local system administrator's group. Your credentials are used by Setup for authentication on the SQL Server instance that will host the Reporting Services databases, ReportServer and ReportServerTempDB. Your credentials are also used to install these databases to the SQL Server, so you will need the following permissions: create logins, create roles, create databases, and assign permissions to users.

- **Start the ReportServer service**   This service primarily manages subscriptions and scheduled report executions. If you want to use either of these features, the service must be running. However, you can continue to use other Reporting Services features if this service is not running. During Reporting Services installation, you need to specify an account that will be used to start the ReportServer Windows service. You can choose between a built-in account or a domain user account.

> ▶ **Important**   If you're running Windows 2000, Microsoft recommends that you use the Local System account, also known as the NT AUTHORITY/SYSTEM built-in account. Otherwise, you won't be able to use stored credentials or prompted credentials with external data sources. There are no similar restrictions if you're using Windows XP or Windows 2003. Any built-in account or domain user account can be used. (Using credentials with data sources is explained in Chapter 8, "Managing Content.")

- **Connect to the Reporting Services databases** The Report Server must be able to access the Reporting Services databases. You can create a dedicated user account for this purpose, either as a service account, a domain account, or a SQL Server login. During installation of Reporting Services, you must provide the credentials for this account. (If you choose to use a SQL Server login, this account will be created in the SQL Server instance if it doesn't already exist.) Setup will assign the account to the RSExecRole and public roles on the ReportServer, ReportServerTempDB, master, and msdb databases.

▶ **Important** You can use the same credentials that you use to start the ReportServer service, but if you do, and the Report Server is on a Windows Server 2003 machine, you need to install the SQL Server Hotfix 859 before you begin the Reporting Services installation. You can download the hotfix at *http: //support.microsoft.com/default.aspx?scid=kb;en-us;821334&Product=sql2k*. This hotfix will not be required if you have installed Reporting Services SP1 (which has not yet been released at the time of this writing).

If you choose to use a domain user account to connect to the Reporting Services databases, you must configure SQL Server Agent to use a user account in the same domain. The account used by SQL Server Agent does not need to be the same account used to connect to Reporting Services databases. Because schedules are created as SQL Server Agent jobs using the Report Server's domain account, SQL Server Agent needs permissions to access scheduled jobs owned by a domain account.

In this procedure, you will add a service account that will be used for running the ReportServer service and for connecting to the Reporting Services databases.

Add a service account for Reporting Services

1 Open the Computer Management console.

2 Expand the Local Users and Groups folder.

3 Right-click the Users folder and select New User.

4 Enter a user name: **ReportServer2000**.

5 Add a description: **Account used for running the ReportServer service**.

6 Provide a strong password.

7 Clear the User Must Change Password At Next Logon check box.

8   Select User Cannot Change Password.

9   Select Password Never Expires.

The New User dialog box looks like this:

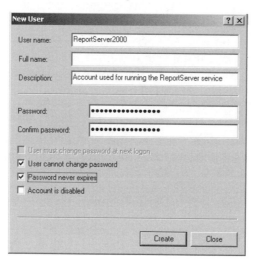

10   Click the Create button.

11   Click the Close button, and then close the Computer Management window.

Installing Reporting Services

You have the option to install Reporting Services using a setup wizard or by running a command-line executable. Setup can be launched from a CD, a local folder, or a file share that is specified using Universal Naming Convention (UNC) format. If you use the wizard, you select options on each page of the wizard to set property values for the installation. If you use the command-line executable, you can use command-line arguments or a template file to set property values. You must perform the installation locally, although you can choose which components to install if you're distributing components across computers.

▶ **Note**   For more information about installing other editions, see the Reporting Services Setup help file, rssetup.chm, which is packaged with the Setup executable.

How to Install Reporting Services by Using Setup

When using the setup wizard to install Reporting Services, you progress through a series of pages that are dependent on your selection of features to install. If you install all components, you will need to specify credentials for the ReportServer Windows service, define virtual directories for the Report Server and Report Manager, and name the SQL Server instance and database used by Report Server and provide connection credentials. You can optionally specify e-mail delivery options for subscriptions. If you choose to install the sample database, you need to select a SQL Server instance on the local computer as a host. Finally, you need to specify licensing options.

Launching Setup

The setup wizard steps you through the process of selecting components, providing credentials, and specifying other configuration settings needed to complete the Reporting Services installation. The pages of the wizard that you see depend on the features that you choose to install.

▶ **Important**   If you plan to install Reporting Services on a Web server that is hosting Windows SharePoint Services, you will need to perform several tasks after you install Reporting Services. These tasks include configuring SharePoint to avoid conflicts with Reporting Services, adding the session state module to SharePoint, and separating the application pools of each server in IIS. You can find detailed instructions at *http://msdn.microsoft.com/library/ default.asp?url=/library/en-us/RSinstall/htm/gs_installingrs_v1_9fdy.asp.*

In this procedure, you will launch the Reporting Services setup wizard.

Launch the setup wizard

1   Run Setup from the installation CD or a network share that contains the contents of the installation CD.

When you run Setup, the first page that appears is the Supplemental End User License Agreement.

2   After reviewing the agreement, select the I Accept The Licensing Terms And Conditions check box.

3   Click the Next button.

The Component Update portion of the installation will begin and might take a minute or two. The components to be installed will be listed separately on this page.

4   Click the Next button.

The System Prerequisites Check will begin. If this check passes, you will be able to continue. Otherwise, you will need to stop and fix the problem.

5   Click the Next button.

After a moment, you will see the introduction page.

6 Click the Next button.

7 Type a name and optionally a company name on the Registration Information page.

8 Click the Next button.

The Feature Selection page is displayed:

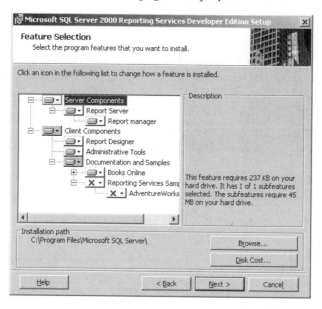

Now you will need to select the components that you want to install.

Choosing the Components

Reporting Services includes several components that are installed on both client and server computers. These components include the Report Server, the Reporting Services databases, Report Manager, Report Designer, and several command prompt utilities for administrative tasks.

In this procedure, you will add the Reporting Services Samples to the default selection of components to be installed.

Select components to install

1 Click the button icon next to Reporting Services Samples and then click Entire Feature Will Be Installed On Local Hard Drive.

▶ **Note** You can skip this step if you don't want to use the samples that ship with Reporting Services. You can always use Setup later to install the samples individually if you change your mind.

The Feature Selection page of the setup wizard is displayed:

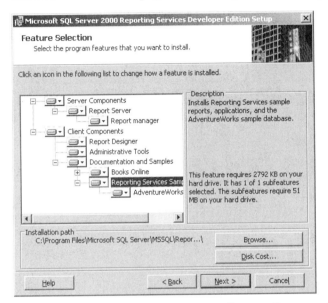

Notice that you can change the installation directory for some features. If you click a feature and the Browse button is dimmed, you're not allowed to change the location. Also, when you click a feature, the disk space required to install the selected feature is displayed. Use the Disk Cost button to see the total space required for all the Reporting Services you selected to verify that you have enough space available in the specified installation locations.

2 Click the Next button.

Selecting the Service Account

The ReportServer Windows service needs to run under a Local System or domain user account as explained earlier in this chapter. If you're installing Reporting Services on Windows Server 2003, you can also choose to run the service using either the LocalService or NetworkService account. The options that you can choose from will depend on the local operating system. You can also decide whether you want the ReportServer service to automatically start when the server starts.

In this procedure, you will assign the ReportServer2000 account as the service account for the ReportServer Windows service.

Select a service account

1   On the Service Account page, click Use A Domain User Account.
2   Enter **ReportServer2000** as the user name, and then enter the account password that you created earlier in this chapter and enter the domain name.

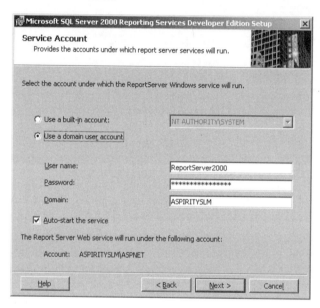

▶   **Note**   If you need to change this account or its start options later, you can use the Services console.

Notice that the service account for the Report Server Web service is displayed on this page. You are not allowed to specify a different account.
3   Click the Next button.

Specifying the Report Server and Report Manager Virtual Roots

Virtual directories are used to access Report Server and Report Manager. These virtual directories are created on the Default Web Site in IIS. If your Web Server is dedicated to Reporting Services, you should redirect the home page to the Report Manager's home page, although this is not required. You can also secure data sent to browser or client applications with SSL encryption, but you must have an SSL certificate installed before starting the Reporting Services installation.

In this procedure, you will specify names for the virtual directories assigned to Report Server and Report Manager.

Configure virtual directories

1   Keep the default settings on the Reporting Services Virtual Directories page, except clear the check box Use SSL (Secure Sockets Layer) Connections When Retrieving Data On These Virtual Directories.

    The Reporting Services Virtual Directories page of the setup wizard looks like this:

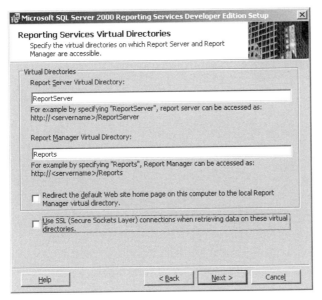

    You don't need to enter the http:// part of the URL if you replace the virtual directory name.

2   Click the Next button.

Specifying the Report Server Database

You need to select a local or remote SQL Server instance that will host the Reporting Services database. You can use an existing Report Server database or provide a unique name if you want to create a Report Server database. You also need to specify an account that Reporting Services will use to connect to this database at run time. The default account is the service account used to run the

ReportServer Windows service, but you can also specify a domain user account or a SQL Server login to conform to existing security practices for your SQL Server instance.

In this procedure, you will specify the SQL Server instance and the name of the database used by the Report Server.

Configure the Report Server database

1   On the Report Server Database page, keep the default settings.

The Report Server Database page of the setup wizard looks like this:

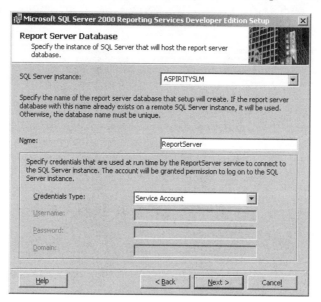

The ReportServer and the corresponding ReportServerTempDB databases are created using your credentials. You need to have permissions to create a database on the SQL Server instance that you specify on this page.

▶   **Note**   If you need to use different credentials to create the Reporting Services databases, you can use the command-line executable Setup.exe instead of the setup wizard to pass those credentials to the installation process.

If you enter the name of an existing database and are not using the Standard Edition, the Report Server you are currently installing can be added to a Web farm. The subsequent page in the setup wizard will allow you to enter values needed to add the Report Server to the Web farm. This page will not appear if you don't assign an existing name for the database or if you are using the Standard Edition.

2   Click the Next button.

Specifying Report Delivery Options

If you will be using e-mail delivery of subscriptions, you need to specify the name of the e-mail server that Reporting Services should use to send reports. You can also specify an e-mail account that will be added as the From address of the e-mail message. Specifying the report delivery options on this page is not required at this time because you can always edit Reporting Services configuration files later. However, by adding the information now, your Report Server will be ready for e-mail delivery right after installation is complete.

In this procedure, you will specify e-mail delivery information for your Reporting Services installation. (You can skip this procedure if you don't want to perform the e-mail delivery procedures in Chapter 13, "Managing Subscriptions.")

Configure e-mail delivery

1   Enter an SMTP server address: **localhost**.

▶   **Note**   The procedures that you will use later in this book to learn about e-mail delivery assume that you have SMTP on your local server if you follow this procedure as written. You can alternatively enter the server address of an existing SMTP server on your network or the SMTP gateway of your Exchange server if you prefer.

2   Enter an e-mail address to be used as the sender for report deliveries: **postmaster@adventure-works.com**.

The Report Server Delivery Settings page of the setup wizard looks like this:

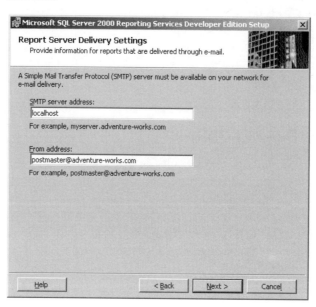

The e-mail address that you enter doesn't need to be valid. This address becomes the default reply-to address. When you set up e-mail delivery for a report, you can override this default.

3   Click the Next button.

Choosing a Samples Location

If you opted to install the Reporting Services samples, you need to specify the SQL Server instance to which the AdventureWorks sample database will be attached. This database can be attached only to a local SQL Server instance and it cannot already exist in that instance. If it does, you will not be able to complete the installation unless you delete the sample database, or return to the Feature Selection page of the setup wizard to remove the AdventureWorks database selection as a feature to install.

▶ **Tip**   If you want to install the AdventureWorks database on a remote SQL Server instance, you can run Setup on the remote computer as a local process. Another way to install this database elsewhere is to copy the database from the installation folder Setup\Report Server\Reporting Services\Samples\Databases, clear the read-only attribute, and then attach the database manually to the SQL Server instance.

In this procedure, you will specify the local SQL Server instance as the host for the AdventureWorks sample database.

Select a SQL Server instance for the AdventureWorks database

1   Select a local SQL Server instance.

This is the SQL Server instance used to install the AdventureWorks database.

▶ **Note**   You won't see this page of the setup wizard if you skipped the step to select this feature for installation.

2   Click the Next button.

Selecting Licensing Options

Licensing options for Reporting Services conform to licensing options for SQL Server. Reporting Services supports per seat or per processor licensing. With *per seat licensing*, you must have a license for each computer running Reporting Services and a Client Access License (CAL) for each user or device that accesses reports (including workstations installed with Report Designer). If you're using Reporting Services in an Internet or extranet deployment, you must purchase a *per processor* license for each CPU in the server running Reporting Services. You can also use per processor licensing if it's more cost effective than purchasing CALs.

In this procedure, you will specify per seat licensing for one device.

Choose a licensing type

1   Type **1** device.

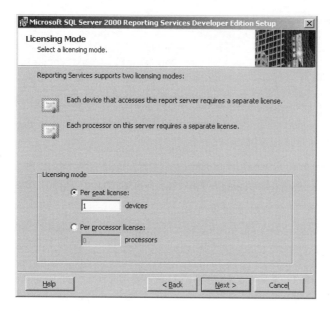

▶ **Note**   Because the installation procedures are intended for educational purposes, per seat licensing for one device is used as an example. You should specify the licensing options that are applicable to your site.

2   Click the Next button.

Now the official installation begins!

3   Click the Install button.

You will see a status bar that indicates the progress of the installation. Be patient—this process will take several minutes before the status bar begins moving.

4   Click the Finish button when the installation is complete.

Verifying the Installation

To verify that your installation of Reporting Services was successful, you should perform several tests. First, to test the Report Server, you can either check that the ReportServer service is running by using the Services console or you can use your browser to navigate to the Report Server virtual directory, which by default is *http://servername/ReportServer*. To test Report Manager, use the application to add a new folder.

In this procedure, you will confirm that the Report Server service is running and that Report Server and Report Manager are working.

Test Report Server and Report Manager

1   From the Administrative Tools program group, open the Services console and scroll to ReportServer to confirm that the service is running.

The Services console looks similar to this:

2   Open Microsoft Internet Explorer and type the server name and virtual directory name of Report Manager: **http://**_servername_**/Reports**.

The Home page of Report Manager is displayed:

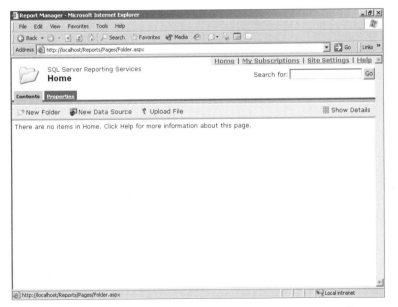

3   Click the New Folder button on the Report Manager toolbar.

The New Folder page is displayed.

4   Type a name for the folder: **Adventure Works**.

Your screen looks like this:

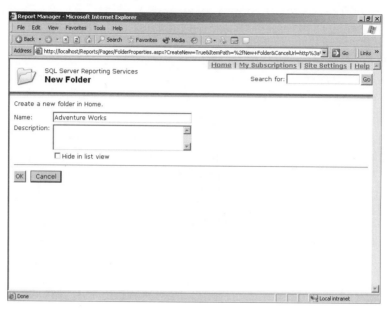

By creating a new folder, you are testing that the Report Manager is able to access the Report Server, which passes instructions to the ReportServer database.

5   Click the OK button.

Your screen looks like this:

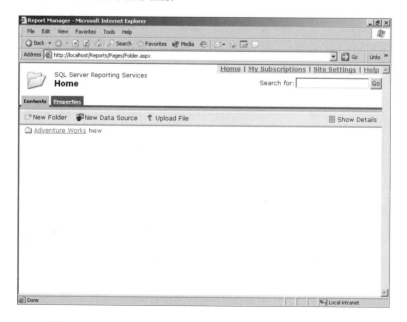

Your new folder is now ready for reports to be added. You'll add a report to this folder when you finish Chapter 3, "Building Your First Report."

Chapter 2 Quick Reference

To	Do this
Test features of Reporting Services before making a purchasing decision	Use the Evaluation Edition in a single or multiple server deployment.
Use Reporting Services in a single server deployment	Use Standard Edition for production and Developer Edition for development and testing.
Use Reporting Services in a multiple server deployment	Use Enterprise Edition for production and Developer Edition for development and testing.
Prepare a server for installation of Report Server or Report Manager	Install IIS 5.0 or later on each server that will host either of these Reporting Services components. Additionally, install .NET Framework 1.1 or later and MDAC 2.6 or later.
Prepare a server or client workstation for installation of Report Designer	Install Visual Studio .NET 2003.
Configure a computer for a Reporting Services installation	Enable the Distributed Transaction Coordinator service prior to running Setup.
Configure IIS in preparation for a Reporting Services installation	Enable the IWAM_*computername* account. Map the Default Web Site to (All Unassigned). Optionally, install an SSL certificate and associate the certificate with the Default Web Site.
Configure e-mail delivery	Install SMTP on the Web Server, or have available the name of a SMTP or POP3 server on your network.
Establish Reporting Services credentials	Use the Local System account or a local system administration account that is a domain user (or LocalService or NetworkService for the service account if running Windows 2003) to start the ReportServer Windows service. Use a service account, domain account, or SQL Server login for Report Server to use to connect to the Reporting Services databases.
Install Reporting Services	Double-click Setup.exe in the installation to launch the setup wizard. *or* Run the *setup* command-line executable. Specify options using command-line arguments or a template file.

Building Your First Report

In this chapter, you will learn how to:

- Use the Report Designer wizards to create a simple tabular report.
- Publish a report solution.
- Use Report Manager to manage report properties.
- Use the HTML Viewer to access and export a report.

In Chapter 1, "Understanding Enterprise Reporting," you learned about the three stages of the reporting life cycle: authoring, managing, and accessing reports. In Chapter 2, "Installing Reporting Services," you learned how to install and configure Reporting Services, so you should be ready to go exploring now. In this chapter, rather than review each component of Reporting Services in detail, you take a tour of it. You visit each stage of the reporting cycle as you build, manage, and review your first report, and learn about the key components of Reporting Services.

You start your tour by authoring a simple report using wizards in the Report Designer, which will enable you to set up and design the report. You also use the Report Designer to polish up and publish your report. Then, you move on to the management stage by using Report Manager to update the report's description and execution properties. Finally, you wrap up your tour in the access stage by using Report Manager to explore the report online and to export it as a Microsoft Excel file. When finished, you wind up with a high-level understanding of the various components of Reporting Services and the way they work together to create a powerful reporting platform.

Authoring a Report

The process of authoring, or building, a report consists of several steps. The first step is to define a Reporting Services *data source*, which packages information about where the data to be used in your report is stored, and ensure that the credentials needed to access that data have the right security clearance to get the data out. To create a data source, you need to know which server hosts the data and which database or file stores the data, as well as have the credentials with permission to retrieve that data. Each report that you author must have at least one data source defined. Data sources are covered in more detail in Chapter 4, "Developing Basic Reports."

The second step in building a report is to create a *dataset* for the report. An important component of the dataset is a query, which requires that you know the language and syntax used to retrieve data. For example, if your report will use data from a Microsoft SQL Server database, you will need to be able to create a Transact-SQL query (or know someone who can write it for you!). A dataset also includes a pointer to the data source and other information that is used when the query executes. When you use the Report Project Wizard, you can define only one dataset, but you'll learn how to work with multiple datasets in a single report in Chapter 7, "Building Advanced Reports."

The third and final step in the construction of your report is the creation of a *report layout,* which is the design template used by Reporting Services to arrange and format the data. The report layout includes the structure, or *data region*, into which data is placed when the report is processed, such as a table or matrix. You can set properties for each section of a data region to define style properties, such as font, color, and format. Additionally, you can set these properties for report items, such as the report title in a textbox or the report background, which gives you enormous flexibility to control the look and feel of your report.

How to Prepare a Report

In this chapter, you use the Report Project Wizard and the Report Wizard to help you start and build a new report. (In Chapter 4, you'll learn another way to begin a report.) These wizards, which are provided within the Report Designer, are handy tools that walk you through each of the steps described in the preceding section. As part of the report preparation, you create a data source to locate the database for Reporting Services, and then define the query that is used to populate the report with data.

Starting a New Report

When you start a new report using the Report Project Wizard, you are creating Microsoft Visual Studio containers to hold your report, a project, and a solution. You must name these containers and provide a storage location for them on your computer's hard drive or on a network file share.

In this procedure, you create a new report project called Adventure Works and specify a storage location for the project.

Start the Report Project Wizard

1   Start Visual Studio.

2   On the File menu, point to New, and then click Project.

The New Project dialog box appears. Templates are organized by Project Type, represented as folders in this dialog box.

▶ **Note**   If this is your first time working with Visual Studio, you might not be familiar with the way that items are organized in this environment. A report is placed inside a project, which you can think of as a folder that organizes many reports into a collection. Because you're using the Report Project Wizard, you can work with only one project right now. However, you'll be adding reports to this project as you progress through this book. When you publish all reports in a project, they are automatically organized into the same folder on the Report Server.

3   If the Business Intelligence Projects folder isn't open, click this folder to display the available templates.

4   Click the Report Project Wizard.

5   If necessary, click the More button at the bottom of the dialog box.

You can skip this step if the Less button is displayed at the bottom of the dialog box.

6   Type a name for the project: **Adventure Works**.

Notice that as you type, the text in the New Solution Name box of the New Project dialog box changes to match the project name. You have the option to change the solution name later if you change your mind.

▶ **Note**   In the same way that a project is a container for a report, a solution is a container for one or more projects. Visual Studio lets you work with only one solution at a time, but you have free access to any project within the open solution.

7   Type a location for the project: **c:\rs2000sbs\Workspace**.
The New Project dialog box looks like this:

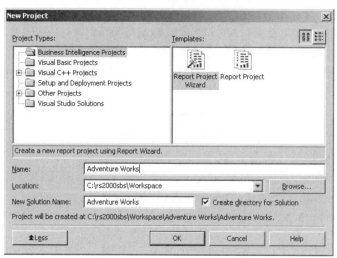

8   Click OK to continue.

The Welcome page of the Report Wizard is displayed. Note that this wizard is different from the Report Project Wizard. The Report Project Wizard lets you create a solution, a project, and a report in one step, and then launches the Report Wizard. You can use the Report Wizard any time you want to add a report to an existing project using a wizard interface. (This is explained in Chapter 4.)

If you want to bypass this page of the Report Wizard in the future, you can select the check box here to disable the Welcome page.

9   Click Next.

Connecting to a Data Source

The next step of the Report Wizard allows you to specify connection information. Here you identify the server and database hosting the data. If necessary, you can also supply credentials information to be used by Reporting Services for authentication when querying the database.

In this procedure, you create a data source that defines a connection to the rs2000sbsDW database in your SQL Server using Microsoft Windows authentication.

Select a data source

1   Type a name for the data source: **rs2000sbsDW**.

2   Click Microsoft SQL Server in the Type list box.

The Select The Data Source page of the Report Wizard now looks like this:

You can choose from four connection types: SQL Server, OLE DB, Oracle, or ODBC. After you select a connection type, you can type a connection string manually, or you can click the Edit button to use the Data Link Properties dialog box to generate the connection string automatically. By default, the data source you create here will be available only to the current report, which allows you to manage its usage separately from other reports. Select the check box at the bottom of the dialog box to allow this data source to be shared with other reports, which simplifies the management of data sources in general.

3   Click Edit.

The Data Link Properties dialog box is displayed. Because you selected Microsoft SQL Server as the connection type on the Select The Data Source page of the Report Wizard, the data provider defaults to Microsoft OLE DB Provider for SQL Server.

4   Type **localhost** or the name of the SQL Server instance in the Select Or Enter A Server Name box.

5   Click Use Windows NT Integrated Security.

6   Select rs2000sbsDW in the Select The Database On The Server list box.

The Data Link Properties dialog box looks like this:

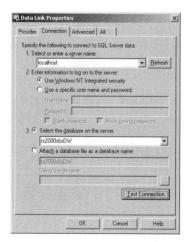

7   Click Test Connection to make sure you can connect to the rs2000sbsDW database, and then click OK to close the confirmation dialog box.

8   Click OK to close the Data Link Properties dialog box.

The current page of the Report Wizard looks like this:

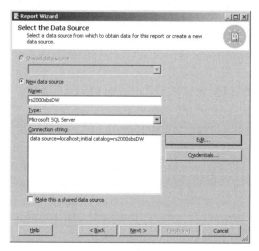

Notice the connection string generated for your SQL Server data source: `data source=localhost;initial catalog=rs2000sbsDW`. Remember that you can also type a connection string for a data source, but it must use the syntax of the database to which Reporting Services will connect.

Now you have defined a data source that contains the information that Reporting Services needs to connect to the database it will use to retrieve data for your report. The data source includes a connection type, a connection string, and the credentials that will be used when the database is queried.

By leaving the Make This A Shared Data Source check box cleared, you are creating a data source that can be used only with the report you are currently building. That's okay for now. In Chapter 4, you'll learn more about the difference between report-specific data sources and shared data sources.

9 Click Credentials.

The Data Source Credentials dialog box is displayed:

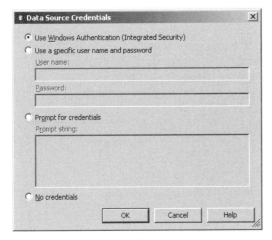

You can click the applicable option to override the authentication method that you specified in the Data Link Properties dialog box. Authentication methods include Windows Authentication, a single user's credentials, a prompt at runtime for the user's credentials, or no credentials at all. (You learn more about credential management in Chapter 8, "Managing Content.")

10 Click Cancel.

11 Click Next.

Getting Data for the Report

In this next step of the Report Wizard, you design the query that will be displayed in the report. The query must conform to the relational database syntax that you defined in the data source. You must get this query correct, or you won't be able to continue with this wizard.

In this procedure, you paste in a query that summarizes the Adventure Works sales for each employee by year, sales territory group, and sales territory country.

Design a query

1   Start Microsoft Notepad.

2   On the File menu, click Open.

3   Open the Sales Summary.txt file in the C:\rs2000sbs\chap03 folder.

4   Copy the following query entirely:

```
SELECT
    SUM(FactResellerSales.SalesAmount) AS ActualSales,
    DimTime.CalendarYear,
    DimSalesTerritory.SalesTerritoryGroup,
    DimSalesTerritory.SalesTerritoryCountry,
    DimEmployee.FirstName + ' ' + DimEmployee.LastName AS Employee
FROM
    FactResellerSales
    INNER JOIN DimEmployee ON
        FactResellerSales.EmployeeKey = DimEmployee.EmployeeKey
    INNER JOIN DimTime ON
        FactResellerSales.OrderDateKey = DimTime.TimeKey
    INNER JOIN DimSalesTerritory ON
        FactResellerSales.SalesTerritoryKey =
DimSalesTerritory.SalesTerritoryKey            AND
        DimEmployee.SalesTerritoryKey =
DimSalesTerritory.SalesTerritoryKey
GROUP BY
    DimTime.CalendarYear,
    DimSalesTerritory.SalesTerritoryGroup,
    DimSalesTerritory.SalesTerritoryCountry,
    DimEmployee.FirstName + ' ' + DimEmployee.LastName
```

5   Paste the copied query into the Query String box on the Design The Query page of the Report Wizard.

Now the current page of the Report Wizard looks like this:

▶   **Note**   Instead of typing or pasting in a query string, you can also click the Edit button to open the Query Builder to create a SELECT statement using a graphical interface. If you've used the Query Builder in SQL Server Enterprise Manager, you will be in familiar territory here. If you haven't used it, you can learn more about the Query Builder in Chapter 7.

This query will be used to retrieve data from the defined data source for use in your report. The format of the query depends on the data source you selected. For this procedure, because you selected a Microsoft SQL Server data source, you use Transact-SQL to build your query.

The query that you create is just one of several items stored in a dataset. As you learned earlier in this chapter, a dataset is a container for a pointer to the data source and the query you design. (You learn more about designing queries to create a dataset in Chapter 4.) In general, you can type a query directly into the Query String box, use the Edit button to open the Query Builder, or paste in a query that has been tested first in Query Analyzer or saved in a file.

6   Click the Next button.

When you click the Next button, the query is validated against the data source. If there is any problem, such as an invalid column name, an error message will be displayed in the bottom section of the Design The Query page. You will not be able to continue past this page of the wizard until you correct the error.

How to Design a Report

After defining the data source and the dataset, you're ready to move on to design considerations. Now you select a report type that defines how the data is structured in the report. You also arrange the data within the selected structure and finish the design by applying a style template. These steps make it easy to create a nice-looking report without a lot of effort, but you'll still have an opportunity to make adjustments to the layout and style before you publish the report.

Structuring Data in the Report

This step of the Report Wizard requires you to select a report type that defines how the data will be structured in the report. You can choose between a tabular or a matrix report type.

In this procedure, you select the tabular report type for your report.

Choose a report type

1   Click Tabular.

The Report Wizard page looks like this:

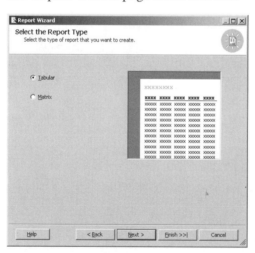

Notice that the Finish button is now enabled. You have, at this point, created a basic report that is ready for publishing. Now you can decide how you want to proceed. You could click the Finish button and make modifications using the Report Designer. However, to find out everything you can do with this tool, you'll continue designing your report with the wizard.

The report type defines the structure, or data region, of the data that is returned by the query you design. The Report Wizard allows you to present this information as either a table or a matrix. (You do have more options, but the Report Wizard limits you to these two data regions, referred to as report types in the wizard.) The main difference between these two types of data regions is the number of columns. A table has a fixed number of columns, whereas a matrix has a variable number of columns that is determined by the query results. You'll find more information about these and other data regions in Chapter 6, "Organizing Data in Reports."

2   Click the Next button.

Placing Data in the Report Structure

In this step of the Report Wizard, you arrange the data within the report type that you selected. This process determines how data is grouped and the order in which it is displayed. You can think of grouped data as the vertical sections of a report (although groups can be displayed next to each other), and the data order as the sequence in which the data is presented in the same row, vertically for groups and horizontally for columns.

In this procedure, you arrange the five fields produced by the query to build a report that displays the *ActualSales* amount for each *Employee* as details, in groups by *SalesTerritoryGroup* and *SalesTerritoryCountry*, with a page break for each *CalendarYear*.

Arrange data on the report

1   Click *CalendarYear*, and then click the Page button to place the CalendarYear field in the Page section of the Displayed Fields list.

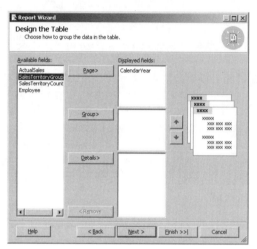

When you place a field in a display section, the corresponding section in the sample table is highlighted to show you where the field will appear in your report. Each column of data returned by the query is linked, or mapped, to a report field that is displayed in the Available Fields list until assigned to a section of the data region. When assigned to a data region's section, the report fields appear in the Displayed Fields list. The section to which you assign the field determines whether you see detail rows, aggregated rows, or both types of rows, in the report. Assignment of fields to data regions and the use of aggregations are discussed more thoroughly in Chapter 4 and Chapter 5, "Working with Expressions."

Because you are using a tabular report type, you can assign fields to the page, group, or details section of the report. For example, a field assigned to the page section will not be included in the table in the report, but will instead be placed in a textbox positioned at the top left corner of the report. Each distinct value for a page field creates a page break in the report. Fields added to the group section of the report are used to break the table into separate sections, which can include subtotals by section.

The table rows are built from the values for the fields assigned to the details section of the report. There is one table row for each row returned by the defined query. A numeric field in the details section is

summed up into the subtotals if you select the option to include subtotals. You can decide later whether you want to hide the details in
the report if you prefer to display just summary information.

▶ **Note**   If you choose a matrix report type, the field assignment is slightly different. The wizard still includes the page and details sections, but the group section is replaced by sections for columns and rows. You will need to assign at
least one field to each of these sections to build a matrix, which is also known
as a crosstab. Matrix reports are covered in Chapter 6.

2   Click *SalesTerritoryGroup*, and then click the Group button to place
the field in the Group section. Repeat for *SalesTerritoryCountry*.
Alternatively, you can use the drag-and-drop feature to move a field
from the list of available fields to the appropriate section.

▶ **Note**   The order in which you add fields to each section determines the
sequence in which the data displays in the report. The fields in the Group section will be displayed in order from top to bottom or from left to right, depending
on the style template that you select in a later step in the wizard. Fields in the
Details section will be displayed in columns in order from left to right.

3   Drag *ActualSales* to the Details section, which is the bottom section of
the Displayed Fields list, and then drag *Employee* to the same section.
The Design The Table page of the Report Wizard looks like this:

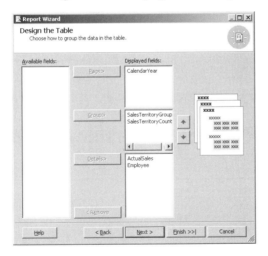

▶ **Tip**   Even after the fields are placed into the Displayed Fields list, you can still
rearrange them to affect their order in the respective sections.

If you had selected the Matrix option on the previous page, Select The Report Type, you would see the Design The Matrix page here instead of the Design The Table page.

4   Click *Employee*, and then click the Up button to move *Employee* above *ActualSales*. You can also use drag-and-drop to rearrange fields within a data region.

Now the page looks like this:

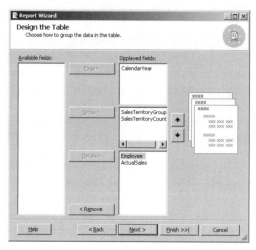

5   Click the Next button.

Applying a Style Template

In this step of the Report Wizard, you make your last design decision for your report. When you apply a style template, you define the "look and feel" of the report.

In this procedure, you define a block layout for the table, which includes group subtotals, and select the Bold style template.

Select a report style

1   Click Block.

▶   **Note**   This page of the wizard will not be displayed if you selected a matrix report type.

Notice that the sample layout changes to give you a preview of the block layout. Here, you are choosing a layout style for the tabular report that controls the placement of detail rows relative to aggregated rows on the report. You can also choose to include subtotals or enable drilldown. The difference between the layout options will become clearer when you can actually view your report. At that time, you'll see examples of the other layout styles for comparison.

On this page of the Report Wizard, you must select either a stepped or block report layout style. In the stepped layout, each distinct group value is arranged on its own row and in its own column. The drilldown option (which displays hidden detail data) is available only for the stepped layout. By contrast, the block layout is more compact—you place data in each column, and start a new row only for additional detail rows within the same group or for a new group value.

2   Select the Include Subtotals check box to include subtotals in your report.

3   Click the Next button.

4   Click each table style to preview the style in the Choose The Table Style page.

The assignment of a style template to a tabular or matrix report sets the overall color theme and font usage for the report.

5   Click Bold to set the style for your report.

6   Click the Next button.

How to Complete the Wizard

You're almost finished building your report by using the wizard. You've defined where to find the data, what data to include in the report, and how the data will look in the report. All that remains is to specify a location on the Report Server that will be the ultimate destination of your report when it is published, and to give your report a name.

Finishing the Report Wizard

In the last step of the Report Wizard, you enter information for your report that you need for deployment. You also have an opportunity to review a summary of the selections that you made throughout the wizard and to proceed to a preview of your report.

In this procedure, you provide the URL for your local Report Server, specify the Adventure Works folder for deployment, and name your report. When you're finished with the wizard, you will be able to preview the report.

Set report and project properties

1 Confirm that the current page of the Report Wizard looks like this:

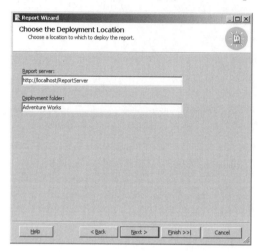

The deployment location is a URL to the Report Server that will host the report as well as the folder into which the report will be placed on the server. This step of the Report Wizard simply sets the project properties and does not actually *deploy*, or publish, the report to the Report Server. Notice that the default folder has the same name as your project. If this folder does not already exist, the folder will be created when you deploy the report. Otherwise, the report will be deployed to the existing folder.

▶ **Important** The server name will not be validated in this step. If you enter an incorrect server name, deployment fails. You can update the project properties in the Solution Explorer if this occurs. You'll learn how to do this in Chapter 8.

2 Click the Next button.

3 Type **Sales Summary** in the Report Name box.

▶ **Important** If you use the name of a report that has already been deployed to the Report Server, you will overwrite the published report during deployment of the report in Visual Studio—but only if you deploy the report to the same folder as the existing folder. There will be no warning message during deployment stating that you are about to overwrite an existing report, so be careful when assigning names and folder locations to reports.

4   Scroll through the information in the Report Summary box to review your selections.

5   Select the Preview Report check box to preview your report.

The final page of the Report Wizard now looks like this:

At the completion of the Report Wizard, you can immediately preview the report. Sometimes you might prefer to make some additional changes to the report before you display the preview. If you do not select the Preview Report check box, the Report Designer displays your report in layout mode. If the report is in layout mode, you can easily switch to preview mode by clicking the Preview tab in the Report Designer.

▶   **Tip**   An important reason to preview the report is to check the size of the columns. The columns will all default to the same size and will probably not be wide enough for data. Also, you might need to adjust formatting for numeric values. You can fix these problems using the layout mode and then review the fixes using the preview mode.

6   Click the Finish button.

How to Publish a Report

When you finish designing your report, you need to preview it to check the layout and make some corrections to improve its appearance. When you finish making these corrections, you'll wrap up this authoring stage of the reporting life cycle by publishing the report to the Report Server, where it can be accessed by users.

Checking the Report Layout

Previewing your report is important so that you can check the layout after finishing the design steps. You need to make sure that you get the data you expected and that the data is formatted correctly.

In this procedure, you explore your report in preview mode so that you can see the results of the selections you made in the Report Wizard.

Preview a report

1   If you selected the check box to preview the report on the last page of the Report Wizard, you will see your report in preview mode. If not, just click the Preview tab in the Report Designer.

When you display a report in preview mode, the query is executed and the query results are stored in a dataset and assigned to fields. The report is then rendered according to the assignment of the fields to data regions that you specified as well as the layout and style that you selected. At this point, the report format and the report data are merged to produce the preview that you can see in the Report Designer. In preview mode, you can interact with the report just as if it were published to the server so that you can test the results before making it available on the Report Server.

Your screen now looks like this:

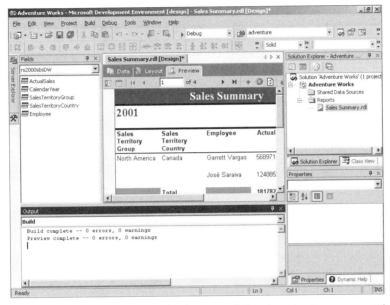

Take a moment to review the layout of the data in the report. The *CalendarYear* field is displayed in the top left corner. Just below the *CalendarYear*, you can see the column names in the table header with the details displayed in rows by groups. The first group is *SalesTerritoryGroup*, and the second group is *SalesTerritoryCountry*. Because these fields are defined as groups, their values are displayed only in the first row of details within that group. In the example, you can see actual sales amounts for employees Garrett Vargas and José Saraiva for Canada in North America. The row beneath these details is the group subtotal for Canada.

After the wizard is closed, you can't return to the wizard to make layout changes. Instead, you must create a new report, which you might find easier to do than making changes to the layout directly in the Report Designer. If you were to use the wizard to create a stepped report with subtotals (on the Choose The Table Layout page) using the same query, the report would look like this:

Sales Summary (Stepped)			
2001			
Sales Territory Group	**Sales Territory Country**	**Employee**	**Actual Sales**
North America			$9,665,054
	Canada		**$1,817,824**
		Garrett Vargas	$568,971
		José Saraiva	$1,248,853
	United States		**$7,847,231**
		David Campbell	$608,546
		Fernando Caro	$1,499,400
		Michael Blythe	$903,230

Notice that North America is now in its own row, and its subtotal is included on the same row. Then Canada appears by itself on the next row, followed by the detail rows. This report style is longer than the block layout.

If you had instead used the wizard to create a report with a stepped layout with drilldown selected, the report—with North America and Canada expanded to show the detail rows—would look like this:

Sales Summary (Stepped - Drilldown)			
2001			
Sales Territory Group	**Sales Territory Country**	**Employee**	**Actual Sales**
⊟ North America			$9,665,054
	⊟ Canada		**$1,817,824**
		Garrett Vargas	$568,971
		José Saraiva	$1,248,853
	⊞ United Stat		**$7,847,231**

With drilldown, the user can, at will, click the plus sign to expand the report and click the minus sign to collapse the report. By default, the report is completely collapsed when it is opened.

2   Scroll down to the bottom of the first page. Notice the group subtotal for United States. Beneath this group subtotal, you can see the group subtotal for *SalesTerritoryGroup*, which is the subtotal for Canada and the United States.

3   Click the Next Page button on the Preview toolbar to view the page for 2002.

Because you assigned *CalendarYear* to the Page data region of the report, each page contains data for a separate year. You can use the page buttons on the Preview toolbar to navigate between pages, or you can type in the page number that you want to view:

4   Scroll to the bottom of the second page to see the layout when there are multiple values for SalesTerritoryGroup, and then scroll back to the top of the page.

5   If you can't see the full width of the report, scroll horizontally to see the Actual Sales column.

The top of your report looks like this:

2002

Sales Territory Group	Sales Territory Country	Employee	Actual Sales
Europe	France	Ranjit Varkey Chudukatil	1028496.7453 06
	Total		1028496.7453 06
	United Kingdom	José Saraiva	925011.83907 1001
	Total		925011.83907 1001

Notice that the text is wrapping in several columns: *SalesTerritory-Country*, *Employee*, and *ActualSales*. In addition, the format of the ActualSales values can be improved.

Correcting Report Layout Issues

Preview mode in Report Designer allows you to see where you need to clean up your report, but you need to switch to layout mode to fix the problems. In layout mode, you can adjust every property of every element in the report, giving you complete control over everything that you can see. You can easily switch back and forth to test the results of your changes to the report in layout mode.

In this procedure, you use layout mode to improve the appearance of the report, and check the results by again previewing the report.

Fix column sizes and data formatting in the report layout

1   Click the Layout tab.

The report is displayed in layout mode:

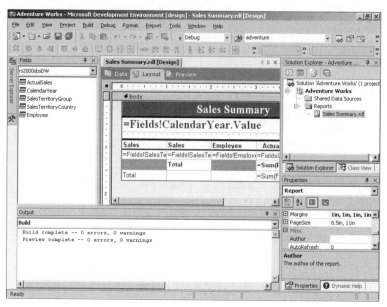

Notice the rulers that appear both above and to the left of the report layout. You can use these rulers as a visual guide when making changes to the report, such as when resizing report items or positioning new report items.

2   Click any cell in the table to display the column and row handles.

The table now looks like this:

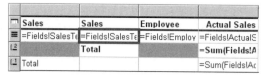

The column handles are the shaded cells that appear above the table, and the row handles are the shaded cells with icons that are shown to the left of the table. You use these handles to modify the table properties.

3   Position your cursor between the second and third column handles, and then click and drag to widen the second column, Sales Territory Country, to approximately 1.5 inches.

Now the table looks like this:

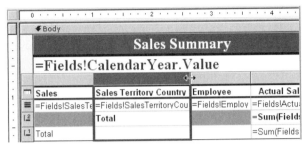

You can drag the column only when the cursor is properly positioned and the cursor changes to a double-headed arrow. Making the column bigger eliminates the text-wrapping problem, but it also requires you to have some idea of the maximum length of the data that could appear in that column.

4   Position the cursor between the third and fourth column handles, and then click and drag to widen the Employee column to approximately 1.75 inches.

5   Right-click the fourth column handle, above Actual Sales, to select the entire column, and then click Properties.

The Properties window for the selected column, named TableColumn4, is displayed in Visual Studio:

6 You might need to scroll through the Properties window to find the *Format* property, and then type **C0** in the *Format* property field to format the field as currency with no decimal places.

▶ **Note**   Use .NET formatting strings to control the display of the data. You can find more information about formatting numeric strings online at *http: //msdn.microsoft.com/library/default.asp?url=/library/en-us/cpguide/html /cpconstandardnumericformatstrings.asp*. Information about formatting date strings is located at *http://msdn.microsoft.com/library/default.asp?url=/library /en-us/cpguide/html/cpconDateTimeFormatStrings.asp*.

7 Click the Preview tab to preview the modified report.

The newly formatted report is displayed:

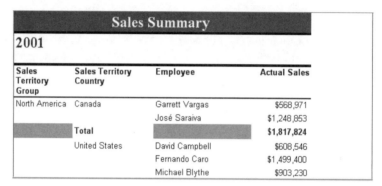

Sales Summary			
2001			
Sales Territory Group	Sales Territory Country	Employee	Actual Sales
North America	Canada	Garrett Vargas	$568,971
		José Saraiva	$1,248,853
	Total		**$1,817,824**
	United States	David Campbell	$608,546
		Fernando Caro	$1,499,400
		Michael Blythe	$903,230

The text-wrapping problem is solved, and the format of the Actual Sales column is improved. Your first report is ready for publishing!

Publishing a Report

Now you'll wrap up the authoring stage of the reporting life cycle by publishing the report to the Report Server, where it can be accessed by the user community.

In this procedure, you deploy a report solution that enables you to publish your report to your local Report Server.

Deploy a report solution

1 On the File menu, click Save All.

2 In the Solution Explorer window, right-click the Adventure Works solution (not the project) at the top of the tree, and then click Properties.

The Solution 'Adventure Works' Property Pages dialog box is displayed.

3 Click the Configuration Properties folder in the left pane.

The project contexts is displayed in the right pane.

4 Verify that the Deploy check box is selected.

The Solution 'Adventure Works' Property Pages dialog box looks like this:

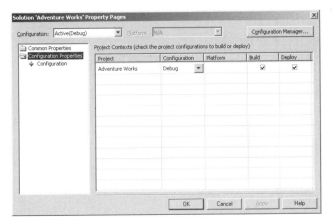

5 Click the OK button.

6 On the Build menu, click Deploy Solution.

The Output window displays the progress of deployment. Deployment of the solution is complete when you see messages in the Output window announcing that the build and deploy operations succeeded:

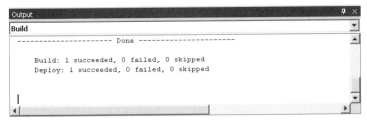

In addition to deploying an entire solution, you have the option to deploy a single report or multiple reports within a project or solution. A report is published by using one of these deployment options to transfer it from Visual Studio to the Report Server. There are other ways to publish a report that you will learn about in Chapter 8.

Managing a Report

You can manage published reports by using the Web application called Report Manager, which is supplied by Reporting Services. Management of reports includes such activities as setting report properties and execution properties; managing content in folders; and applying security on the Report Server to control how users interact with reports.

How to Change Report Properties

You perform only a few management tasks in this chapter. (You'll learn about all the management tasks in the chapters in Part 3, "Managing the Report Server.") You take a look at the current settings of some of the report properties, and then add a description so that a user knows what your report contains before she opens it.

Reviewing Report Properties

Each report has a set of properties pages that you must manage. You need to know how to use the Report Manager to find these properties and to review the types of properties you can manage.

In this procedure, you navigate from the Home page of Report Manager to the Properties page of your report.

Open the report's Properties page

1 Open Internet Explorer.
2 Type the URL **http://localhost/Reports** to open the Report Manager. The Home page of Report Manager is displayed:

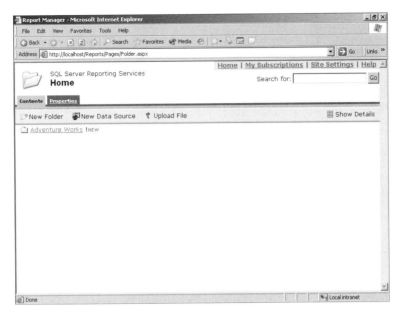

3   Click the Adventure Works folder link.

The folder contents are displayed:

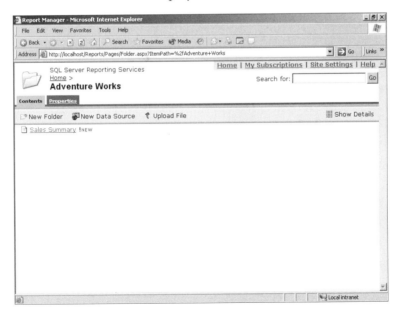

Notice that this page has a Properties tab in addition to the Contents tab. (You learn more about managing folder properties in Chapter 8.) Currently, the Adventure Works folder contains only one report, the Sales Summary report that you just published.

4   Click the Sales Summary report link.

Reporting Services generates and displays the Sales Summary report:

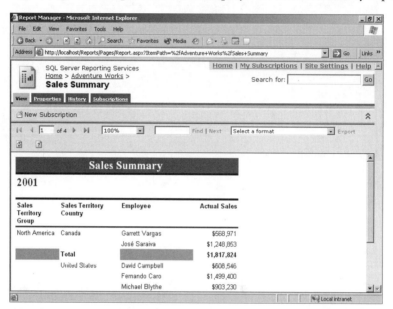

The View tab displays by default when you open a report. Three other tabs are available for this report: Properties, History, and Subscriptions. In this section, you review the Properties page. Later, in Chapter 7, you learn more about the other tabs.

▶ **Tip**   You don't have to wait for the report to display before clicking another tab.

5   Click the Properties tab.

The Properties page for the Sales Summary report is displayed:

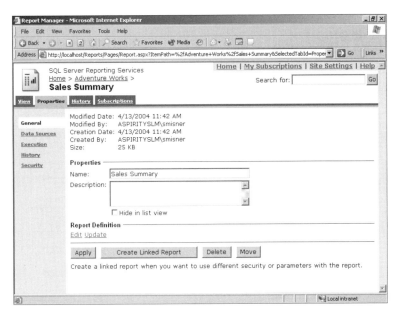

On this page, you can see the author and also the date the report was created. The modification author and date of modification match the creation information until the report is subsequently modified.

Notice that you can change the name of the report on this page and add a description. The other tasks that you can perform on this page covered in Chapter 8.

Notice the links in the left frame of the browser window. There are many types of report properties, which are logically organized into separate pages where you can apply changes to current settings. Properties determine, for example, how the report appears in Report Manager, how users can interact with the report, and how the Report Server connects to the data sources. You'll review report properties in greater detail in Chapter 7.

Changing Report Properties

Often, you will want to add a description so that a user knows what your report contains before opening it. This property is accessible on the main properties page of the report.

In this procedure, you add a description and observe how a description is displayed on the Contents page of a folder.

Add a description

1   In the Description box, type **Actual sales by year, territory, and salesperson.**

Your screen looks like this:

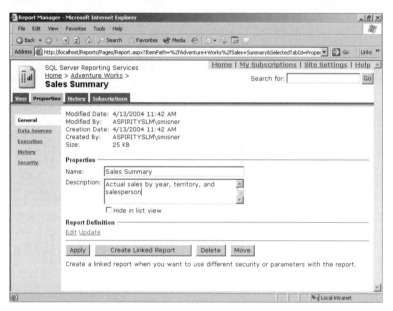

This report description is displayed on the Contents page and, importantly, is visible only to users who have been granted permission to view the report.

2   Click the Apply button.

Clicking the Apply button doesn't appear to change anything. However, the report description is now visible on the Contents page of the Adventure Works folder.

3   Click the Adventure Works folder link at the top left corner of the browser window.

Your screen looks like this:

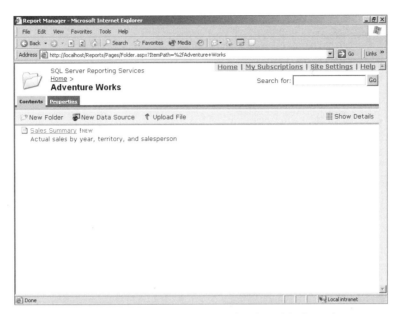

Notice how the report description is displayed below the report name.

How to Change Execution Properties

Execution properties allow you to manage reports by balancing system resources and performance with the users' information requirements. For example, you set up caching to achieve a reasonable balance when data used in the report is not changing rapidly at the source. To use caching, you first need to change the data sources properties so that you can assign logon credentials that will be used to execute the report for the cache. Separate logon credentials are required by Reporting Services to implement report caching to make a single report available to many users.

Reviewing Execution Properties

Execution properties are a subset of the report properties maintained for each report. When you understand the implications of the execution property settings, you can choose the most appropriate property setting for your reporting environment.

In this procedure, you open the Execution Properties page for your report to review the available options.

Open the report's Execution Properties page

1   Click the Sales Summary report link.

Assume for a moment that you've just started a new browser session. Just like the previous time you opened this report, a message is displayed to let you know that several activities are occurring: "Report is being generated." Each time a report executes on demand, as you initiated in this step, a query is executed to retrieve data from the rs2000sbsDW database. The data is processed with the report, which is then rendered into the HTML display in your browser window.

2   Click the Properties tab.

3   Click the Execution link in the left frame of the page.

The Execution Properties page is displayed:

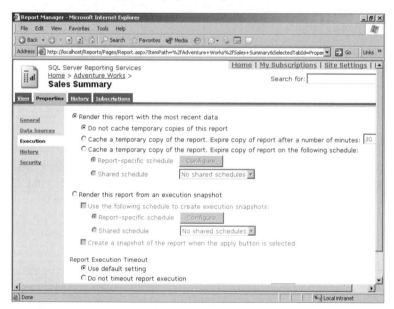

Notice that you can render the report either on demand or on a scheduled basis. When rendered on demand, the report typically displays the most recent data and might or might not use caching. By default, a report renders on demand without caching. When rendered on a scheduled basis, the report is stored as an execution snapshot, which captures data for the report at a point in time.

Execution properties control when processing of the report occurs. When a report executes on demand, which occurs every time another user opens the report, the defined query runs, and the query results are merged with the report definition to produce the HTML output format. You can alternatively set the execution properties to process the report at a scheduled time so that the report is ready when accessed. However, if you choose to do this, let users know that the data in the report is not current. Another option is to cache a report temporarily to make the same output available to several users for the duration of a specified time frame. The key difference between a snapshot and a cached report is that the snapshot is stored permanently until physically deleted, whereas the cache is stored temporarily with a predetermined expiration. The options you have for specifying execution properties are covered in Chapter 8.

Changing Data Sources Properties

Data sources properties define the connection to be used for query execution. You can change these properties to override the credentials used for authentication when the report executes. Queries that run unattended, such as when a report is cached or scheduled for execution, require stored credentials. These credentials are encrypted when stored in the ReportServer database. (You'll learn more about using secured credentials in Chapter 8.) To set up a cache for your report, you need to change the credential information in the data sources properties.

Use secured credentials

1   Click the Data Sources link in the left frame of the page.

2   Click the Credentials Stored Securely On The Report Server option.

3   Type **ReportExecution** as the user name.

4   Type **ReportExecution** as the password.

▶   **Important**   In a production environment in which you are using stored credentials, it's important to test the report to ensure that you have entered the user name and password correctly. The credentials will not be validated until the report executes.

Your screen now looks like this:

5   Click the Apply button.

Changing Execution Properties

You might want to temporarily cache a report to improve performance. When a user first opens the report, a copy of the report is placed in temporary storage and made available to other users who open the same report. You can also assign a time limit for the cache so that the report can be periodically refreshed with more current data.

▶ **Note**   The type of caching discussed in this chapter refers to the access of a single report by multiple users. When you open a report, the report is automatically cached for you as part of your browser session. You can then return to this report repeatedly during the same session without having to wait for the query to execute again, regardless of the current setting of the report's execution properties. When you close the browser window, the report is removed from this cache. You learn more about session caching in Chapter 8.

In this procedure, you change the report execution properties to cache your report, and set the cache to expire after 60 minutes.

Define a report cache

1 Click the Execution link.

2 Click the Cache A Temporary Copy Of The Report. Expire Copy Of Report After A Number Of Minutes option to cache the report and expire after a specified number of minutes. Change the number of minutes to **60**.

Your screen looks like this:

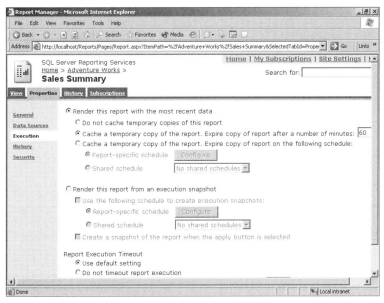

3 Click the Apply button at the bottom of the page.

The next time this report is opened, a temporary copy of it will be placed in the cache to speed up its display for any later requests by other users within the same hour. At the end of 60 minutes, the temporary copy is removed from the cache. A new copy is placed in the cache only when a user requests the report again.

As mentioned earlier, by using the caching option, you can improve performance for the next user who opens the same report. Any subsequent request for a report results in the display of the cached copy of the report rather than in the execution of the query and processing of the report. That is, any subsequent request displays the cached report until the cache expires. The purpose of expiring the cache on a periodic basis is to force the report to be refreshed with the most current data when the next user accesses the report. The result is a new cached instance of the report until the next scheduled expiration.

▶ **Tip**   This feature is useful when you have a query that takes a few minutes or more to execute and many people want to see the same report. It minimizes the demand for resources on the database server, reduces the level of network traffic associated with transporting the data from the database server to the Report Server, and speeds up the display of reports when requested. For more details about report caching, refer to Chapter 8.

Accessing a Report

Each published report has its own URL on the Report Server. Instead of using the Report Manager to navigate through folders to find a report, you can enter the report's URL address into your browser. You can also use this URL in a hyperlink that you add to a custom HTML page. In fact, you could even include additional characters in the URL to control the behavior of the report, such as formatting the report with a different rendering extension, but you learn how to do that in Chapter 16, "Building Custom Reporting Tools." For now, it's easiest to use the Report Manager to find and view a report online, and to export the report to another format. (Chapter 16 can be found on the companion CD.)

How to Explore a Report

Now that you successfully authored and managed your report, you are ready for the access stage of the reporting life cycle. When you access a report online, you can use a toolbar in the viewer to help you explore your report. After opening the report, you can navigate through its pages or search for specific text so that you can jump forward in it.

Displaying a Report

At this point, you're ready to use the Report Manager to launch the applicable viewer to display your report online. By default, the report is displayed with the HTML Viewer.

In this procedure, you explore each page of your report and review the Help page for the HTML Viewer.

View report pages

1 Click the View tab.

2 The first page of the report, for calendar year 2001, is displayed. This presentation of the report is nearly identical to the version you saw in the Report Designer. You now have the HTML Viewer that includes a report toolbar to help you explore and interact with the report. For example, you can use controls in the toolbar to page through the report, to search for a string in the report, or to export the report to another format. The HTML Viewer is covered in more detail in Chapter 11, "Accessing Reports." Click the Next Page button on the View toolbar to view the sales data for each year.

3 Click the Help button on the View toolbar to review the documentation for the HTML Viewer, and then close the new browser window that was opened.

The documentation for the HTML Viewer includes descriptions of each icon or control, the export formats available by default, and advanced report features such as parameter fields and credentials fields.

Searching a Report

Sometimes the information you're looking for can be difficult to find in a lengthy or multi-page report. The HTML Viewer provides a feature to help you find a text string anywhere in the report, from your current position to the end of the report.

In this procedure, you use the search feature to locate specific text in the report.

Find text in a report

1 In the search box, located in the center of the View toolbar, type **Linda**. Click the Find link.

Your screen looks like this:

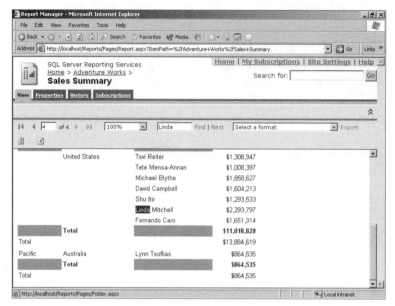

The Find link is not enabled until you type a string into the associated search box. When you click this link, the report scrolls to the first occurrence of this string in the report.

2   Click the Next link to find the next occurrence of the string.

The search operation begins in the currently selected page or section and continues across each page of the report until the end of the report is reached.

▶ **Tip**   You don't need to worry about using the correct case, because the search operation is not case-sensitive. However, you are limited to a string length of 256 characters.

How to Export a Report

The HTML format is not the only format you can use to view your report. You can also export the report to another format that allows you to create a file that you can open immediately or save to your computer. (Reporting Services includes several export formats, also referred to as rendering formats, which you'll review more closely in Chapter 12, "Rendering Reports.") In the next procedure, you export your report to the Excel format to see how easy it is to export a report to another format and to see the quality of the exported report.

Exporting a Report

The HTML Viewer toolbar provides a list box from which you can choose an export format. This feature gives you the flexibility to produce several versions of your report from a single platform.

In this procedure, you complete your tour of Reporting Services by exporting your report to an Excel format, opening the generated Excel workbook, and examining each sheet in the workbook, comparing them with the rendering of your report as HTML.

Export to Excel

1   Click Excel in the list box at the far right of the View toolbar.

Your screen now looks like this:

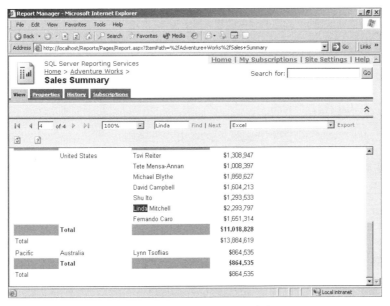

As mentioned earlier, the Export feature of the HTML Viewer gives you the ability to view the report in a different format. When you export the report, if a viewer is available for the selected format, a new browser window opens. For example, to export to the Excel format, you must have Microsoft Excel installed on your computer.

2   Click the Export link.

A new browser window opens and the File Download dialog box is displayed:

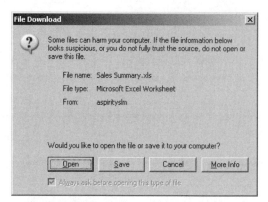

You can open the file to view it now, or you can save the file to view later.

3   Click Open.

The Report Server renders the report as an Excel file that downloads to your computer. The Excel application opens, and the report is displayed:

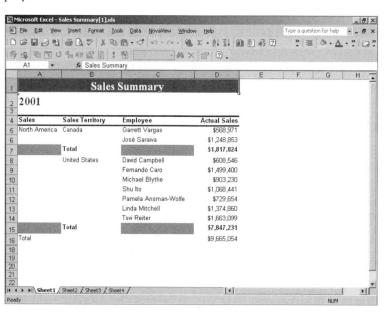

Notice that the report style in Reporting Services is closely reproduced in the Excel version of the report. Much of the color style, font style, and layout that you see in the HTML version of the report also appears in the Excel version. Each page has been placed on a separate sheet in the Excel workbook.

4 Click each sheet tab to review the sales data for each year.

With the report in this format, you can take advantage of all of Excel's features to interact with the report data and perform additional analysis that was not possible using the static report in the browser.

Chapter 3 Quick Reference

To	Do this
Start the Report Project Wizard	Start a new project in Visual Studio and select Report Project Wizard from the Business Intelligence Projects folder. You must provide a name for the project and solution, and designate a folder location for the solution.
Add a data source using the Report Wizard	On the Select The Data Source page, enter a name for the data source; select a connection type; and enter a connection string, or use the Edit button to access Data Link Properties dialog box to generate the connection string automatically. For example: `data source=localhost;initial catalog=rs2000sbsDW`
Add a query string using the Report Wizard	On the Design The Query page, enter or paste in a query string, or click the Edit button to open the Query Builder.
Select a report type using the Report Wizard	On the Select The Report Type page, click either the Tabular or Matrix option.
Arrange the data using the Report Wizard	On the Design The Table page, assign fields to the Page, Group, and Details sections. In the Design The Matrix table, assign fields to the Page, Columns, Rows, and Details sections.
Select a table layout using the Report Wizard	On the Choose The Table Layout page, select Block or Stepped, or optionally include subtotals. If you choose the stepped layout, you can enable drilldown.
Apply a style template using the Report Wizard	On the Choose The Table Style page or the Choose The Matrix Style page, click a style name. A preview of the style will be displayed.

To	Do this
Assign a deployment location and a report name using the Report Wizard	On the Choose The Deployment Location page, enter the URL for the Report Server to host the report. For example: `http://localhost/ReportServer`. Optionally, enter a folder name. The folder will be created on deployment if it does not already exist. This page requires a report name.
Preview a report	In Visual Studio, click the Preview tab.
Adjust the size of a column in a table	In Visual Studio, click the table to display the column and row handles. Then drag the column handle to the left to make the column smaller or to the right to make it larger.
Publish a report solution	On the Build menu of Visual Studio, click Deploy Solution.
Open Report Manager	Enter the URL in your browser. For example: `http://localhost/Reports`.
View a report	In Report Manager, navigate the folder hierarchy to the report, and then click the report link.
Manage report properties	With the report open in Report Manager, click the Properties tab. Use the applicable link in the left frame to access the set of properties to be managed. Set a property by clicking an option or selecting a check box, and then clicking the Apply button.
Export a report	With the report open in Report Manager, select the export format from the list box, and click the Export link.

Authoring Reports

Developing Basic Reports

In this chapter, you will learn how to:

- Add a new report to a project.
- Define data for a report.
- Add a table to a report.
- Group data in a table.
- Add items to a report.
- Edit properties of report items.

In Part 1, "Getting Started with Reporting Services," you learned how the activities of enterprise reporting are fully supported by the Reporting Services platform. You also explored the reporting life cycle by using Reporting Services to author, manage, and access a simple report. In the four chapters of Part 2, you'll focus on the authoring stage of the reporting life cycle by developing a variety of reports that use the range of features provided by the report design environment. In Part 3, "Managing the Report Server," you learn how to manage the reports you create.

This chapter shows you how to use the Report Designer in Microsoft Visual Studio so that you can prepare, structure, and format a tabular report. This chapter begins by explaining the output of the authoring stage—a report definition file.

Understanding a Report Definition File

Reporting Services generates a report by using a *report definition*, which describes the report's data, layout, and properties. Rather than build a report by using a programming language to create a series of instructions, you can use

Reporting Services to define exactly how you want the report to look. The use of a definition, as contrasted with a series of instructions, is known as a *declarative model*. Regardless of the language later used to generate the report from this definition, the result is the same and can be produced in many different formats.

The declarative model used by Reporting Services is constructed as a collection of XML elements that conform to a specific XML schema definition known as *Report Definition Language* (RDL). RDL is an open schema that can be extended by third parties, such as application developers and commercial software companies, to support specialized features. Microsoft developed RDL to promote the exchange of report definitions between report producers and report consumers.

A *report producer* is an application that is used to create a report definition. This application typically has a graphical user interface (GUI), allowing the report developer to create a report definition without writing any code. A developer could also build a custom application to generate a report definition completely from code—ultimately, it's the report definition that counts, not the means by which it is produced.

A report definition is transformed into the desired output format by an application known as a *report consumer*. The report consumer's job is to use the query embedded in the RDL to get data for the report and to merge the results with the set of instructions that define the report's layout and properties. Most commercial reporting applications produce reports in a proprietary format that can be used only within the vendor's report execution environment. By separating production and consumption, reports can be ported easily from one vendor's reporting platform to another, such as Reporting Services.

Preparing a Report by Using Report Designer

In Chapter 3, "Building Your First Report," you built a simple report by using some of the features of Report Designer. As you recall, Report Designer is integrated with Visual Studio. Because Report Designer generates a report definition, it is therefore a report producer. The integration of Report Designer into Visual Studio allows you to take advantage of a fully featured programming environment to develop many types of reports, from the most basic reports to quite complex ones. Many people find Report Designer easier to use than Microsoft Access to build reports. As you work in Visual Studio, the Report Designer automatically converts your report layout into RDL.

Even if you don't know any programming languages or XML, the Report Designer is easy enough to use to create attractive and information-rich reports. If, however, you're already an experienced programmer, you'll find that Report Designer has all the tools you need to extend the capabilities of your reports.

You can learn how to add custom development to your reports in Chapter 14, "Report Authoring with Custom Development," which can be found on the companion CD.

In this section, you use the Report Designer to prepare a report by creating a report project and adding a report to this new project. You then add a data source to the project to define the connection information that Reporting Services will use to get data for the report. To finish preparing the report, you create a dataset to define the data that will be displayed in the report.

How to Prepare a Report by Using Report Designer

You do all the authoring of the report using the three report views in the Report Designer rather than using the wizards that you used in Chapter 3. You use the Report Project template to create a new project, to which you add a blank report based on the Report template. Then you prepare the report by defining the data source and dataset to be used in the report.

Creating a New Report Project

In Chapter 3, you learned how to create a new project using the Report Project Wizard. Here, you use the Report Project template to create a project to contain your report.

In this procedure, you add a new project, My Adventure Works, not by using the wizard but by using the Report Project template.

Use the Report Project template

1   If necessary, start Visual Studio.
2   On the File menu, point to New, and then click Project.
3   In the New Project dialog box, click the Report Project template in the Business Intelligence Projects folder.
4   Type in a name for the project: **My Adventure Works**.
5   If necessary, type the following location for the project: **c:\rs2000sbs\Workspace**.
6   Click the OK button.

Creating a New Report

Now you're ready to add a report to your project. You still have the option to use the Report Wizard to help you set up a new report. However, in this section, you create a blank report without using the wizard. As you progress through this chapter, you'll add items to this report.

In this procedure, you add a new item to your project using the Report template.

Add a new item to a project

1   In Solution Explorer, right-click the Reports folder, point to Add, and then click Add New Item.

▶   **Note**   Notice that Add New Report is an available option. If you click Add New Report, the Report Wizard that you learned how to use in Chapter 3 is launched.

2   In the Add New Item dialog box, click the Report template.

Notice that you can launch the Report Wizard from this dialog box as well.

3   Type a report name: **Product Profitability.rdl**.

▶   **Important**   You must include the .rdl extension in the name of the report to ensure that Report Designer interacts properly with the report definition file.

4   Click the Open button.

Your screen looks like this:

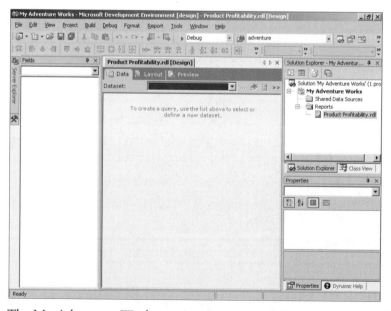

The My Adventure Works project now contains the new report. The Document window displays the report in the Data view.

Connecting to a Data Source

You already learned in Chapter 3 that a data source must include location information for the data that will be used in the report. At minimum, the data source includes the server, database name, and user credentials for authentication. The specific information contained by the data source depends on the type of database in which the data is stored.

A data source can be report-specific or shared. In Chapter 3, you created a report-specific data source that cannot be used in other reports in the project. Now you learn how to create a shared data source that can be used by several reports. By using a shared data source, you can more easily manage changes when the location of data or authentication information changes—you need to update only the shared data source instead of update each report that uses a report-specific data source.

In this procedure, you create a shared data source to define the connection to the rs2000sbsDW database in your SQL Server using Windows authentication.

Add a shared data source

1   In Solution Explorer, right-click the Shared Data Sources folder, and then click Add New Data Source.

The Connection tab of the Data Link Properties dialog box is displayed. By default, the data provider is Microsoft OLE DB Provider for SQL Server. Reporting Services can work with any OLE DB .Net data provider; you simply select the appropriate provider on the Provider tab as you build the data source.

2   In the Data Link Properties dialog box, type a server name: **localhost.**

▶   **Note**   This book assumes that you have all Reporting Services components and SQL Server installed on one computer. In a real-world environment, there are advantages to using localhost instead of a SQL Server instance, because you can easily reuse the data source when moving from development to production if everything is similarly contained in a single machine. However, if you maintain separate instances of SQL Server, this strategy will not be useful.

3   Click Use Windows NT Integrated Security.

4   Click rs2000sbsDW in the database list box.

5   Click OK.

The Solution Explorer window looks like this:

The Shared Data Sources folder now contains a shared data source item, rs2000sbsDW.rds.

Working with Datasets

A report definition can include one or more datasets. Each dataset is essentially a query used to gather data for the report, but it also contains a pointer to the data source and other information about the data, such as collation and case sensitivity. Each column from the dataset query becomes a field that can be used in the report. In Chapter 3, you used the Report Wizard to add a single dataset to your report. (You'll learn how to use multiple datasets in Chapter 7, "Building Advanced Reports.") In this section, you work with just a single dataset in your report, but you create it without the help of the wizard.

In this procedure, you enter a SQL query that returns data from a view that summarizes costs, sales amounts, and order quantities by product, product subcategory, and product category in January, 2003.

Add a dataset

1 On Dataset toolbar, click <New Dataset. . .> in the Dataset list box, as shown here:

The Dataset dialog box is displayed:

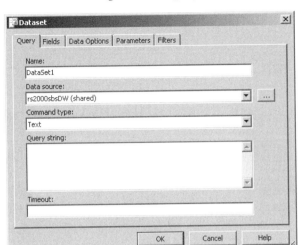

Notice that the data source defaults to the shared data source you created earlier, labeled rs2000sbsDW (shared). You can also create a new private data source for the report by clicking <New Data Source. . .> in the Data Source list box. Creating a new private data source opens the Data Link Properties dialog box, just like creating a shared data source did.

2 Replace the name of the dataset with **DataDetail**.

▶ **Important** The name of the dataset cannot contain a space.

3 Type the following SQL statement to define a query string for the dataset:

```
select * from vProductProfitability

where Year = 2003 and

MonthNumberOfYear = 1
```

This query uses a view in the rs2000sbsDW database, which was prepared specifically to provide data for reporting.

▶ **Tip** It's a good idea to use a view rather than a table when extracting data for reporting purposes. If business rules change for the reports, you can make the necessary updates to the view rather than modify each report using a the table—avoiding a maintenance nightmare. Another way to manage future changes to the report is to use a stored procedure, which you'll learn how to do in Chapter 7.

4   Click the OK button.

5   Click the Run button on the Dataset toolbar to test the query and see the result set.

The Run button is represented as an exclamation point in the Dataset toolbar. You might need to resize the Document window to view the entire toolbar.

The Document window now looks like this:

The Data view page shows the dataset in the Generic Query Designer layout. The query is displayed in the top section of the page, and the query results are shown in a grid in the bottom section. The query results are not stored with the report definition, but they are displayed here to help you validate that you are retrieving the expected data.

Each column in the grid becomes a field available for use in the report. These fields do not change over time unless you change the query in the dataset. Of course, as the data changes in the source database, the rows that appear in this grid, and eventually in the report, change when the query is executed.

6   Click the Generic Query Designer button (to the left of the Run button) to toggle the Query Builder on.

You can use the Query Builder to help you create a query using a graphical interface rather than simply typing a completed query as you did in this procedure. The Query Builder uses the same query interface available in Enterprise Manager. You'll learn how to use the Query Builder in Chapter 7.

7   Right-click the grid.

8   On the File menu, click Save All.

Structuring a Report by Using Report Designer

After you complete the preparatory steps to define a data source and to create a dataset, you are ready to work on the structure of your report. As you learned in Chapter 3, a data region is a report structure that contains the data. You'll learn how to use the matrix, list, chart, rectangle, and subreport data regions in Chapter 6, "Organizing Data in Reports." In this chapter, you work only with the table data region. You start by placing the table in the report body. Then you add fields to the table and define groups to organize the data into logical sections.

How to Add a Data Region

So far, you've used Solution Explorer to add a blank report and a shared data source to your project. You've also used the Data view of your report to add a dataset. Now you're ready to use the Layout view to structure data in your report. You use the Toolbox window to select a data region, and then you select a location for the data region on the design grid. After the data region is in place, you select fields from the Fields window and add them to the data region.

Adding Items from the Toolbox

The Toolbox window contains all the *report items* available. Report items can be data regions, graphical elements, and freestanding text. You can choose from six data regions: table, matrix, rectangle, list, subreport, and chart. Graphical elements you can add include a line and an image. You can add one or more of these report items to your report. You can even add multiple data regions, which you'll learn how to do in Chapter 6. You'll learn how to add the other types of report items later in this chapter.

In this procedure, you add a table to the design grid.

Add a table

1   Click the Layout tab.

2   In the Window toolbar on the left side of your screen, hover the pointer over the Hammer and Wrench icon to open the Toolbox window.

If the Toolbox window is not visible and the Hammer and Wrench icon is not in the Window toolbar, you will need to click Toolbox on the View menu to show it.

3   In the Toolbox window, click Table.

4   Point to the intersection of the top row and first column of grid lines in the body of the report, and then click to add a table.

If you are using the Visual Studio default layout for Windows, your screen looks like this:

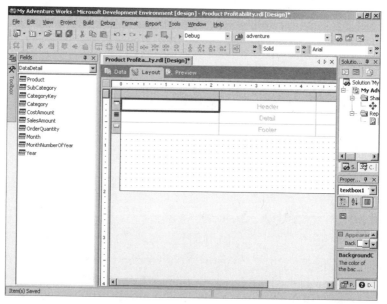

You'll learn how to place the other items in the design grid later in this chapter and in Chapter 6.

▶   **Tip**   You can also drag an item from the Toolbox window and drop it on the design grid in the desired location.

Notice that the initial layout of the table has three columns and three rows. Each row handle—the shaded area on the left border of the table—has a unique icon to represent the row type. The first row is a table header, the second row is a detail row, and the third row is a table footer. The detail row repeats for each row in the dataset. The header and footer rows each appear only once in the table.

Working with Table Rows

A *table* is a collection of cells. Each cell of the table is initially filled with a textbox. A textbox can contain either static text or a formula. The formula can refer simply to a field from a dataset, or it can include more complex calculations.

In this procedure, you add fields to each row of the table.

Add fields to a table

1   In the Fields window, click Product and drag the field to the first cell of the detail row.

Your table looks like this:

Notice that the field name is automatically placed in the table header of the first column as static text. An expression is added to the first column's detail row:

```
=Fields!Product.Value
```

This expression is evaluated when the report is processed and replaced with values in the Product column of the dataset that you created. Expressions that place a field value into a textbox always use this syntax. If you prefer to type a field expression into a textbox directly, just place the field name between the exclamation point and the period. However, using drag-and-drop is safer because it ensures proper spelling of the expression.

▶   **Tip**   Because the field name can be used in the table header row, build your query to give columns a report-friendly name. For example, if the table column in the database is labeled vProduct, consider writing your query as follows:

```
Select vProduct as Product...
```

Reporting Services automatically converts underscores to spaces and adds a space before capital letters in the middle of a word. For example, both Product_Name and ProductName would appear as Product Name.

Each row of the dataset becomes a separate detail row in the table when the report is processed. The size of the table adapts dynamically to the number of rows returned by the dataset's query. By default, the table is added with three columns. You'll add an additional column to this report in Chapter 5.

2   Make sure the first column is approximately 2 inches wide. If necessary, position your pointer between the first and second columns and drag to widen the column to 2 inches.

3   In the Fields window, click *SalesAmount* and drag to the second cell of the detail row.

Notice that the field name *SalesAmount* is automatically changed to Sales Amount in the table header. Notice also that the string in the table header and the expression in the detail row of the second column are right-justified. The field *SalesAmount* is a numeric column to which Report Designer automatically applies right justification.

4   Resize the second column to approximately 1.25 inches.

5   In the Fields window, click *OrderQuantity* and drag to the third cell of the detail row.

6   Resize the third column to approximately 1.25 inches.

7   In the Fields window, click *SalesAmount* and drag to the second cell of the table footer.

Your table now looks like this:

Product	Sales Amount	Order Quantity
=Fields!Product.Value	=Fields!SalesAmour	=Fields!OrderQuanti
	=Sum(Fields!SalesA	

When you add a numeric field to a table header or table footer, the Report Designer automatically adds a *Sum* function to the expression to aggregate the values in the column to which the field was assigned. In this case, when the report is processed, the sum of *SalesAmount* is calculated from the detail rows in the dataset and is displayed in this table footer cell.

8   In the Fields window, click *OrderQuantity* and drag to the third cell of the table footer.

9   Click the first cell of the table footer, and then type **Grand Total**.

You can enter a string into any cell. The string is treated as a constant when the report is processed.

▶ **Tip**   It's good practice in report design, when using aggregate functions like *Sum* in a table header or table footer, to add descriptive text to the same row so that the reader understands what the value represents.

10 On the File menu, click Save All.

11 Click the Preview tab.

The top of your report looks like this:

Product	Sales Amount	Order Quantity
AWC logo cap	477.5895	85
Cable lock	720	48
Full-finger Gloves, L	4228.761875	176
Full-finger Gloves, M	2129.56744	87
Full-finger Gloves, S	197.548	8
Half-finger Gloves, M	704.0898	46
Half-finger Gloves, S	336.7386	22
HL Fork	2547.339	15

There is one row for the table header, which shows the field names in the header row, and one detail row for each row in the dataset.

12 Click the Next Page button in the Preview toolbar.

13 Scroll to the bottom of the page.

The table footer displays the string Grand Total and the sum of the detail rows for *SalesAmount* and *OrderQuantity*.

How to Group Data in a Table

When a report has many detail rows, it is often helpful to organize the detail rows into groups. You now insert groups into the table to improve the arrangement of data. After adding the groups, you add fields to the group headers and a function to subtotal the detail rows within each group.

Grouping Data in a Table

A group is a set of detail rows that have something in common. For example, in your report's dataset, each detail row has a unique product name, but many products share the same product category. If a group is added to the report based on a product's category, all products for one category are arranged together and then followed by another set of detail rows with a different category. You can also nest a group within a group. Because each product category has several product subcategories, you can add another group to further divide the detail rows into smaller sets.

In this procedure, you add two groups to the table to organize detail rows by Category and SubCategory.

Add groups to the table

1   Click the Layout tab.

2   Click the table to display the row and column handles.

3   Right-click the row handle for the detail row, and then click Insert Group.

The Grouping And Sorting Properties dialog box is displayed:

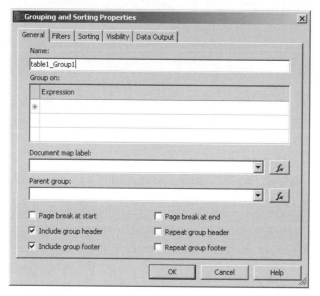

A default name is assigned to the group: table1_Group1. Every item, including a group, that you add to a report is assigned a name. The table you are working with is table1, so the first group added to this table is named table1_Group1. You have the option to keep this name or supply a new name.

▶ **Tip**   Assigning a new name to a group makes it easier to remember how the group is being used. For example, you could use the field name by which the table detail rows will be grouped.

4   Change the name to **table1_Category**.

5   Click =Fields!Category.Value in the first Expression list box.

When you display the Expression list, the Grouping And Sorting Properties dialog box looks like this:

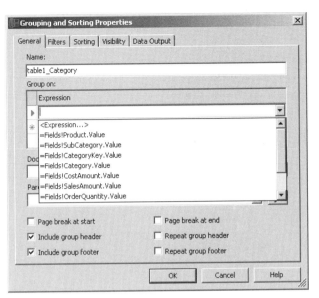

Notice that each item in the list is an expression formed from each field in the dataset. For each unique value of the selected expression, there is a group in the table.

Also notice from the checked options that, by default, the group header and group footer are included. When a group header and group footer are included in a table, the result is the Stepped layout that you reviewed in Chapter 3. Excluding the group header and group footer results in a table with the Block layout that you saw in that chapter.

The Grouping And Sorting Properties dialog box contains several tabs that you can use to manage properties for a group. You'll learn more about using the other properties in Chapter 5 and Chapter 6.

6   Click the OK button.

7   Right-click the row handle for the detail row, and then click Insert Group.

▶ **Note**   The placement of the new group relative to the existing group is determined by the row you right-click. When you select the detail row, the new group is nested between the existing groups and the detail row. If you select an existing group, the new group is added between the selected group and either the other existing groups, if any, or the detail row when there are no other existing groups.

8   Change the name to **table1_SubCategory**.

9   Click =Fields!SubCategory.Value in the first Expression list box.

10 Click the OK button.

11 On the File menu, click Save All.

12 Click the Preview tab.

The top of your report looks like this:

Product	Sales Amount	Order Quantity
AWC logo cap	477.5895	85
Full-finger Gloves, L	4228.761875	176
Full-finger Gloves, M	2129.56744	87
Full-finger Gloves, S	197.548	8
Half-finger Gloves, M	704.0898	46
Half-finger Gloves, S	336.7386	22

Now you can see that products are arranged in groups, but you cannot determine from the report how each group is defined. You need to add more information to the report.

Adding Group Headers

A group header gives context to the set of detail rows associated with each group. As with any other textbox in a table, the group header can contain static text, a field value, or a calculation that might reference a field. Usually, group headers include the same expression used to define the group.

In this procedure, you add the *Category* and *SubCategory* fields to the respective group headers.

Use field names as a group header

1 Click the Layout tab.

2 In the Fields window, click *Category* and drag to the first cell in the table1_Category header, which is the row just below the table header. Your table now looks like this:

Product	Sales Amount	Order Quantity
=Fields!Category.Value		
=Fields!Product.Value	=Fields!SalesAmour	=Fields!OrderQuanti
Grand Total	=Sum(Fields!SalesA	=Sum(Fields!OrderC

When the report is processed, the group header displays the value of the field that you placed in this row. All detail rows with the same value for the field that are selected in the Grouping And Sorting Properties dialog box will be organized together in the report between the group header and footer rows. This means that you could group detail rows by one field and display a header, or caption, for the group using another field. However, more commonly you'll use the same field in both places.

3   In the Fields window, click SubCategory and drag to the first cell in the table1_SubCategory header, which is the row just above the detail row.

4   Click the Save All button on the toolbar.

5   Click the Preview tab.

The top of your report looks like this:

Product	Sales Amount	Order Quantity
Clothing		
Cap		
AWC logo cap	477.5895	85
Gloves		
Full-finger Gloves, L	4228.761875	176
Full-finger Gloves, M	2129.56744	87
Full-finger Gloves, S	197.548	8

Now you can see the category and subcategory displayed in separate rows above each group of detail rows.

Computing Group Subtotals

Subtotals can be created for each group by placing a function to sum the detail rows into either a group header or group footer. You can also use other aggregate functions in these rows, such as an average, which you'll learn how to do in Chapter 5.

In this procedure, you add static text as a caption in each group footer row, and then insert the *Sum* aggregate function in the group footer cells for *SalesAmount* and *OrderQuantity*.

Add the *Sum* function to group footers

1   Click the Layout tab.

2   Click the first cell of the table1_Category footer, which is the row just above the table footer, type **Category Total**.

3 Click the second cell of the table footer, and then, while pressing Ctrl, click the third cell of the same row to select both cells.

4 Right-click one of the selected cells, and then click Copy.

5 Right-click the second cell of the table1_Category footer, and then click Paste.

The table now looks like this:

Product	Sales Amount	Order Quantity
=Fields!Category.Value		
=Fields!SubCategory.Value		
=Fields!Product.Value	=Fields!SalesAmour	=Fields!OrderQuanti
Category Total	=Sum(Fields!SalesA	=Sum(Fields!OrderC
Grand Total	=Sum(Fields!SalesA	=Sum(Fields!OrderC

Even though the same formula now appears in the table1_Category footer and the table footer, the results will be different because of the context of the rows. The table footer sums all detail rows in the table, whereas the table1_Category footer sums detail rows for each category separately.

6 Click the first cell of the table1_SubCategory footer, which is the row below the detail row, and type **SubCategory Total**.

7 Right-click the second cell of the table1_SubCategory footer, and then click Paste.

8 On the File menu, click Save All.

9 Click the Preview tab.

You can see that on the first page of the report, several SubCategory subtotals are interspersed between groups. You need to scroll about halfway down the page to find the first Category subtotal. However, the group headers and footers aren't noticeably different from detail rows, which make them difficult to pick out.

Formatting a Report by Using Report Designer

After defining the data to be gathered for the report and structuring the data within the report, the next step in authoring a report is to apply formatting and set properties for each report item. This step is necessary to control the appearance and behavior of the items in your report. You start with basic formatting to display numeric values properly and to set font styles and colors for different sections of the report. You continue adjusting the formatting of your report by designing your report for the printed page and controlling the visibility of selected report items across pages. Then you finish your report by adding graphical elements to make it more attractive.

How to Apply Basic Formatting

Report Designer provides a wide array of formatting options. In this section, you perform only the most common formatting tasks. You start by changing the formatting of numeric values, and then you change the appearance of selected report items using first the Format toolbar, and then the Properties window.

Setting the *Format* Property

Sometimes you might want to change the format of the data retrieved for your report. Often, numeric and date or time values require a change from the default format. The *Format* property in the Properties window can be edited to adjust the format of a string in a textbox.

In this procedure, you format the SalesAmount column of the table as Currency, and the OrderQuantity column as a number with no decimals.

Format numeric values

1 Click the Layout tab.

2 Click the column handle for the second column that contains Sales Amount values.

   All cells in the column are selected when you click the column handle.

3 In the Properties window, find the *Format* property, and then type C0.

   Properties in the Properties window are arranged alphabetically, first by property category and then by name.

▶ **Note** The Report Designer uses Visual Basic .NET formatting strings. The first character represents the data format. The most common data formats you're likely to use are C for currency, N for numbers, and P for percents. The digit following any of these characters specifies the number of decimal places, or precision. You can omit the digit if you want to use the system default for the specified data format. You can find out more about the system defaults for numeric data formats at *http://msdn.microsoft.com/library/default.asp?url=/library/en-us/cpref/html /frlrfsystemglobalizationnumberformatinfoclassinvariantinfotopic.asp.*

When you select multiple cells, such as all cells in a column, the property setting that you apply affects all selected cells. You can also change several properties at once to update the cells while they remain selected.

4   Click the column handle for the third column that contains Order Quantity values.

5   In the Properties window, find the *Format* property and type **N0**.

6   On the File menu, click Save All.

7   Click the Preview tab.

The numeric values are now formatted correctly.

Applying Styles

You can edit style properties for every item in a report, such as background colors, border styles, font styles and colors, and padding values. Like the *Format* property, style properties can be edited in the Properties window. Not all style properties are available to every report item. For example, only items that can contain text have font style properties. The easiest way to apply common styles is to use the Report Formatting toolbar.

In this procedure, you use the Report Formatting toolbar to set the background color of the detail row and the font styles of the headers and footers for the table and groups.

Use the Report Formatting toolbar

1   Click the Layout tab.

2   Click the row handle of the detail row to select the entire row.

3   On the Report Formatting toolbar, click the Background Color button. The Background Color button looks like this:

▶   **Note**   If the Report Formatting toolbar is not visible, right-click any Visual Studio toolbar, and then click Report Formatting. You might need to rearrange the toolbars to view the entire Report Formatting toolbar.

4   On the Web tab, click Silver, and then click the OK button. The new background color is applied to the detail row.

5   Click the row handle for the table header, and then while pressing Ctrl, click the table footer row handle to select both rows.

▶ **Tip** When you want to apply the same formatting styles to several rows, select each row handle while pressing Ctrl.

6 On the Report Formatting toolbar, click 12 in the Font Size list box, click the Bold button, then click the Background Color button.

7 On the Web tab, click Black, and then click the OK button.

8 On the Report Formatting toolbar, click the Foreground Color button, which is to the left of the Background Color button.

9 Click the Web tab, click White, and then click the OK button.

▶ **Note** Alternatively, you can set these properties directly in the Properties window. The Background Color button sets the *BackgroundColor* property, and the Foreground Color button sets the *Color* property.

Expand the Font category to access the font properties. The Font Size list box selection sets the *FontSize* property. The Bold and Italic buttons set the *FontWeight* and *FontStyle* respectively. Finally, the Underline button sets the *TextDecoration* property, which is not categorized with the other font properties.

10 Click the table1_Category header row handle, and then click the table1_Category footer row handle while pressing Ctrl to select both rows.

11 On the Report Formatting toolbar, click 12 in the Font Size list box, click the Bold button, then click the Background Color button.

12 On the Web tab, click Gainsboro, and then click the OK button.

13 Click the table1_SubCategory header row handle, and then click the table1_SubCategory footer row handle while pressing Ctrl to select both rows.

14 On the Report Formatting toolbar, click 11 in the Font Size list box, and then click the Bold button.

15 On the File menu, click Save All.

16 Click the Preview tab.

The top of your report looks like this:

Product	Sales Amount	Order Quantity
Clothing		
Cap		
AWC logo cap	$478	85
SubCategory Total	**$478**	**85**
Gloves		
Full-finger Gloves, L	$4,229	176
Full-finger Gloves, M	$2,130	87
Full-finger Gloves, S	$198	8
Half-finger Gloves, M	$704	46
Half-finger Gloves, S	$337	22
SubCategory Total	**$7,597**	**339**

By applying different format styles to each section of the report, the distinctions between the table headers and footers, the group headers and footers, and the detail rows are more clear.

Editing Properties

The Report Formatting toolbar contains only some of the properties available for editing. To access all formatting properties, use the Properties window. For example, you might want to adjust the padding within a textbox. *Padding* is the white space between the sides of a textbox and the text inside the textbox, just like a margin is the white space between the sides of a page and the text on the page. You can adjust the amount of padding on any side of the textbox: top, bottom, left, or right. The default padding of each side of the textbox is 2 points.

In this procedure, you adjust the padding in the first column of the detail row and the table1_SubCategory group header and footer to indent the column values in these rows.

Indent a column

1   Click the Layout tab.

2   Click the first cell in the detail row, which is the Product cell.

3   In the Properties window, click the plus sign to expand the Padding category.

4   In the *Padding Left* property field, type **22pt**.

Your Properties window looks like this:

▶ **Note**   In the Properties window, some properties, such as *Padding* properties, are arranged in categories. The category name appears in the Properties list with a plus or minus sign so that you can expand or collapse the category. By default, the category is collapsed to make finding a property easier. When the category is expanded, you can modify any individual property that category contains. The field to the right of the category name has the values of all properties in the category. If you know the position of the property that you want to change, you can edit the category values.

In the example in this procedure, you can replace 2pt, 2pt, 2pt, 2pt, with **22pt, 2pt, 2pt, 2pt**. The sequence of values from left to right in the category field corresponds to the properties grouped in the category from top to bottom. So, for the *Padding* category field, the sequence of values corresponds to *Padding Left*, *Padding Right*, *Padding Top*, and *Padding Bottom*.

5   Click the first cell in the table1_SubCategory header, and then click the first cell in the table1_SubCategory footer cell while pressing Ctrl to select both cells.

6   In the Properties window, type **12pt** in the *Padding Left* property field.

7   On the File menu, click Save All.

8   Click the Preview tab.

The top of the report now looks like this:

Product	Sales Amount	Order Quantity
Clothing		
Cap		
AWC logo cap	$478	85
SubCategory Total	$478	85
Gloves		
Half-finger Gloves, S	$337	22
Half-finger Gloves, M	$704	46
Full-finger Gloves, S	$198	8
Full-finger Gloves, M	$2,130	87
Full-finger Gloves, L	$4,229	176
SubCategory Total	$7,597	339

How to Enhance the Report Layout

Now that you've used style properties to control the appearance of items in the report, you improve the report layout by using other item properties to define pagination, add a static title, and control the appearance of report items across pages. Also, you add visual interest to your report by adding graphical elements.

Triggering Page Breaks

When the report was added to the project, the *PageSize Width* property of the report was set by default to 8.5in and the *PageSize Height* property was set to 11in. When you render the report to preview it, the rendering engine determines the number of rows that can fit on a page and creates page breaks automatically. However, you can specify your own trigger for a page break, such as a change in a group value or following a selected report item. You learn how to design pages for other rendered formats in Chapter 12, "Rendering Reports."

In this procedure, you add a page break to the table1_Category group.

Add pagination

1   Click the Layout tab.

2   Click the blank area in the Document window below the design grid.

The report properties display in the Properties window. Note the default settings for the *Margin* and *PageSize* properties.

3   Click the table to display the row and column handles.

4   Right-click the table1_Category footer row handle, and then click Edit Group.

5   Select the Page Break At End check box.

6   Click the OK button.

7   On the File menu, click Save All.

8   Click the Preview tab.

Your report now has four pages, one for each category. Notice that the number of detail rows per page is different. The rendering engine still inserts a page break if there are more detail rows within a category than will fit on a single page. However, the group page break forces a new page when the category changes, regardless of the number of detail rows.

▶   **Note**   If Reporting Services followed the page break instruction literally, it would put a page break after the last category, putting the Grand Total on a page by itself. However, Reporting Services doesn't do this.

Adding a Textbox

So far, you've been working with textboxes that are organized as a table. A textbox can also be placed into the report as a separate report item. For example, to add a static title, or report header, to the report, you can add a textbox. You'll learn other uses for an independent textbox in Chapter 5 and Chapter 6.

In this procedure, you add a textbox to the design grid and insert static text to create a report header.

Add static text

1 Click the Layout tab.

2 Click the handle in the top left corner to select the entire table. If you can't see the table handles, click the table first.

3 Drag the table down to place the top of the table approximately 1.5 inches from the top of the report body.

4 In the Toolbox window, click Textbox.

5 Click the top left corner of the report body, and then drag the corner of the textbox to the right and down to create a textbox approximately 2.5 inches wide and 1.25 inches high.

▶ **Note** You can also use the *Size Width* and *Height* properties in the Properties window to set the size of the textbox once it is placed in the report body. Another option is to drag the sides of the textbox to resize it as desired.

Your screen now looks like this:

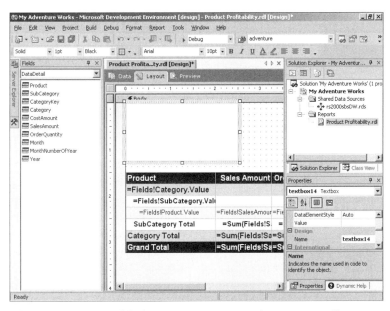

The textbox was added as a report item and automatically assigned a name, similar to textbox14.

6 Click inside the textbox, and then type **Adventure Works Product Profitability Report**.

▶   **Note**   Text will wrap to a new line automatically to fit the width of the textbox, but will never expand the textbox horizontally. In the rendered report, the textbox will expand vertically to display all text contained in the textbox if its *Can-Grow* property is set to True, which is the default. You can force a new line in the text by pressing Shift+Enter at the desired position.

7   Make sure the textbox is still selected in the design grid, click 20 in the Font Size list box, and then click the Bold button in the Report Formatting toolbar.

▶   **Note**   Unlike the way you apply formatting in a word processing application, you don't need to select the text in the textbox before applying the formatting styles. You need to have only the textbox selected.

8   On the File menu, click Save All.

9   Click the Preview tab.

The top of the report looks like this:

**Adventure Works Product
Profitability Report**

Product	Sales Amount	Order Quantity
Clothing		
Cap		
AWC logo cap	$478	85
SubCategory Total	$478	85

Notice that the text does not get truncated.

10   Click the Next Page button.

The textbox that you added does not appear on this or any other page because you added it above the table. In this usage, the textbox acts as a report header because it is not contained within a repeating region and consequently appears only once. (You'll learn more about repeating regions in Chapter 6.) Also, notice that the table header is not repeated. Even though the table header is a collection of textboxes that *is* contained in a repeating region, its designation as a table header results in rendering that is different from other rows in the same table. By default, the table header is displayed only on the first page.

Setting Table Properties

As you learned in the previous procedure, a table header is displayed only on the first page that contains the table. If you want to repeat the table header on every page, you can edit the *RepeatOnNewPage* property for the row. The table header will then be repeated, but only on the pages that include the table.

In this procedure, you edit the *table* property to force the table header to repeat on each page of the report.

Repeat the table header

1 Click the Layout tab.

2 Click the table, and then click the table header row handle.

   The properties for this item, TableRow1, display in the Properties window.

3 Scroll to the bottom of the Properties window to locate the *Repeat-OnNewPage* property in the Layout section.

4 In the Properties window, click True in the list box for the *Repeat-OnNewPage* property.

▶ **Note** Similarly, group headers and footers appear only at the beginning or end of a group. You can edit the group to set options in the Grouping And Sorting Properties dialog box so that you can force the group header or footer to repeat on each page, or you can select the group row in the table and set the *RepeatOnNewPage* property in the Properties window.

5 On the File menu, click Save All.

6 Click the Preview tab.

7 Click the Next Page button.

   The top of the second page of your report looks like this:

Product	Sales Amount	Order Quantity
Accessory		
Locks		
Cable lock	$720	48
SubCategory Total	$720	48
Pumps		
Mini-pump	$636	53
SubCategory Total	$636	53

Working with Page Headers

When you want to repeat the same content at the top of every page, you can use a page header. A page header can contain textboxes and images, but it cannot contain data regions, subreports, or any item that directly references a field.

In this procedure, you add a page header containing a textbox that will be suppressed on the first page, but printed on every other page.

Add a page header

1   Click the Layout tab.

2   Right-click the blank area in the Document window to the left of the report body, and then click Page Header. Alternatively, on the Report menu, you can click Page Header.

Your screen looks like this:

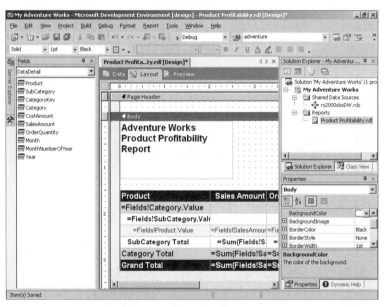

3   In the Toolbox window, click Textbox.

4   Click the top left corner of the page header section, and then drag the corner of the textbox to the right and down to create a textbox approximately 4.5 inches wide and 0.25 inches high.

5   In the Properties window, click Right in the *Text Align* property list box.

The page header will now align with the right edge of the table. If you add more columns or additional items later that increase the width of the report, you will also need to adjust the location of the textbox in the header.

6   Click the textbox to select it, and then type **Product Profitability Report**.

▶   **Tip**   If the right edge of the report is hidden by Solution Explorer, you might not be able to see the text as you type. In that case, simply use the horizontal bar to scroll the Document window to the right, or resize windows to confirm the text is entered properly. Another option is to Auto Hide the Solution Explorer and Properties windows.

7   In the Properties window, click *PageHeader* in the report item list box at the top of the window (or click anywhere in the page header's design grid), and then scroll to the bottom of the window to find the properties in the Misc group.

▶   **Tip**   Type **P** after opening the Properties report item list box to jump to the report items beginning with that letter instead of scrolling. This list can get long when you're building complex reports.

8   Click False in the *PrintOnFirstPage* property list box.

9   Make sure True is the current setting for the *PrintOnLastPage* property.

10   On the File menu, click Save All.

11   Click the Preview tab.

12   Click the Next Page button.

The page header appears only on pages 2 through 4.

Working with Page Footers

Like a page header, you can use a page footer to repeat content on every page of the report. The same rules regarding what can be placed in this area of the report apply. You can also choose whether to suppress the page footer from the first or last page of the report.

In this procedure, you add a page footer with static text that will print on every page of the report.

Add a page footer

1   Click the Layout tab.

2   Right-click the blank area in the Document window to the left of the report body, and then click Page Footer.

   You might need to close the Output window to view the newly added page footer.

3   In the Toolbox window, click Textbox.

4   Click the top left corner of the page footer section, then drag the corner of the textbox to the right and down to create a textbox approximately 1.5 inches wide and 0.25 inches high.

5   Click the textbox to select it, and then type **Company Confidential**.

6   In the Report Formatting toolbar, click the Italic button.

7   In the Properties window, click PageFooter in the report items list box.

   The *PrintOnFirstPage* and *PrintOnLastPage* properties are both set to True by default.

8   On the File menu, click Save All.

9   Click the Preview tab.

   The page footer is displayed on the first page.

10 Click the Next Page button to check the existence of the page footer on all other pages.

Adding Graphical Elements

Lines and images are graphical elements that you can use to give your report an attractive, professional appearance. These report items are added to the report from the Toolbox window like the other report items you've learned how to use. You can use the graphical interface to resize the graphical elements as desired, or you can use the Properties window to edit properties.

In this procedure, you add a line to the top of the report to separate the report body from the page header.

Add a line

1   Click the Layout tab.

2   In the Toolbox window, click Line.

3   Click the top left corner of the report body, and then drag the line to the right to match the width of the table.

▶   **Tip**   Adding a line to the design grid is easier if, before you start, you make the window large enough to show the beginning and end of the line. If you do not, you'll spend time moving and resizing your line to get it right.

Your screen looks similar to this:

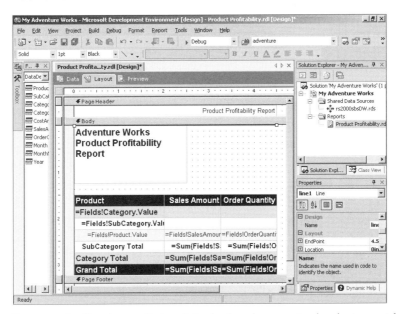

Because the line is small, it might be hard to see in the design grid right now. You should be able to see the line handles at each end. You can use these to lengthen or shorten the line as needed. In the Properties window, you can view the properties for the new report item, line1.

4   In the Properties window, scroll up to find the *LineWidth* property in the Appearance category, and then change the property value to **12pt**.

5   If the line covers some of the text in the textbox containing the report title, drag the textbox a little lower on the design grid.

As you add report items to the design grid, you will probably need to tweak their arrangement to prevent one item from obscuring another.

6   On the File menu, click Save All.

7   Click the Preview tab.

The top of the report looks like this:

**Adventure Works Product
Profitability Report**

Product	Sales Amount	Order Quantity
Clothing		
Cap		
AWC logo cap	$478	85
SubCategory Total	$478	85

Because the line was added to the report body, it is displayed only on the first page. If you want a line to repeat, you must add it to a repeating section of a data region, such as a group header, a group footer, or a detail row.

Adding Images

In addition to containing data regions and freestanding textboxes, a report can contain logos and other types of graphical images. You can embed an image within the report itself, or reference an image that is stored on the Report Server. Often, an image is included in a report as a freestanding item, like the report header you added earlier in this chapter. However, you can also use images in detail rows if you have stored images in a database, such as product images for a catalog.

In this procedure, you will add the Adventure Works logo as an embedded image at the top of the report.

Use the Image Wizard

1   Click the Layout tab.

2   In the Toolbox window, click Image.

3   Click the top right corner of the report body just below the line and to the right of the textbox you created as a report header.

   The Image Wizard is launched.

4   Click the Next button.

The Select The Image Source page of the Image Wizard is displayed:

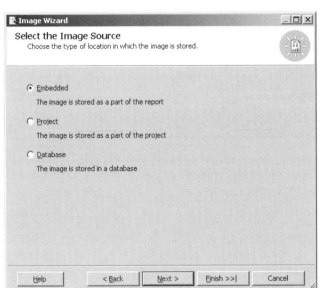

Here you specify where the image to be added to the report is stored: embedded, project, or database.

■ An embedded image is converted to a Multipurpose Internet Mail Extension (MIME) object, which allows the image to be stored as text in the report definition file. Using an embedded image ensures that the image is always available to the report, but it also makes the report definition file much larger.

▶ **Important**   ASP.NET imposes a 4 MB-limit on items that are posted to the server. Report definition files rarely exceed this limit unless you use embedded images. You can increase this limit by changing the *maxRequestLength* element in the Machine.config file, but by doing so you also increase the vulnerability of the server to denial of service attacks. Editing this file is beyond the scope of this book. If you need to use multiple images in a report, include them as shared resources in the project, or store them in a database field.

■ A project image is an image that is stored as an item in the project. You can choose an image that was already added to the project, or you can use the wizard to add an image. When publishing the project, the report definition and the image files are placed on the Report Server separately. As a result, the report definition file is smaller than it is when using an embedded image. Using project images is a good strategy when you want to use the same image within several reports, such as a company logo.

■ A database image is retrieved as binary data by the query in the dataset and is included in the detail row. You specify the dataset, the column of query results containing the image, and the MIME type. Because the image is part of the dataset, the images are not stored in the report definition file.

5 Click Embedded.

6 Click the Next button.

7 Click the New Image button.

8 Open the image at C:\rs2000sbs\chap04\logopart.jpg.

9 Click the logopart name in the Name column and type **Logo** to replace the default name.

▶ **Tip**   Choose a name for the image with care so that you can find it more easily when working with your report.

10 Click the Next button.

11 Click the Finish button.

The image is now embedded in the report as an independent report item.

▶ **Tip**   You can also use an image with any item in the report that has the *Back-groundImage* property. For example, you can use an embedded image as a background for a table or textbox.

12 Click the image, and then drag down and to the right so that the height of the image matches the height of the report header textbox and the width extends to the right edge of the table.

The top of the design grid looks like this:

13 On the File menu, click Save All.

14 Click the Preview tab.

The top of the report looks like this:

**Adventure Works Product
Profitability Report**

Product	Sales Amount	Order Quantity
Clothing		
Cap		
AWC logo cap	$478	85
SubCategory Total	**$478**	**85**
Gloves		
Full-finger Gloves, L	$4,229	176
Full-finger Gloves, M	$2,130	87
Full-finger Gloves, S	$198	8
Half-finger Gloves, M	$704	46
Half-finger Gloves, S	$337	22

The Adventure Works logo appears only on the first page because it was added to the report body, not to the page header.

Chapter 4 Quick Reference

To	Do this
Create a new report project	On the File menu in Visual Studio, point to New, and then click Project. Choose the Report Project template to create an empty report project. Enter a name and a physical folder location for the project.
Add a blank report to a project	In Solution Explorer, right-click the Reports folder of a project, point to Add, and then click Add New Item. Type a report name with an .rdl extension, and then click the Open button.
Add a shared data source	In Solution Explorer, right-click the Shared Data Sources folder, and then click Add New Data Source. In the Data Link Properties dialog box, select a provider and enter a server name and credentials for authentication, if needed, and select a database name.
Add a dataset	In the Document window, click <New Dataset. . .> in the Dataset list box, change the name of the dataset if desired, enter a query string, and then click the OK button.

To	Do this
Add a data region	Open the Toolbox window, click the desired data region, point to the target destination in the report body, and then click to place the data region.
Add fields to a table	In the Fields window, click the field to be added and drag to a data region cell or textbox. You can also type a field expression directly into the cell or textbox. For example: **=Fields!Product.Value**
Add a group to a table	Click the table to display the row handles. Right-click a row, and then click Insert Group. Change the name of the group, if desired, and select one or more expressions from the list box to use for grouping detail rows.
Include subtotals in a table	Copy an expression that returns a numeric value from the table footer, and paste into a group header or group footer row. Alternatively, you can type in an aggregate expression into a group header or group footer cell. For example, to compute a subtotal: **=Sum(Fields!SalesAmount.Value)**
Format a numeric value	Click the textbox (or multiple textboxes) containing the numeric expression to format and edit the *Format* property in the Properties window. Use Visual Basic .NET formatting strings, such as C2, N0, or P1.
Apply formatting styles to text	Click the textbox (or multiple textboxes), then click the applicable style button in the Report Formatting toolbar or edit the applicable style property in the Properties window.
Add a page break	To insert a page break between report items, such as between a report and a chart, click a report item, and then edit the *PageBreakAtEnd* or *PageBreakAtStart* property in the Properties window to apply the page break accordingly. To insert a page break in a table, click the table to display the row handles. Click the row you want to use to trigger a page break when the value changes, and then edit the *RepeatOn-NewPage* property in the Properties window.
Add a page header or page footer	Click the empty space in the Document window surrounding the design grid, right-click, and then click either Page Header or Page Footer.
Add a freestanding textbox	Open the Toolbox window; click Textbox; point to the target destination in the report body, page header, or page footer; and then click to place the data region.

To	Do this
Suppress page headers or page footers from the first or last page	Click Page Header or Page Footer in the report item list box of the Properties window, and then set the *PrintOnFirstPage* or *PrintOnLastPage* property to False.
Repeat table rows across pages	Click the table to display row handles, click the table row to repeat on each page, and then, in the Properties window, set the *RepeatOnNewPage* property to True.
Add a graphical element	Open the Toolbox window, click the graphical element (either Line or Image), and then point to the target destination in the report body, page header, or page footer. If adding a line, drag the cursor across the page to the desired length. If adding an image, click to place the image in the report and use the Image Wizard to locate the image and define the storage for the image.

Working with Expressions

In this chapter, you will learn how to:

- Use global object collections in expressions.
- Create expressions with aggregate functions.
- Change the report appearance with expressions.

In the previous chapter, you started a report project to which you added a report containing a table data region and other report items. You also edited properties of these report items to manipulate their appearance and behavior in the report. In this chapter, you expand the same report. You build some expressions that perform calculations on values in the dataset, and build others that use information that is available only after the report is processed. You also use aggregate functions in various places in the report to learn how the location of a function affects the context of the aggregate. Finally, you change properties by using expressions that are based on conditions or values in the report. Because these expressions are evaluated at run time, the appearance and behavior of the report can dynamically change.

Using Expressions to Calculate Values

You started working with expressions in Chapter 4, "Developing Basic Reports," by adding fields to the table. When you drag a field from the Fields window and drop it into a cell, the Report Designer inserts a field expression into that cell. For example, the first cell of the detail row in your report contains the following expression: `=Fields!Product.Value`. An expression that points to a field is the simplest expression of all. Like all expressions, it starts with an equal sign (=) and is written in Microsoft Visual Basic. This expression refers to the *Product* field by using standard Visual Basic collection syntax, in which

Fields is the name of the object collection, *Product* is the name of an object in the collection, and *Value* is the property of the object. In this case, for each row, the expression returns the value of the *Product* field in the *Fields* collection for the current row.

You can create more complex expressions by using functions or by combining field expressions with mathematical operators to perform a calculation. The expression in the second cell in the table footer, `=Sum(Fields!SalesAmount.Value)`, is an example of an expression that uses an aggregate function, which you learn more about later in this chapter. Expressions are commonly used to display field values and calculated values in a report.

How to Use Expressions in a Report

After you have data for your report, you often need to perform additional calculations using this data to derive values that aren't stored in the database. For example, you might need to include the product margin in the report. The *margin* is the difference between the amount for which the product sold and the cost of making or acquiring it. Even though margin isn't stored as a value in the database, it can be derived from other values that are stored in the database by building an expression that subtracts CostAmount from SalesAmount. An expression can be added as a calculated field to the dataset, and then used in a table as if it were part of the original dataset.

Not all expressions are based on fields in the dataset. Another type of expression that you might want to use in a report can be created using a global variable. Reporting Services makes available certain information about a report, such as page numbering, which you can access through the *Globals* collection. For example, to keep track of the number of pages in a report, you can use the *PageNumber* and *TotalPages* global variables to access the numbering that Reporting Services stores for you. You can create a calculated field to store a global variable expression, or you can type the expression directly into a textbox. In this way, you can avoid writing code to access page numbering.

A third type of expression that is handy to use in reports is a report item expression. To create a report item expression, you use the *ReportItems* collection to access the value stored in a textbox. A value in the textbox, if derived from a field expression like the margin example discussed earlier in this section, doesn't come directly from the dataset but is stored there to be displayed in the report or for use in another expression. You can think of the textbox as not just a display item, but also as a holding area for a value that can be used as part of another calculation.

Creating Calculated Fields

The Fields window initially displays the list of database fields contained in the dataset that you create. You can add expressions as calculated fields to this list. Once a calculated field is created in the dataset, you can use it in a report just like a database field. It's evaluated the same way, too, for each row in the dataset. If an expression needs to be used in several places, create a calculated field so that, if you need to change the expression, you can edit the expression in one place. However, you can also enter an expression directly into a textbox when it's used in only one or two places in a report.

In the following procedure, you create a field to compute each product's margin. After you finish creating the calculated field, you will carry out another procedure to add the calculated field to a new column in the report.

Create a field to compute *Margin*

1   Start Microsoft Visual Studio, and open the solution My Adventure Works that you saved in the C:\rs2000sbs\Workspace\My Adventure Works folder.

▶   **Note**   If you skipped Chapter 4, open the solution My Adventure Works in the C:\rs2000sbs\Answers\chap04\My Adventure Works folder.

2   Open the Product Profitability report, if it isn't already open, by double-clicking the report name in Solution Explorer.

3   Right-click anywhere in the Fields window, and then click Add to display the Add New Field dialog box. Remember that when you add a field to a cell in a heading row, the name of the field, and not the field expression, is inserted.

▶   **Tip**   If you right-click when pointing to an existing field, and then click Edit, you can make changes to that field. For example, if the name of a database field isn't user-friendly, you could change the name directly in the *Fields* collection. Recall from Chapter 4 that the name of the field is automatically added to a table header. Although you can override the name in the table header textbox, you might find it more efficient to rename the field in the *Fields* collection if you reuse this field several times in the same report.

4   Type a name for the field: **Margin**.

5   Click the Calculated Field option, and then click the Expression button that appears to the right of the Calculated Field textbox.
    The Edit Expression dialog box is displayed:

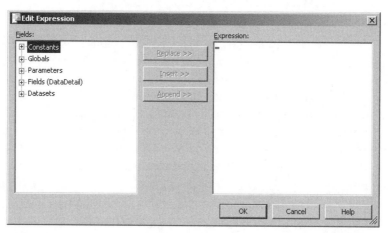

Notice five object collections in the Fields pane: *Constants*, *Globals*, *Parameters*, *Fields (DataDetail)*, and *Datasets*. You'll be working with the *Fields (DataDetail)* collection in this procedure, and with the *Globals* collection later in this section. Each collection contains objects that you can use in an expression.

6   Click the plus sign (+) in front of *Fields (DataDetail)* to expand this collection and view its members.

7   Click *SalesAmount*, and then click the Append button to add it to the Expression pane.

The Append button adds the field to the end of the expression, without regard to the current location of the cursor in the expression.

8   In the Expression pane, place the cursor after =Fields!SalesAmount.Value and then type – (minus sign).

9   Click the *CostAmount* field in the Fields pane, and then click the Append button to finish the expression so that the Edit Expression dialog box looks like this:

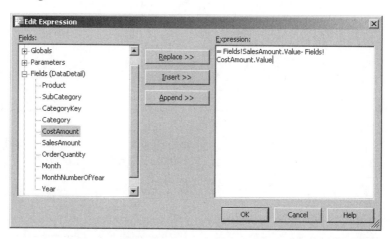

Alternatively, you can type the expression in the field directly. By using the buttons to insert the field names, you can be sure that you're not introducing a spelling error.

▶ **Important** When multiple database fields are used in the same expression, all the fields must come from the same dataset. Also, Microsoft Visual Basic .NET is case-sensitive, so you must use field names correctly. If you don't use the proper case, the field name is not recognized, and you won't be able to view the report because of the resulting compilation error.

10 Click the OK button to close the Edit Expression dialog box.

The expression is inserted into the Calculated Field textbox, as shown here:

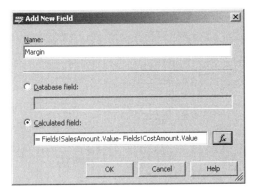

11 Click the OK button to close the Add New Field dialog box.

The *Margin* field is now part of the dataset and appears in the Fields window, as shown here:

Notice the *Margin* field has a different icon, which identifies it as a calculated field.

12 Save your report.

In the next procedure, you add a new column to the table in your report, into which you add the calculated field—*Margin*—to the detail row, and an expression to compute margin subtotals in the footer rows.

Add *Margin* to the table

1   Click the table to display its handles. right-click the column handle for the third column (Order Quantity), and then click Insert Column To The Right.

Your screen looks like this:

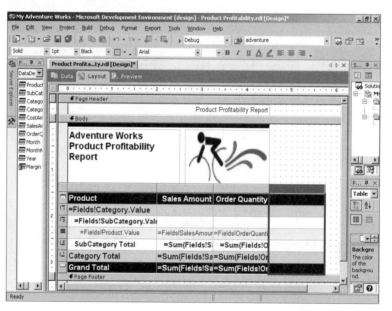

A new column appears in the table. The new column has the same formatting properties as the column you selected. In this case, the *Format* property of the Order Quantity column is set to N0, which is the value automatically assigned to the *Format* property for the new column. Notice that the style formatting of each row of the Order Quantity column is also duplicated in the new column.

▶ **Note**   You can also insert rows into a table by right-clicking a row handle, and clicking Insert Row Above or Insert Row Below. The inserted row becomes the same row type as the selected row, such as a detail or footer row.

2   Click *Margin* in the Fields window and drag the field to the last cell in the detail row.

Notice that the field name is added to the table header automatically. Also, the expression placed in the detail row is an expression that references the *Margin* field and is not the underlying expression that you assigned to the field.

3 Drag *Margin* from the Fields window to the last cell in the table1_SubCategory footer, just below the detail row.

The *Sum* function is added automatically to the field expression because this row is a footer row.

4 Press Enter to select the expression in this cell. Copy this expression to the Clipboard, click the cell beneath it in the table1_Category footer twice so that the cursor appears in the textbox, and then paste the contents of the Clipboard (the expression itself) into the cell.

▶ **Note** Copying an expression is different from copying a cell. Copying an expression does not copy the formatting to the destination cell. Copying a cell, by contrast, also copies the formatting to the target cell.

5 Click the last cell in the table footer twice, and then paste the expression that is still in the Clipboard into that cell.

6 Click the column handle for the Margin column to select all cells in the column, and then type **C0** in the *Format* property in the Properties window to display margin values as currency without decimals.

7 Save the solution files, and then preview the report to confirm that the top of your report looks like this:

Adventure Works Product Profitability Report

Product	Sales Amount	Order Quantity	Margin
Clothing			
Cap			
AWC logo cap	$478	85	$33
SubCategory Total	**$478**	**85**	**$33**
Gloves			
Full-finger Gloves, L	$4,229	176	$1,471
Full-finger Gloves, M	$2,130	87	$766
Full-finger Gloves, S	$198	8	$72
Half-finger Gloves, M	$704	46	$257
Half-finger Gloves, S	$337	22	$123
SubCategory Total	**$7,597**	**339**	**$2,689**

Using Global Variables

Global variables are members of the *Globals* collection, in which Reporting Services tracks information unique to a report. You can display this information in the report by including a global variable in an expression placed in a textbox. Six global variables are available for you to use. They are especially useful for embedding report information in printed reports.

The global variables *PageNumber* and *TotalPages* can be used only in the page header or footer. However, the other global variables can be used anywhere that you can place a report item. You can use *ExecutionTime* to include the date and time that the report was executed so that users know how fresh the report is. To help users locate the report online, you can include the report name and location information by using *ReportName*, *ReportServerUrl*, and *ReportFolder* (which includes the full path to the report without the URL).

Global variables are different from fields. Reporting Services does not have values for the global variables until *after* the report is processed, but it can access these values *before* the report is rendered. Fields, on the other hand, are populated with values *during* processing and then are no longer accessible by Reporting Services once processing has completed. As you learned in Chapter 4, the report data is independent of the report layout to enable rendering in any format. Consequently, some information is simply not available until the query is processed and merged into the report layout. Take, for example, page numbering. A report rendered for online viewing in HTML has a different page numbering system than the same report rendered for print. Until the report has been processed and prepared for rendering, neither the current page number nor the total number of pages are available as global variable values.

In this procedure, you edit expressions in textboxes displayed in the page header and report body to incorporate the global variable, *ReportName*, in the report title.

Add global variables to the report

1   Click the Layout tab, right-click the textbox in the page header, and then click Expression.

2   Expand the *Globals* collection in the Fields pane, click *ReportName*, and then click the Replace button.

    The Replace button clears the previous value, Product Profitability Report, from the Expression pane, and replaces it with an expression referencing the selected item, as shown here:

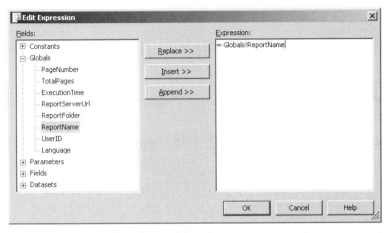

Notice the other global variables that you can use in an expression.

3 Type **+ " Report"** at the end of the expression so that the edited expression looks like this:

```
=Globals!ReportName+" Report"
```

▶ **Note** Be sure to include the space between the quotation mark and word *Report* to properly separate the text when the expression is evaluated and displayed in the report.

4 Click the OK button.

5 Right-click the textbox that contains the report title in the body of the report, and then click Expression.

6 Replace the existing expression by typing this: =**"Adventure Works "+**.

7 Expand the Globals collection in the Fields pane, click *ReportName*, and then click the Append button to add the global variable to the expression.

The Append button inserts the global variable at the current position of the cursor.

8 To finish the expression, type **+ "Report"** at the end of it. The complete expression looks this:

```
="Adventure Works "+ Globals!ReportName+" Report"
```

9 Click the OK button.

10 Save your report, and preview it to check the results.

Notice that the current title of the report is Adventure Works Product Profitability Report.

11 Click the Next Page button to confirm the report title in the page header.

12 In Solution Explorer, right-click Product Profitability.rdl, click Rename, and then type a new name for the report: **Product Sales and Profitability.rdl**.

13 Close the report, and then reopen the report to reset the session cache.

14 Click the Preview tab, and then click the Next Page button to check that the title of the report is updated appropriately, as shown in this illustration:

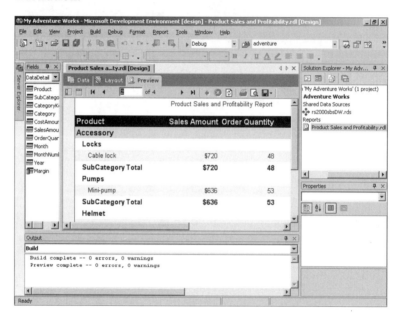

▶ **Tip** The *ReportName* global variable is useful for reusing report items in many reports to retain a consistent appearance.

Using the *ReportItems* Collection

The *ReportItems* collection contains the report's textboxes as objects. You can use a report item expression to display the value of a textbox in a separate text-box or to use a textbox's value as part of a separate calculation. Report item expressions are similar to global variables because they are evaluated by Reporting Services after processing completes but before rendering. Field expressions in detail and aggregated rows must be evaluated first from the dataset so that a textbox has a value that can be used by the report item expression.

Report item expressions, therefore, are useful in situations in which a calculation can be performed only after the dataset is aggregated, and the calculation cannot be derived directly from the dataset. For example, to calculate subtotals in the table, the *Sum* function is used with a field expression. However, if the field expression evaluates as a percentage, the *Sum* function is no longer applicable because percentages are not additive. Specifically, a percentage value in the table footer cannot be calculated by summing percentage values in the detail rows. When working with non-additive values like ratios or percentages, you must perform the division on aggregated values. To accomplish this, you can use a report item expression to summarize percentage values in rows in which you are using subtotals.

A report item expression used in a textbox that is inside a data region can retrieve the value of a textbox that is either on the same level or on a higher level if the data region has grouping defined. This means that you cannot use an expression in a summary row that refers to a textbox in a detail row. Essentially, this is because the report item expression in a data region is acting as a pointer to *one* other textbox at a time, and therefore can retrieve only one result. Because multiple rows can be on a lower level, there is no way to identify which one of those rows contains the value that the report item expression should retrieve.

In this procedure, you add report item expressions to calculate the margin percentage in the detail and summary rows of the table.

Add report item expressions to the table

1   Click the Layout tab, click the table, right-click the Margin column handle, and then click Insert Column To The Right.

2   In the last cell of the table header, type **Margin %**.

3   Click the Margin % column handle to select all cells in the column, and then type **P1** in the *Format* property to display the expression as a percentage with one decimal place.

4   Right-click the last cell in the detail row, click Expression, enter the following expression in the Expression pane, and then click the OK button.

    ```
    =ReportItems!Margin.Value/ReportItems!SalesAmount.Value
    ```

▶   **Tip**   You can also type the expression directly into the textbox, but the width of the textbox often makes it difficult to see what you're doing when working with longer expressions. Another way to edit the expression is to click <Expression...> in the *Value* property for the textbox in the Properties window.

This expression retrieves the value from the Margin textbox, and then divides the value by the value in the SalesAmount textbox. This calculation is performed for each detail row of the report. You could also use the expression =Fields!Margin.Value/Fields!Sales-Amount.Value to get the same result, but for now use the *ReportItems* collection so that you can learn something about its behavior in the next steps.

5   Enter the following expression in the last cell of the table footer:

```
=Sum(ReportItems!Margin.Value)/Sum(ReportItems!SalesAmount.Value)
```

▶   **Note**   This expression is *not* valid, but is introduced here to force an error for you to look at in a few more steps.

6   Click the Preview tab. Your screen looks like this (although the sequence of errors might differ):

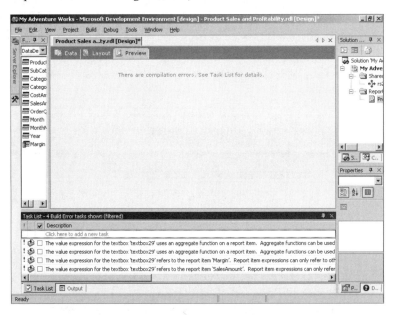

▶   **Note**   There is no error-checking function in Layout mode. To test an expression, you must preview the report.

7   Position the mouse pointer over each message in the Task List window to view the entire message.

Two messages refer to the use of an aggregate function in a report item. The same message displays twice because the expression that you just added contains two instances of *ReportItems*. Because the textbox is in a table in the report body, and not in a page header and footer, you cannot use the *Sum* function in its expression.

The other two messages refer to the use of grouping scope with report items. Here the message displays twice but references the two report items separately, Margin and Sales Amount. In this case, the error is caused because the expression belongs to an item positioned in a summary row but references an item in a detail row. To avoid this error, the report item expression in this textbox can refer only to another textbox that is in the table footer.

8 Click the Layout tab, click the Sales Amount cell in the table footer, and then change the *Name* property to **SalesAmount_Total** in the Properties window.

9 Click the Margin cell in the same row and change its *Name* property to **Margin_Total**.

10 Enter the following expression for the last cell of the table footer:

```
=ReportItems!Margin_Total.Value/ReportItems!SalesAmount_Total.Value
```

This expression uses the summarized value of margin divided by the summarized sales amount. Importantly, the report item expression refers only to textboxes in the same grouping scope—the table footer—and does not use the aggregate function. The referenced textbox values for *Margin_Total* and *SalesAmount_Total* are already aggregated, so there's no need to apply another aggregate function.

11 Click the Sales Amount cell in the table1_Category footer, and then change the *Name* property to **SalesAmount_Category**.

12 Click the Margin cell in the same row and change its *Name* property to **Margin_Category**.

13 Add the following expression to the Margin % cell in the table1_Category footer:

```
=ReportItems!Margin_Category.Value/
ReportItems!SalesAmount_Category.Value
```

14 Click the Sales Amount cell in the table1_SubCategory footer, change the *Name* property to **SalesAmount_SubCategory**, and then click the Margin cell in the same row and change its *Name* property to **Margin_SubCategory**.

15 Add the following expressions to the Margin % cell in the table1_SubCategory footer:

```
=ReportItems!Margin_SubCategory.Value/
ReportItems!SalesAmount_SubCategory.Value
```

16 Save the solution, and then preview your report.

The top of your report looks like this:

Adventure Works Product Sales and Profitability Report

Product	Sales Amount	Order Quantity	Margin	Margin %
Clothing				
Cap				
AWC logo cap	$478	85	$33	6.9 %
SubCategory Total	**$478**	**85**	**$33**	**6.9 %**
Gloves				
Full-finger Gloves, L	$4,229	176	$1,471	34.8 %
Full-finger Gloves, M	$2,130	87	$766	36.0 %
Full-finger Gloves, S	$198	8	$72	36.5 %
Half-finger Gloves, M	$704	46	$257	36.5 %
Half-finger Gloves, S	$337	22	$123	36.5 %
SubCategory Total	**$7,597**	**339**	**$2,689**	**35.4 %**

The margin percentages are now correctly displayed in the report.

Using Aggregate Functions in a Data Region

When you add a field to a table, the group footer rows in the table use the default aggregate function, *Sum,* with that field to total up the rows in each group. The same function is also used to calculate a grand total for the table in the table footer. In the report body, an aggregate function operates on a set of rows defined by an expression, such as a field, and returns a value, such as a total. Usually, an aggregate function operates on numeric values, but some aggregate functions work with string values. In the page header and page footer, an aggregate function can operate only on report item expressions.

Because the expressions in the report body are evaluated when the report is processed, an aggregate function in the report body has access to the dataset and thus can use a field expression as an argument. However, expressions in the page header and footer are evaluated after the report body is processed, and before the report is rendered. If you try to use =Sum(Fields!SalesAmount.Value) in the page footer, the report will not compile. Here's where a report item expression comes to the rescue, because it can access information for the processed page and return a value that is displayed in the rendered page. Thus, you can use =Sum(ReportItems!SalesAmount.Value) to total the value of all the textboxes labeled SalesAmount on the page.

Reporting Services supports 13 standard aggregate functions, which are shown in the following table:

Use this aggregate function	To do this
Avg	Average non-null numeric values in the set
Count	Count values in the set
CountDistinct	Count the distinct values in the set
CountRows	Count the number of rows in the set
First	Get the first value in the set
Last	Get the last value in the set
Max	Get the highest value in the set
Min	Get the lowest value in the set
StDev	Find the standard deviation of all non-null numeric values in the set
StDevP	Find the population standard deviation of all non-null numeric values in the set
Sum	Total the numeric values in the set
Var	Find the variance of all non-null numeric values in the set
VarP	Find the population variance of all non-null numeric values in the set

These functions are typically used in footer rows of a table or a matrix, but can also be used in freestanding textboxes.

Two running aggregate functions are often used in detail rows to display accumulating values. The running aggregate functions are shown in the following table:

Use this running aggregate function	To do this
RowNumber	Show the current row count in an accumulating count of rows in the set
RunningValue	Show the current value in an accumulating aggregation of the set

How to Use Aggregate Functions in a Report

Even though the *Sum* aggregation function is added by the Report Designer as you drop a field into a header or footer row of a table, you can also type an aggregate function directly into the table—for example, when you need to show cumulative values in the detail rows of a report or display averages in the footer row.

Aggregates can also be used outside a data region in a freestanding textbox, either in the report body or in the page header or footer. For example, you might want to show a grand total on the first page of a report or display a page total in the footer of each page. In the case of non-numeric data, such as an employee directory, you might want to show the first and last employee name in a page footer.

Using Aggregate Functions in a Table

When using aggregate functions in a data region, such as a table, you need to consider the scope of the function. *Scope* in the context of a data region determines which rows are included when calculating the aggregated value. Scope can refer not only to a grouping in the data region, but also to an entire data region or even to an entire dataset.

Most aggregate functions use the syntax *Function(Expression,Scope)*, but the *RunningValue* function is constructed using the following syntax: *RunningValue(Expression,Function,Scope)*. In this function, *Expression* cannot itself contain an aggregate function; *Function* is the aggregate function to apply (which cannot be *RunningValue* or *RowNumber*); and *Scope* is the name of data region or a grouping in a data region and is encased in quotation marks.

In this procedure, you use the *RunningValue* function to show how many products in a subcategory contribute to 80 percent of product sales in each subcategory.

Add a running total to the table

1   Click the Layout tab, right-click the Sales Amount column handle, and then click Insert Column To The Right.

2   Type **Cumulative** in the new cell in the Category group header (the second row of the table).

3   Click the Align Right button on the Report Formatting toolbar.

4   Add the following expression to the Cumulative cell in the detail row:

```
=RunningValue(Fields!SalesAmount.Value,Sum,"table1_SubCategory")
```

This expression calculates a running total of *SalesAmount* that is reset each time the *Scope*, which in this case is name of the grouping based on the *SubCategory* value, changes.

5   Save the solution, and then click the Preview tab to verify that the top left section of your report looks like this:

**Adventure Works Product
Sales and Profitability
Report**

Product	Sales Amount		Order Quantity
Clothing		Cumulative	
Cap			
AWC logo cap	$478	$478	85
SubCategory Total	**$478**		**85**
Gloves			
Full-finger Gloves, L	$4,229	$4,229	176
Full-finger Gloves, M	$2,130	$6,358	87
Full-finger Gloves, S	$198	$6,556	8
Half-finger Gloves, M	$704	$7,260	46

Notice that the Cumulative value increases with each detail row in every subcategory section. The Cumulative value for the last detail row is equivalent to the subtotal for the subcategory. Then the Cumulative value is reset to zero and increases with each detail row in the next group. Because the Cumulative value is related to the Sales Amount column, you can place a label above the column to better explain what value is accumulating in the Cumulative column.

In this procedure, you merge the cells in the table header to center the Sales Amount label above the Actual and Cumulative columns.

Merge cells

1   Click the Layout tab, and then type **Actual** in the Category Header (the second row) of the Sales Amount column.

2   Click the Align Right button on the Report Formatting toolbar.

3   Click the Sales Amount header cell in the table header (the first row), press Ctrl and click the cell to its immediate right, right-click either of the selected cells, and then click Merge Cells.

   Merging cells is useful for centering text labels over multiple columns in a columnar data region, such as a table or matrix.

4   Click the Center button on the Report Formatting toolbar to center the text across the two cells.

The first three columns of the table in the design grid now look like this:

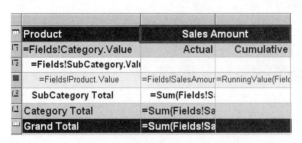

Using Aggregate Functions in a Textbox

Sometimes you might want to display the result of an aggregate function independently of the data region containing the data used by the function. You can place an aggregate function in a freestanding textbox and place it anywhere in your report. If you choose to do this, include a text label, either in a separate textbox or as part of the expression in the same textbox, to indicate the meaning of the value in the report. When using an expression to concatenate a string value with a numeric value, like an aggregate, you need to wrap the *Format* function around the aggregate function to convert the numeric value to a string and apply the proper formatting. The syntax for the *Format* function is *Format(Expression, FormatString)*, where *FormatString* is the same string you would use in the *Format* property.

As stated earlier in this section, the expression used with an aggregate function depends on its location in the report. When using an aggregate function in the report body, you must use a field expression. In the report body, the scope of an aggregate function is always a dataset, which must be specified only when there is more than one dataset in the report. In case you add a dataset later, get into the habit of including the dataset in the *Scope* argument to save edits later. An aggregate function in the page header or footer must instead use a report item expression. *Scope* is never used in this context, because the dataset is no longer accessible.

In this procedure, you use the *Sum* function to show total product sales for all categories in the report body rather than in a table.

Add a *Sum* aggregate function to the report body

1   Click the Layout tab, click Textbox in the Toolbox window, and then click the design grid in the spot just right of the image's top right corner.

2   Use the textbox handles to resize the textbox to approximately 2.5 inches wide and 0.25 inches high so that the design grid now looks like this:

3   Add the following expression to the new textbox:

```
=Sum(Fields!SalesAmount.Value,"DataDetail")
```

▶ **Note**   In this example, only one dataset is in the report, so no *Scope* argument is required in the expression. You could enter =Sum(Fields!Sales-Amount.Value), but if you add another dataset to the report later, you will need to modify the expression to refer to the appropriate dataset in the *Scope* argument.

4   Click the Preview tab, and then scroll to the right of the report, if necessary.

You can see that the format of the value needs to be fixed and a label should be added to explain what the value represents. Since the scope of the aggregate function in the report body is the dataset, the sum represents the total of all product sales in the report.

5   Click the Layout tab, and then modify the expression in the textbox as follows:

```
="Total Product Sales: "+Format(Sum(Fields!SalesAmount.Value), "c0")
```

This expression is an example that illustrates how to concatenate an aggregate function with a text label.

6   On the Report Formatting toolbar, click the Italic button.

7   Save the solution, and preview your report to confirm that the top of your report looks like this:

Adventure Works Product Sales and Profitability Report   *Total Product Sales: $1,582,470*

Now you can have a grand total for all products in the dataset.

In this procedure, you use the *First* and *Last* function to show total product sales for all categories in the report body.

Add a *First* and *Last* aggregate function to the page footer

1   Click the Layout tab, click Textbox in the Toolbox window, click the page footer to the right of the existing textbox, and then resize the textbox to about 2 inches in width and .25 inches in height, and position the textbox so that its left edge is aligned with the 2" mark on the horizontal ruler.

2   Click the first cell of the detail row, and then verify that the *Name* property of this textbox in the Properties window is Product.

The name of the textbox should have been assigned automatically when you dropped the *Product* field into this cell. If for some reason the name is not correct, note the current name for use in the next step.

3   Click the textbox that you added to the page footer, and enter the following expression:

```
=First(ReportItems!Product.Value)
```

This expression will find the name of the product in the first detail row on this page and display the result in the page footer.

▶ **Note**   If the name of the textbox that represents the first cell of the detail row is not *Product*, you will need to modify this expression to reference the current name. For example, if the textbox name is *Product_1*, the expression here should be =First(ReportItems!Product.Value).

4   Click the textbox with the *First* aggregate function, and then click the Align Right button On the Report Formatting toolbar.

5   Click the same textbox, and then, while pressing Ctrl, drag the cell to the right to make a copy of the textbox whose left edge aligns with the right edge of the original textbox and aligns with the 4" mark on the horizontal ruler.

6   Edit the second textbox containing the aggregate function so that the expression now looks like this:

```
=" - " +Last(ReportItems!Product.Value)
```

▶ **Note**   If the name of the textbox that represents the first cell of the detail row is not *Product*, you will need to modify this expression to reference the current name. For example, if the textbox name is *Product_1*, the expression here should be =" – " +Last(ReportItems!Product_1.Value).

This expression includes a dash as a visual separator between the first and last value displayed in the footer. Reporting Services doesn't let you use two report item expressions in the same textbox, but you can place two textboxes side by side to get the same effect.

7   Click the textbox with the *Last* aggregate function, and then click the Align Left button on the Report Formatting toolbar.

8   Save the solution and preview the report, scrolling to the bottom of the page.

The bottom of the page looks like this:

Tights		
Women's tights, L	$4,484	$4,484
Women's tights, S	$3,997	$8,481
SubCategory Total	**$8,481**	
Category Total	**$32,680**	
Company Confidential	AWC logo cap - Women's tights, S	

Using Expressions to Change an Object's Behavior

Even though expressions are often used to display the results of calculations in a report, you can also use them in report item properties to control appearance such as font color. You can even use expressions to control behavior such as sort order. You can set many of the properties in the Properties window by using an expression instead of a single value. This feature of Reporting Services provides endless flexibility in designing your reports.

How to Use Expressions to Control Report Behavior

Not every report will need to include expressions to change its appearance or behavior. However, in some situations, you will find this capability useful. For example, you can find potential problem areas (or highlight areas that are performing well!) by using an expression instead of a value in the *Color* property of a report item. You can also change the color of a detail row when a field value in that row falls below a defined threshold.

In addition to using expressions to modify the appearance of a report item, you can use expressions to alter the sort order of rows or groups in a table. If you want to sort rows by a derived value rather than by an existing value in the row, you can easily add the expression to the sort definition.

Using Conditional Formatting

Conditional formatting is used to change the font or background color of an item based on the result of evaluating a Boolean expression, which returns either True or False. Often, conditional formatting is used to identify values, known as *exceptions*, that fall outside a specified range to make them easier to locate in a big report. You can also use conditional formatting to create rows with alternating colors.

Conditional formatting is commonly implemented using the *IIf* function, which evaluates an expression to determine whether it's true or false. For example, an expression to change the font color when the margin expression is below 15 percent might look like this:

```
=IIf(ReportItems!Margin_Percentage.Value<0.15, "Red", "Black").
```

The first argument of the *IIf* function, `Margin_Percentage.Value<0.15`, is the condition that is evaluated. If the value is true, the second argument, "`Red`" in this case, is the result of the expression and becomes the value of the *Color* property. If the condition is false, the third argument, "`Black`", becomes the value of the *Color* property.

In this procedure, you use conditional formatting to display detail rows using a red font whenever the margin percentage is below 15 percent.

Highlight exceptions

1   Click the Layout tab, click the Margin % cell in the detail row, click Expression in the *Color* property list box, and then replace the default expression with the following expression:

```
=IIf(Me.Value<0.15, "Red", "Black")
```

▶   **Tip**   Use the special word "Me" to refer to the current item so that you can reuse the same expression in several textboxes. If you don't, you will have to create a unique expression for each textbox, even when the expressions are performing the same task. For example, if you wanted to conditionally format the Margin Percentage textbox, you would use
`=IIf(ReportItems! Margin_Percentage.Value<0.15, "Red",`
`"Black")`, but you would need to use
`=IIf(ReportItems!Margin_Percentage_Total.Value<0.15, "Red",`
`"Black")` to conditionally format the Margin_Percentage_Total textbox. Although both of these expressions are valid, your work is simplified by using Me.

2   Copy the expression to the Clipboard, and then click the OK button to close the Edit Expression dialog box.

3   Click the Margin % cell in the table1_SubCategory Footer, press the Ctrl key and click the Margin % cells in the table1_Category footer

and the table footer, and then paste the copied expression into the *Color* property in the Properties window to update all three cells in one step.

4   Click the Margin % cell in the table footer, click Expression in the *Color* property list box, and edit the expression to replace Black with **White**, as shown here:

```
=IIf(Me.Value<0.15, "Red", "White")
```

5   Click the OK button to close the Edit Expressions dialog box.

6   Save your report, and then check the results by clicking the Preview tab.

Confirm that the Margin % for AWC logo cap and the Cap SubCategory Total are both 6.9% and that they are displayed as red text.

Sorting

The sort order of rows in the table is determined by the order of rows in the dataset. You can use an ORDER BY clause in your query if you want to control the sort order on the database server. Alternatively, you can use a field expression for setting the sort order in Table Properties to change the query's default sort order by using the Report Server. If you need to sort rows by a value that is not in the dataset, you can use an expression.

Specifying a sort order in Table Properties affects only the order of the detail rows. If you want to sort the groups, just right-click a group header or footer, and then click Edit Groups to access the Grouping And Sorting Properties dialog box. On the Sorting tab, you can select a field expression or enter your own expression to define a sort order for each level of grouping.

In this procedure, you sort the detail rows by using an expression that calculates the margin percentage.

Sort detail rows using an expression

1   Click the Layout tab; click the table to display the handles; right-click the table handle, which is located in the top left corner; and then click Properties.

2   In the Table Properties dialog box, click the Sorting tab, click <Expression.> in the Expression list box, and then replace the default expression with the following expression:

```
=Sum(Fields!Margin.Value)/Sum(Fields!SalesAmount.Value)
```

▶ **Note**   You can't use *ReportItems!Margin.Value* in this expression because the Margin textbox is in a detail row, which is not in scope for table properties. Remember that when using the *ReportItems* collection, you can reference only those report items that are on the same level of grouping or higher.

3   Click the OK button.

4   Click Descending in the corresponding Direction list box.

The Table Properties dialog box looks like this:

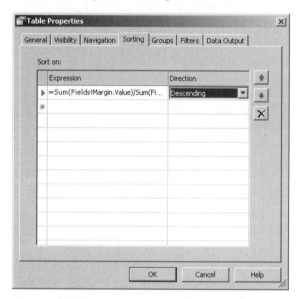

5   Click the OK button to close the Table Properties dialog box.

6   Click the Preview tab to verify that your report looks like this:

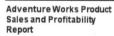

Adventure Works Product Sales and Profitability Report

Total Product Sales: $1,582,470

Product	Sales Amount		Order Quantity	Margin	Margin %
Clothing	Actual	Cumulative			
Cap					
AWC logo cap	$478	$478	85	$33	6.9 %
SubCategory Total	**$478**		**85**	**$33**	**6.9 %**
Gloves					
Half-finger Gloves, S	$337	$337	22	$123	36.5 %
Half-finger Gloves, M	$704	$1,041	46	$257	36.5 %
Full-finger Gloves, S	$198	$1,238	8	$72	36.5 %
Full-finger Gloves, M	$2,130	$3,368	87	$766	36.0 %
Full-finger Gloves, L	$4,229	$7,597	176	$1,471	34.8 %
SubCategory Total	**$7,597**		**339**	**$2,689**	**35.4 %**

The detail rows are now sorted in descending order, but only within each subcategory group. Notice that on the first page of the report, the subcategories are still sorting in the order found in the dataset (the default sort order).

7   Save and close the solution.

Chapter 5 Quick Reference

To	Do this
Add a calculated field	Right-click in the Fields window, and then click Add. Enter a name for the calculated field and click the Calculated Field option. Enter an expression directly into the Calculated Field textbox or click the Expression button to open the expression editor.
Insert a row or column in a table	Right-click the row handle, and then click either Insert Row Above or Insert Row Below. *or* Right-click the column handles, and then click either Insert Column to the Left or Insert Column to the Right.
Copy an expression without copying textbox formatting	Click the textbox containing the expression to copy; press Enter to select the expression, and then press Ctrl+C to copy.
Test an expression	Click the Preview tab.
Merge cells	Click the cells to be merged. You can right-click and then click Merge Cells, or click the Merge Cells button on the Layout toolbar.
Use an aggregate function	Use one of the following: *Function(Expression, Scope)* for a standard aggregation *or* *RunningValue(Expression,Function,Scope)* for a running value aggregation *or* *RowNumber (Scope)* for a running count of rows.
Apply conditional formatting	Use the *IIf* function to test for a condition and assign a property value for true and false conditions. For example, use the following expression to set the *Color* property of a textbox: **=IIf(Me.Value<0.15, "Red", "Black")**.

To	Do this
Sort table rows	Use an ORDER BY clause in the dataset query. *or* Click the table, click the table handle in the top left corner, and then click Properties. In the Table Properties dialog box, click the Sorting tab, and then click an expression in the Expression list box. If you click <Expression.> in this list box, you can open the expression editor to enter your own expression if you want to sort by a value that is not contained explicitly in the dataset.

Organizing Data in Reports

In this chapter, you will learn how to:

■ Represent data in a cross-tabular form by using a matrix.

■ Represent data graphically by using a chart.

■ Represent data in a flexible layout by using a list.

In the previous chapter, you finished your report by adding expressions to enhance the information in it and to affect the appearance and behavior of report items. In this chapter, you expand your report design skills by using the other data regions supported by Reporting Services. You work with a matrix data region to see how both rows and columns can dynamically adjust to the dataset. You also add a chart data region to a report so that you can see how multiple data regions can be combined in a single report and how to manipulate chart properties. To learn how to take advantage of a freeform, repeating data region, you use a list to create grouped sets of a matrix and chart.

Understanding Data Regions

Although a table data region can accommodate most of your reporting needs, you have several other ways to organize data in a report, which you explore in this chapter. Before examining the matrix, chart, and data regions in greater depth, you will compare these data regions with one another and with a table to better understand the general similarities and differences between them. You will also be introduced to some typical applications of these data regions to help you decide which will be appropriate for your next reporting project.

Comparing Types of Data Regions

As you learned in Chapter 3, "Building Your First Report," a data region is a structure in the report in which data from the dataset is arranged. A data region differs from other report items, such as a textbox or a rectangle, because it repeats data. For example, in the table you built in Chapter 4, "Developing Basic Reports," you defined properties by row, such as the detail row, which was repeated for each record in the dataset.

The following table highlights the differences between the four data regions supported by Reporting Services. You already know that a table data region displays the same number of columns every time the report is executed, but as data changes in the source, the number of rows can vary. In the Product Sales and Profitability report, for example, as new products are sold by Adventure Works, more rows of data are added to the report. Grouping isn't required in a table, but you did add two grouping levels to the table, Category and SubCategory, to break the product detail rows into smaller sets for which subtotals could be calculated. In this chapter, you work with a matrix, a chart, and a list.

Data region	Description	Grouping levels	Group on
Table	Fixed number of columns with variable number of repeating rows	From zero to many	Rows
Matrix	Fixed crosstab with variable number of repeating rows and columns of aggregate data only	From zero to many	Rows or columns
List	Freeform layout of repeating report items	One	List
Chart	Graphical display of dataset of aggregate data only	Category, Series	Dependent on chart type

Using Data Regions

When designing your report, you need to select a data region that is appropriate for the data that you expect to be returned in the dataset. Most of the time, a table will probably satisfy your requirements. However, if you want to use data from the query, such as month names, in the column headers, you'll need to use a matrix data region. If you need more flexibility in positioning report items, rather than use the fixed row and column structure of a table or matrix, you can use a list.

You also need to consider whether to use multiple data regions. You can nest data regions to repeat the same data region multiple times by placing a list within a list or a table within a list. This is a great way to design one table that is reused many times in the same report. For example, you could use a separate table for each salesperson when reporting sales data. If you wanted to present alternate views of data side by side—sometimes the best way to communicate information—you could use a table with detail data and a chart with aggregated data.

Using a Matrix

A matrix data region can be compared to a PivotTable or crosstab-style report, because the number of rows as well as the number of columns adapt dynamically. The number or rows or columns can change as the results of the query change or as selections are made in the report to focus attention on certain data. Like a table, the detail rows of a matrix come from the report's dataset. However, a table has the same number of columns every time the report is executed. The number of columns in a matrix, by contrast, can increase or decrease depending on the query results.

Options for Using a Matrix

In its simplest form, a matrix contains a single numeric value that is aggregated by groups added to the rows and columns. Report Designer creates these groups when you drop fields into the Row and Column areas of the matrix.

You can also add a static column to create sets of numeric values that display for each column group. For example, if you create a column group of Months and have static columns for Sales Amount and Order Quantity, you can repeat the static columns for each month.

When you have multiple groups, you might want to include subtotal rows to display intermediate aggregations or a grand total for the matrix. You can create subtotals for either rows or columns, or you can insert subtotals in both directions.

Adding a Matrix Data Region

Adding a matrix data region is as easy as adding any other data region. In the Toolbox window, click Matrix, and then click the report body to position the top left corner of the matrix. Because the rows and columns of the matrix expand according to the dataset, report items below or to the right of the matrix shift when the matrix adjusts.

▶ **Tip**   If, for some reason, the query returns no data to the dataset, the data region is not rendered. You can choose to display a textbox with a message by entering a value in the *NoRows* property of the data region. This value, when displayed, will use the same style properties, such as *Color* and *Font*, that are defined for the data region. Be sure to supply a value for this property if you want something to appear on the report when no data is returned.

In this procedure, you create a new report containing a matrix data region that displays *SalesAmount*.

Add a simple matrix

1   Start Microsoft Visual Studio, and open the solution My Adventure Works that you saved in the C:\rs2000sbs\Workspace\My Adventure Works folder.

▶ **Note**   If you skipped Chapter 5, "Working with Expressions," open the solution My Adventure Works in the C:\rs2000sbs\Answers\chap05\My Adventure Works folder.

2   In Solution Explorer, right-click the Product Sales and Profitability.rdl report, click Copy, click the Reports folder, and then press Ctrl+V to paste a copy of the report into the folder.

3   Right-click the new report, click Rename, and then type a new name for the report: **Product Sales and Profitability by Month.rdl.**

4   Double-click the Product Sales and Profitability by Month.rdl report in Solution Explorer to display the report in the Document window.

5   Click the table in the new report to display the handles, right-click the table handle in the top left corner, and then click Delete.

▶ **Tip**   When you plan to use the same dataset in another report, rather than start with a blank report, copy an existing report and then delete data regions from it. Using this technique, you can also preserve the overall appearance with minimal effort for a consistent look between reports.

6   In the Toolbox window, click Matrix, and then click the left edge of the design grid just below the textbox containing the report title.

Your screen looks like this:

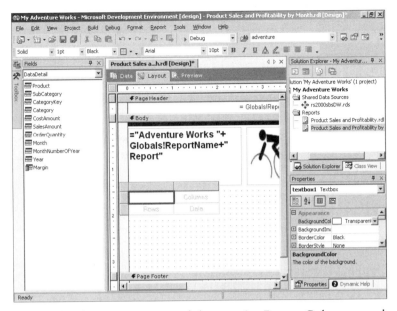

Notice the three main areas of the matrix: Rows, Columns, and Data. These are drop zones for fields from the dataset.

7   In the Fields window, click *SalesAmount* and drag to the Data area of the matrix.

Notice that the *Sum* function was added to the expression.

▶   **Note**   A matrix data region does not have a detail row and always aggregates numeric data based on the intersection of the rows and columns. The default aggregation function is *Sum*, but you can change this if you need to use a different aggregation.

8   In the Properties window for the SalesAmount textbox, type C0 as the *Format* property.

Grouping Rows

You create dynamic row groups by using fields in the dataset. Because both the number of rows in each group and the value displayed as the group row header are determined by the dataset, the table grows or shrinks as the dataset increases or decreases. The group row header cell appears, by default, to the left of the numeric value that appears in the Data area of the matrix. You can nest dynamic rows to create multiple grouping levels for rows. The result is similar to the grouping that you added to the table in Chapter 4.

In this procedure, you will add Category and SubCategory as row groups in the matrix.

Add row groups

1   Drag *Category* from the Fields window and drop it in the Rows area of the matrix.

2   Drag *SubCategory* and drop it in the same cell, placing the mouse pointer on the right side of the cell as you drop the field so that a new column appears between Category and SalesAmount, as shown here:

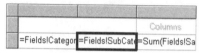

If the drop zone already contains a field, you can still drop another field into the zone. Instead of inserting a column to the right, you can hold the mouse pointer over the left portion of the Row drop zone, and then drop the field to insert a new column to the left of the existing cell.

3   Click the =Fields!Category.Value cell, and then click the Bold button on the Report Formatting toolbar.

4   Save the solution, and then preview the report.

The top of the report looks like this:

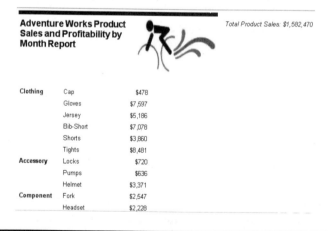

Sorting Rows

Sorting rows in a matrix is similar to setting sorting properties for a table. You can sort by a field value, or you can add your own expression to control sort order.

In this procedure, you edit the matrix properties to apply sorting to each row group.

Define sort order

1 Click the Layout tab, right-click the matrix handle in the top left corner, and then click Properties.

2 In the Matrix Properties dialog box, click the Groups tab, click matrix1_Category in the Rows pane, and then click the Edit button.

3 Click the Sorting tab, click =Fields!Category.Value in the Expression list box, and then click the OK button to close the Grouping And Sorting Properties dialog box.

4 Click matrix1_SubCategory, and then click the Edit button.

5 Click the Sorting tab, click =Fields!SubCategory.Value in the Expression list box, and then click the OK button twice to close all dialog boxes.

6 Save the report, and then preview the report, which now looks like this:

Adventure Works Product Sales and Profitability by Month Report

Accessory	Helmet	$3,371
	Locks	$720
	Pumps	$636
Bike	Mountain Bike	$600,010
	Road Bike	$807,962
Clothing	Bib-Short	$7,078
	Cap	$478
	Gloves	$7,597

By default, a matrix shows values for only the lowest visible level. In this example, the lowest visible level is the SubCategory group. This report resembles a table. It has yet to show off the power of a matrix because no column groups are defined.

Grouping Columns

A dynamic column group is one of the main differentiators between a matrix and a table. Recall that a table has dynamic rows, but a fixed number of columns. Dynamic column groups work like dynamic row groups, but are laid out from left to right across the page instead of from top to bottom. Also, like dynamic rows, both the number of rows and the value displayed as the column header are determined by the dataset. As with row groups, you can nest dynamic columns to create multiple grouping levels for columns.

▶ **Tip**   If you want some of the data columns to appear to the left of the row headers, use the *GroupsBeforeRowHeaders* property of the matrix. This property uses an integer value to control the number of column groups that are displayed in front of the row header column.

In this procedure, you add a column grouping to the matrix to display Sales Amount and Order Quantity by month.

Adding column groupings

1   Click the Data tab, and then change the WHERE clause of the query to the following:

```
WHERE Year = 2003 and MonthNumberOfYear IN (1,2,3)
```

Now the query will return data for January, February, and March of 2003.

2   Click the Layout tab, right-click the matrix handle, and then click Properties.

3   In the Matrix Properties dialog box, click the Groups tab, and then click the Add button in the Columns pane.

The Grouping And Sorting Properties dialog box is displayed.

▶ **Note**   You can also drag a field from the Fields window to the Columns drop zone to add a column. However, by adding a column using the Matrix Properties dialog box, you can also set group properties for the new column right away.

4   Replace the default name of the group by typing **matrix1_Month**.

5   Click =Fields!Month.Value in the Expression list box to define the expression to be used to create a column group.

6 Click the Sorting tab, and then click =Fields!MonthNumberOf-Year.Value in the Expression list box, and then click the OK button.

▶ **Tip** When displaying month names in a report, your query should also include a numeric value of the month that you can use to sort the months in the correct order.

The Matrix Properties dialog box looks like this:

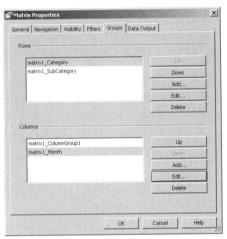

7 In the Matrix Properties dialog box, click the matrix1_Month group, click the Up button to move matrix1_Month above matrix1_ColumnGroup1, and then click the OK button. The matrix now looks like this:

The matrix_ColumnGroup1 group is a static group that consists of a set of columns that will be displayed for each column group. You'll work with the static group later in this chapter. In this case, the static group contains the Sales Amount column. By moving matrix1_Month above the static group, the name of the month is displayed first.

8 Save and then preview your report, which now looks like this:

Adventure Works Product Sales and Profitability by Month Report

		Jan	Feb	Mar
Accessory	Helmet	$3,371	$4,360	$3,932
	Locks	$720	$735	$750
	Pumps	$636	$468	$660
Bike	Mountain Bike	$600,010	$972,136	$698,250
	Road Bike	$807,962	$1,615,294	$934,106
Clothing	Bib-Short	$7,078	$9,183	$7,078
	Cap	$478	$759	$695

Notice that the month names are not centered above each column. You will fix the position of the month names in a later procedure.

Your report can now expand vertically as more products are sold by Adventure Works, and horizontally if the query is modified to include more months. You'll learn how to make the query more dynamic in Chapter 7, "Building Advanced Reports," so that you don't have to change the query string each time you want to view different data in the report.

Using Subtotals in a Matrix

When working with a single row group, the numeric data in each column is already aggregated, so a subtotal is not necessary. However, when working with multiple groups, you might want to add subtotals to see totals by group. Working with subtotals in a matrix is much different from working with subtotals in a table. In a matrix, the same cell is used to manage the properties of the subtotal label and the numeric values that are displayed in the subtotal row. You turn on subtotals by selecting the Subtotal command from the shortcut menu for the group heading cell. You format subtotal data values by selecting a small triangle in the corner of the subtotal cell.

In this procedure, you add a subtotal to the SubCategory and Category groups.

Add subtotals

1   Click the Layout tab, right-click the SubCategory cell, and then click Subtotal to add a new row to the matrix, which now looks like this:

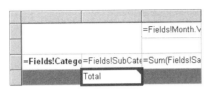

The result of this subtotal will be the sum of each SubCategory within a Category. In effect, it's really the Category total, which you'll see when you preview the report.

2 Click the Total cell, and then click Bold on the Report Formatting toolbar.

Now the label for the subtotal is formatted, but you still have to perform additional steps to format the subtotal values.

3 If necessary, open the Properties window, and then click the small green triangle in the top right corner of the new Total cell.

The Properties window now displays Subtotal in the report items list box.

4 On the Report Formatting toolbar, click the Bold button.

The subtotal values are now formatted, even though you can't see the new format in the matrix.

5 Right-click the Category cell, and then click Subtotal.

Another Total cell appears in the matrix. Because Category is the highest level of the row groups, this subtotal is the equivalent of a grand total.

6 Format the Category Total cell by using the Report Formatting toolbar to set the Font Weight to Bold, the Font Size to 12, the Background Color to Black, and the Foregound Color to White.

7 Click the green triangle in the Category Total cell to format the values, and then use the Report Formatting toolbar to set the Font Weight to Bold, the Font Size to 12, the Background Color to Black, and the Foreground Color to White.

8 Add a subtotal for months by right-clicking the =Fields!Month.Value cell, and then clicking Subtotal.

Now there are two grand total columns to summarize Sales Amount and Order Quantity for all months.

9 Click the Month Total cell, and then click the Bold button on the Report Formatting toolbar.

10 Save and then preview the report, which now looks like this:

Adventure Works Product Sales and Profitability by Month Report

		Jan	Feb	Mar	Total
Accessory	Helmet	$3,371	$4,360	$3,932	$11,663
	Locks	$720	$735	$750	$2,205
	Pumps	$636	$468	$660	$1,763
	Total	**$4,727**	**$5,563**	**$5,341**	**$15,631**
Bike	Mountain Bike	$600,010	$972,136	$698,250	$2,270,397
	Road Bike	$807,962	$1,615,294	$934,106	$3,357,362
	Total	**$1,407,973**	**$2,587,430**	**$1,632,356**	**$5,627,759**
Clothing	Bib-Short	$7,078	$9,183	$7,078	$23,339

Notice that the Month and SubCategory totals are bold, and the Category totals are bold and reversed. You might need to scroll to the bottom of the report to see the Category totals.

Using Static Rows and Columns in a Matrix

You can also add static rows and columns, called static groups, to the matrix. By having such rows or columns, you can have multiple aggregations for a single field. For example, your matrix currently displays the aggregated Sales Amount, but you could also add the aggregated Order Quantity. If you have column groups in your report, each column group will display the set of static columns, that is, Sales Amount and Order Quantity. Static columns in a matrix are similar to the columns in a table data region because there is a fixed number of static columns per column group.

In this procedure, you add the *OrderQuantity* field to the matrix as a static column.

Add static columns

1   Click the Layout tab, right-click the SalesAmount textbox, and then click Add Column.

The matrix now looks like this:

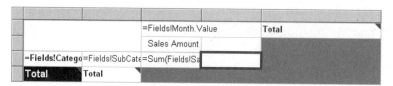

To the right of SalesAmount, another column is added as a static column to the group. Notice that a column label is also automatically added to the SalesAmount column.

▶ **Note** To add a static row, right-click a matrix textbox, and then click Add Row. Similar to a static column, a static row will repeat with each row group.

2 In the Fields window, click *OrderQuantity* and drag the field to the new data column.

3 Change the *Format* property of the Order Quantity textbox to N0.

4 Click the column handle between Sales Amount and Order Quantity columns, and then drag to make the Sales Amount column approximately 1.25 inches wide.

5 Drag the right side of the Order Quantity column handle to extend its width also to approximately 1.25 inches.

6 Click the =Fields!Month.Value cell, and then click the Center button on the Report Formatting toolbar to center the textbox value across the Static Group.

7 Click the Month Total cell. Then click the Center button on the Report Formatting toolbar to center the subtotal label across the Static Group that isn't visible now but will be rendered.

8 In the first cell of the top row of the matrix, type **Product**.

9 Click all three cells in the top row of the matrix while pressing Ctrl, and then use the Report Formatting toolbar to set the Font Weight to Bold, the Font Size to 12, the Background Color to Black, and the Foreground Color to White.

10 Save the report, and preview to verify that the report now looks like this:

Adventure Works Product Sales and Profitability by Month Report

Product		Jan		Feb	
		Sales Amount	Order Quantity	Sales Amount	Order Quantity
Accessory	Helmet	$3,371	$167	$4,360	$216
	Locks	$720	$48	$735	$49
	Pumps	$636	$53	$468	$39
	Total	$4,727	$268	$5,563	$304
Bike	Mountain Bike	$600,010	$488	$972,136	$781
	Road Bike	$807,962	$1,024	$1,615,294	$1,863
	Total	$1,407,973	$1,512	$2,587,430	$2,644
Clothing	Bib-Short	$7,078	$121	$9,183	$157

You can scroll to the right and down to see all the rows and columns on this page. Notice that each month, as well as the month subtotal column, has a column for Sales Amount and Order Quantity.

Using a Chart

You use a chart to display data graphically. Although a chart cannot contain other report items such as a textbox, it does have many attributes that you must manage. Reporting Services supports a wide variety of chart types: column, bar, pie, line, doughnut, area, scatter, bubble, and stock. Standard formatting options allow you to change the chart appearance of the plot and chart areas, the chart axes, and the legend. In addition to choosing colors and styles from a palette, you can use expressions to incorporate conditional formatting into your chart. Many of the chart properties that you might need to change are not accessible in the Properties window, but they are managed in a Chart Properties dialog box associated with the chart.

Options for Using a Chart

A chart can be placed into a report all by itself, but many users like to see the data that supports the chart as a separate data region. You can position a chart above, below, or on either side of a data region. At a minimum, you need to define a data value to display in the chart, which you can then segment into category and series groups if you want. Reporting Services provides plenty of formatting options and property settings to enhance the appearance of the chart.

Adding a Chart

You can click Chart in the Toolbox window and then click the design grid to add a chart of a fixed size to your report body, or you can drag the mouse pointer across the design grid to set a specific size for the chart. It's perfectly fine to create a report that contains only a chart, but often users like to view a chart along with its supporting data. However, whenever you're combining data regions, regardless of type, be sure to account for the vertical expansion of a table, matrix, or list, and the horizontal expansion of a matrix. You might want to place a chart above a data region rather than below it or to its side to avoid problems with placement.

In this procedure, you add a chart to your report, which is displayed with the matrix.

Add a chart to a report

1   In Solution Explorer, right-click the Product Sales and Profitability by Month.rdl report, click Copy, click the Reports folder, and then press Ctrl+V to paste a copy of the report into the folder.

2   Right-click the new report, click Rename, and then type a new name for the report: **Product Sales and Profitability Chart.rdl**.

3   Double-click the Product Sales and Profitability Chart.rdl report to open the report in the Document window.

4   Click the matrix to display the handles, and then drag the matrix to a lower position in the report body so that the top of the matrix is at about 3.5 inches on the vertical ruler.

The design grid is not large enough for you to move the top of the matrix to the 3.5-inch mark, but you can move the matrix there in two drag operations by dragging the matrix as far as you can. The design grid will expand vertically to accommodate the matrix, and then you can drag the matrix into position. The additional space will give you more room in the report for working with a chart.

5   In the Toolbox window, click Chart, and then click to the leftmost part of the body just under the report title and above the matrix to place a fixed-size chart in the report body.

6   In the Properties window, change the Width property of the new chart1 report item to **6in**, and then change the Height property to **2in**.

The screen looks similar to this:

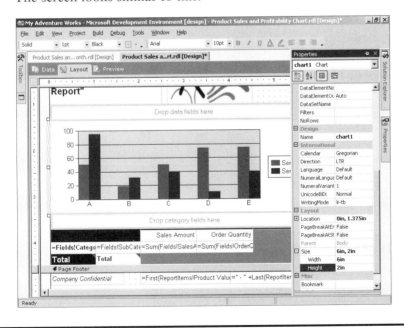

Adding Values and Column Groups to a Chart

A chart must include at least one value. A value is the numeric expression represented by a position in a chart, such as a point in a line chart; or by size, such as the length of a bar or the size of a bubble. Values can be grouped by categories, which are basically labels for the values (like a row header). These category groups can be nested, which allows you to break down groups into subgroups, such as years and quarters.

In this procedure, you add SalesAmount as the chart's value and Year and Month as its category groups.

Add fields to the chart

1   In the Fields window, click the *SalesAmount* field and drag it to the area located above the chart labeled Drop Data Fields Here.

2   Drag the *Year* field from the Fields window to the area located below the chart labeled Drop Category Fields Here.

3   Drag the *Month* field to the same area.

4   Save, and then preview the report.

The chart looks like this:

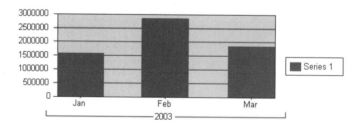

Take a look at how the category groups are arranged. The first group you added, Year, is displayed as the outermost grouping, and includes brackets to indicate how it relates to the next grouping level, Month. If the dataset included another year, you would see the second year as another group in the chart.

Grouping Data by Series

A series group adds more information to the report by differentiating the displayed values by yet another group. For example, if your report had category groups for year and quarter, you see a separate value in the report for each year and quarter available in the dataset. A series group further subdivides the values by using different colors for the members of the series. So, to continue the example, for a single quarter of a particular year, you can see several values for that quarter, such as a value for each employee's sales. The chart legend is used to map the series color with each series member.

In this procedure, you add a series group for SubCategory.

Add a series group

1   Click the Layout tab, right-click the chart, and then click Properties. The Chart Properties dialog box is displayed:

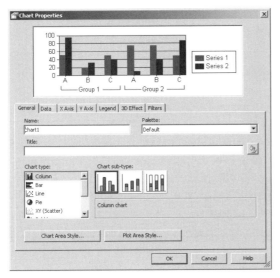

2   Click the Data tab, and then click the Add button to the right of the Series Groups box.

3   In the Grouping And Sorting Properties dialog box, click =Fields!SubCategory.Value in the Expression list box.

The series group is generated dynamically from the *SubCategory* field in the dataset each time the report is rendered.

4   Click =Fields!SubCategory.Value in the Label list box.

Report Designer uses the label that you specified in the Chart Properties dialog box for the series group. The label doesn't have to be the same value used to create the series group.

5   Click the Sorting tab, click =Fields!SubCategory.Value in the Expression list box, and then click OK. Keep the Chart Properties dialog box open for the next procedure.

The series group sorts the SubCategory values in alphabetical order. The Chart Properties dialog box now looks like this:

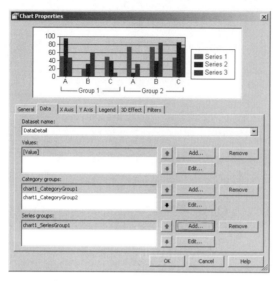

Notice that as you set properties, a generic preview is updated in the Chart Properties dialog box, which helps you see the impact of your changes without previewing the report. Because the preview uses sample data, the chart that you see here is just a guideline to illustrate the current property settings.

Working with the Chart Legend

A chart legend describes the values used in your report. If a series group is not added to the chart, you might want to hide the chart legend. You have complete control over its location and appearance.

In this procedure, you move the chart legend and format the legend's font text.

Format the chart legend

1   Click the Legend tab.

The buttons in the Position area are used to position the chart legend relative to the chart.

2   Click the top button in the right column of the Position section of the dialog box to align the legend at the top right corner of the chart.

The Chart Properties dialog box now looks like this:

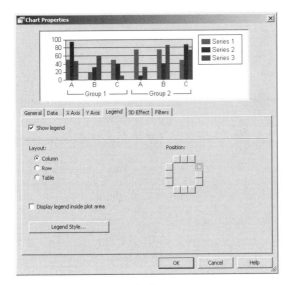

3 Click the Legend Style button.

The Style Properties dialog box is displayed:

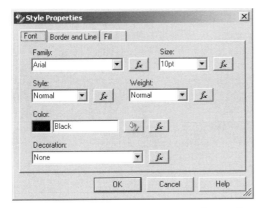

You can use this dialog box to select a font and to set font size, color, and other style properties. The dialog box also includes tabs for specifying border, line, and fill properties. Notice that every property has an Expression button that allows you to enter a conditional expression to set a property value.

4 Click 8pt in the Size list box, and then click the OK button to close the Style Properties dialog box.

5 Click the OK button to close the Chart Properties dialog box and apply the property changes.

6   Save the report, and then preview it to confirm the chart now looks like this:

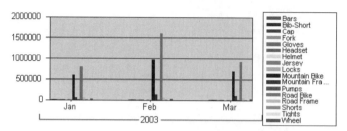

For each month, there is now one column for each member of the series group for which a value exists in that month. The chart legend shows the color assigned to each SubCategory. Now you can continue to refine the chart's appearance by changing some chart properties.

Setting Chart Properties

The Properties window for the chart data region contains the standard background color, border, and size properties that are associated with the other data regions. However, most of the properties that affect the appearance and behavior of the chart are accessible only in the Chart Properties dialog box. To open the Chart Properties dialog box, you right-click the Chart, and then click Properties.

If you've worked with charting in other applications, most of these properties should be familiar. On the General tab, you can specify a name for the chart for reference in expressions and a title to be displayed in the rendered chart. You can also select from a variety of chart types and subtypes, which are alternate versions of a chart type. Style properties can be changed for anything that you can see in the chart: the chart area, the plot area, data values, axis titles, and labels. You can even apply 3-D effects to the chart, if desired.

In this procedure, you format the chart.

Format the chart

1   Click the Layout tab, right-click the chart, and then click Properties. Take a look at the chart type options, but leave the default chart type. In this dialog box, you can also set the Chart Area and Plot Area styles.

2   Click the Y Axis tab, and type **$#,#,** in the Format Code textbox. By using "**$#,#,**", you can format the string as currency in thousands to reduce the amount of space needed to display the label.

3   In the Title box, type a label for the Y axis: **Sales in 1,000s.**

4   Click the Style Properties icon next to the Title box, click 8pt in the Size list box, and then click the OK button.

5   Click the 3D Effect tab, select the check box to enable the 3-D settings, select the Cylinder check box, and then slide the bars to change the settings as follows:

Setting	Value
Horizontal rotation	5°
Perspective	0%
Wall thickness	10%
Vertical rotation	0°

6   Click the OK button.

7   Save and preview the report.

The chart now looks like this:

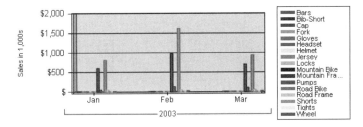

There are, of course, many other properties that you can change to make a really nice-looking chart. The best way to learn about them is to experiment by observing the effect of different property settings on your chart. However, remember that the intent of a chart is to convey information. Most users are satisfied with simple chart effects and won't use a report if the chart is too busy or too complicated to decipher.

Using a List

When you use a list, you can combine different types of report items in an unstructured arrangement within the data region. This type of data region repeats each row from a dataset, just like a table or matrix, but has more flexibility. Instead of arranging data in strict rows and columns, you can place textboxes anywhere you want within the data region, regardless of whether your data is dynamic or static. You can even reproduce a columnar look to simulate a table, but you'll spend more time getting report items lined up properly if you do this with a list.

Options for Using a List

The columnar format of the table and matrix data regions makes aligning data easy. However, apart from offering the *Padding* property, which allows you to shift text away from the edges of the column, this format doesn't provide you with much flexibility when arranging data. Using a list, you can arrange report items freely. You can add a grouping level to the list to define how the report items in the list will repeat. You can also nest other data regions in a list, including nesting a list within a list, to take advantage of repeating data regions. Consider these options as just a starting point for using a list, because its freeform nature gives you unlimited possibilities.

Adding a List

You add a list like you add a chart. You can click List in the Toolbox, and then click the design grid to add a list of a fixed size; or you can drag the mouse pointer across the design grid to create a list of a specific size. The list looks just like a rectangle that is waiting for you to put report items inside it. The difference between a list and a rectangle is that a list repeats for each row of its data set or group when the report is rendered, whereas a rectangle does not repeat. You can also add a list to a report that already contains report items. After adding a list to the design grid, you can drag existing report items into the list.

In this procedure, you create a new report to which you add a list data region and associate the data region with a dataset.

Add a list

1   In Solution Explorer, right-click the Product Sales and Profitability Chart.rdl report, click Copy, click the Reports folder, and then press Ctrl+V to paste a copy of the report into the folder.

2   Right-click the new report, click Rename, and then type a new name for the report: **Product Sales and Profitability List.rdl**.

3   Double-click the Product Sales and Profitability List.rdl report in Solution Explorer to display the report in the Document window.

4   Resize the Document window so that you can see the full width of the chart. You might need to close some Visual Studio windows, which you can open later by using the View menu.

5 Change the *Height* property to **10in** in the Size category of the Body object in the Properties window.

You won't really need all this space for the finished report, but the design grid is now longer, which gives you more room to work with.

6 Click the upper right-hand corner of the matrix to select the matrix, and then, while pressing the Ctrl key, click the chart to select both report items.

7 Drag the report items down so that the top of the chart is at the 6-inch mark on the vertical ruler.

8 Click List in the Toolbox window, and then place your mouse pointer just below the bottom left corner of the report title textbox. Click to create a list of a fixed size.

9 In the Properties window, change the *Width* property to **7.5in** and the *Height* property to **4in**.

10 In the Properties window, scroll to find the *DataSetName* property, and then click DataDetail in the property's list box.

▶ **Note** Each data region is associated with a single dataset. In previous procedures, the *DataSetName* property was updated automatically for you when you added the first field from a dataset to a table or a matrix. However, you need to set this property manually when you add a list to your report. Regardless of the data region, however, if you change the dataset name or remove a dataset from the report, you will need to update the *DataSetName* property or else the report will not render.

Grouping and Sorting a List

A list can display detail rows or a single grouping level, but not both. Further, a list can have only one level of grouping. (As you learn later in this chapter, you can work around that limitation by nesting a list within a list.)

In this procedure, you group data in the list by Category.

Add a grouping level

1 In the Properties window, with list1 selected, click the button with three dots, known as the Ellipsis button, in the *Grouping* property.

2 Replace the default name of the group with **list1_Category**.

3 Click =Fields!Category.Value in the Expression list box, and then click the OK button.

As mentioned earlier, a group in a list works the same way as a group in a table. The difference is that a table can have many groups, whereas a list can have one group.

4   Right-click anywhere inside the list border, click Properties, click the Sorting tab, click =Fields!Category.Value in the Expression list box, and then click the OK button.

The rows in this list will sort alphabetically by Category. At this point, however, a report preview will not render the list because fields have not yet been added to the list.

Working with Fields in a List

Fields in a freestanding textbox can be used anywhere in a list. Just drag the field from the Fields window and position the textbox in the desired position. When you add a numeric field to a list that has grouping applied, the *Sum* function is automatically included in the field expression.

In this procedure, you add Category to the list to serve as a label.

Add a field to the list

1   In the Fields window, click *Category*, drag it to the top left corner of the list, and then drag the right side of the new textbox until it is approximately 2 inches wide.

The list in the design grid looks like this:

2   Click the Bold button on the Report Formatting toolbar.

A basic list data region is created that includes a label to display the current Category when the list repeats the group. Now you're ready to move the chart and matrix into the list.

Nesting Data Regions

To overcome the limitation that a list can have only one grouping level, you can nest a second list inside the first list. Nested lists increase your flexibility by simulating the effect of grouping. You can also nest other data regions inside a list, thereby enabling a variety of report structures that are limited only by your imagination. When nesting data regions in a list, all data regions must use the same dataset.

In this procedure, you nest a chart and a matrix inside the list.

Move a chart and a matrix into the list

1   Click the chart, and then drag the chart into the list just below the Category textbox so that the list data region looks like this:

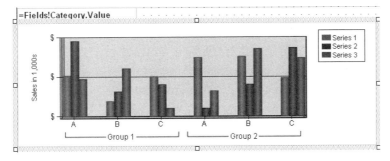

2   Preview the report.

The top of the report should have four separate charts, one for each category. The list is repeating the textbox and the chart for each member of the Category group. The matrix appears below the list just one time, because it is not yet part of the list.

▶   **Note**   If the chart is not repeating, the chart might not be properly positioned within the list. Try moving the chart so that its boundaries are clearly within the boundaries of the list.

3   Click the Layout tab, select the matrix, and then drag the matrix into the list just below the chart.

Now the list should completely surround the chart and matrix.

4   Save and preview the report.

A portion of the first Category of the list is shown here:

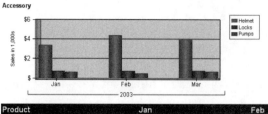

Product		Jan		Feb	
		Sales Amount	Order Quantity	Sales Amount	Order Quantity
Accessory	Helmet	$3,371	167	$4,360	216
	Locks	$720	48	$735	49
	Pumps	$636	53	$468	39
	Total	$4,727	268	$5,563	304
Total		$4,727	268	$5,563	304

Now the scope of each matrix is limited to the Category group, which makes the subtotal for SubCategory redundant. Notice that the bottom two rows of the matrix are identical except for the difference in styles. You can edit the matrix to remove one of the subtotals to fix this duplication.

5 Click the Layout tab, right-click the SubCategory Total cell, and then click Subtotal.

The Subtotal cell disappears from the matrix.

6 Drag the lower edge of the list up to place it just below the lower edge of the matrix to shrink the space between the repeating regions.

7 Save the report, and preview the report to confirm there is now only one subtotal row.

8 Close the solution.

Chapter 6 Quick Reference

To	Do this
Add a data region	Open the Toolbox window, click the desired data region, point to the target destination in the report body, and then click to place the data region.
Add a row group or column group to a matrix	Select a field in the Fields window and drag to the applicable area, marked Rows or Columns, in the matrix.
Add a static row or column to a matrix	Right-click a textbox in the matrix, and click one of the following: Add Row or Add Column.
Add subtotals to a matrix	Click the group cell in a row or column, and then click Subtotal. Format the subtotal value by clicking the green triangle in the new Total cell for the group.

To	Do this
Open the Chart Properties dialog box	Right-click the chart, and then click Properties.
Add values to a chart	In the Fields window, click the field to be used as a value and drag it to the area of the chart labeled Drop Data Fields Here. *or* Open the Chart Properties dialog box, click the Data tab, and then click the Add button next to the Values box. Click an expression in the Expression list box.
Add a category group to a chart	In the Fields window, click the field to be used as a value and drag it to the area of the chart labeled Drop Category Fields Here. *or* Open the Chart Properties dialog box, click the Data tab, and then click the Add button next to the Category Groups box. Click an expression in the Expression list box.
Add a series group to a chart	In the Fields window, click the field to be used as a value and drag it to the area of the chart labeled Drop Series Fields Here. *or* Open the Chart Properties dialog box, click the Data tab, and then click the Add button next to the Series Groups box. Click an expression in the Expression list box.
Add a grouping level to a list	Click the list name in the report items list box of the Properties window. Click the Ellipsis button of the Grouping property. Click an expression in the Expression list box.
Nest a data region	Open the Toolbox window, click the data region, point to the target destination in an existing list, and then click it. Resize and position as necessary. *or* Drag an existing data region into a list while making sure that the data region is completely surrounded by the list.

Chapter

7

Building Advanced Reports

In this chapter, you will learn how to:

■ Create a report parameter to use as a variable for calculating values in a report.

■ Pass a report parameter to a query to filter data at the source.

■ Use a report parameter to filter a dataset or a data region in the report.

■ Use interactive features to navigate within a report or to jump to information located elsewhere.

■ Work with hierarchical data.

In the previous chapter, you created a variety of reports to explore the different ways that data can be organized into data regions. In this chapter, you'll turn your attention to the use of advanced techniques to manipulate data in the report. You'll work with report parameters to allow a user to change a report on demand. You'll also add other interactive features to reports to help users navigate within and across reports. Finally, you'll learn how to work with data that is stored using hierarchical data structures. By successfully completing this and the previous three chapters, your report authoring skills will be complete.

Using Parameters to Change Report Data

You can use report parameters to make reports more flexible in a number of ways. A report parameter can be used alone to calculate values in the report. Such values can be either displayed as content in the report or used to change properties that affect the behavior and appearance of a report. For example, instead of using a fixed value to control conditional formatting in a report, as you did in Chapter 5, "Working with Expressions," you can add a report parameter that prompts the user to enter a value. The report then renders the report using the new value to format the report.

You can also create a single report that provides alternate views of data by using a report parameter in combination with a query parameter. This enables a query to be modified on demand, thus changing the query results. A *query parameter* is a placeholder in the WHERE clause of a SQL query that is linked to a report parameter. Reporting Services replaces the placeholder in a query with a report parameter's value and then executes the query. Each time the value of the report parameter changes, the query executes.

Another way to use a report parameter is to filter data in the report after the query executes. This technique is useful when a user wants to switch quickly between different sets of data in the same report. With a filter in the report, a user does not have to wait for the query to execute after changing the value of a report parameter.

How to Use Report Parameters in Expressions

A report parameter is added to a report in the authoring stage. At a minimum, you must define a name and a data type for the report parameter, and you can optionally create a predefined list from which the user can select a value. You can then add an expression to the report that calculates a value to be displayed in the report or that controls the behavior and appearance of items in the report.

Adding a Report Parameter

Every report parameter that you add to a report must have a unique name and a data type. The report parameter name cannot contain a space or a special character, because its name will become part of an expression used to access the parameter value. If you use a numeric or time data type, be aware that you'll have to use the *Format* function to control the formatting of the value if you want to display the report parameter's value in a textbox.

A report parameter normally has a prompt, which is a label for the input box or list box that the user sees when the report is displayed. If you don't enter text for a prompt, the user can neither see nor change the report parameter. This is actually a good way to hide a parameter if you're providing the value in some other way such as administratively, as you'll learn in Chapter 8, "Managing Content," or programmatically, as you'll learn in Chapter 16, "Building Custom Reporting Tools." (Chapter 16 can be found on the companion CD.)

When you create a report parameter, you have the option to specify the values that Reporting Services will consider valid. Not only can you prevent a user from using a blank or null value, but you can also provide a list of specific values from which the user must choose. You can create this list manually or by using a query from any dataset in the report to build the list. You can even define a default value so that the user can view the report before changing the report parameter value. Like the list of available values, the default value can be entered manually or it can be based on a query.

In this procedure, you will add a report parameter to prompt the user for a margin percentage value that defaults to 0.15.

Add a report parameter with a default value

1 Start Microsoft Visual Studio, and open the solution My Adventure Works that you saved in the C:\rs2000sbs\Workspace\My Adventure Works folder.

▶   **Note**   If you skipped Chapter 6, "Organizing Data in Reports," open the solution My Adventure Works in the C:\rs2000sbs\Answers\chap06\My Adventure Works folder.

2 In Solution Explorer, right-click the Product Sales And Profitability.rdl report, click Copy, click the Reports folder, and then press CTRL+V to paste a copy of the report into the folder.

3 Right-click the new report, click Rename, and then type a new name for the report: **Product Sales and Profitability Parameters.rdl**.

4 Double-click the Product Sales And Profitability Parameters.rdl report in Solution Explorer to display the report in the Document window.

5 Click the Preview tab to view the report.

In Chapter 5, you added conditional formatting to this report to display margin percentage exceptions with a red font color when the value was below 15 percent. Now you'll use a report parameter to allow the user to change the exception definition at execution.

6 Click the Layout tab, and then click Report Parameters on the Report menu.

Currently, no report parameters are defined in this report.

7   Click the Add button to open the Report Parameters dialog box:

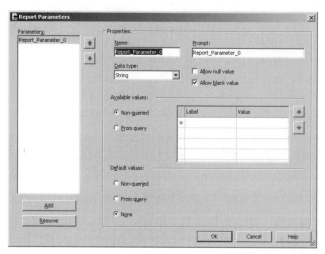

By default, the name of the parameter is also used as a prompt, which as you'll see later is visible to the user when the report is rendered online. Notice the options to control whether the parameter can accept a null or a blank value, or both.

8   Replace the default parameter name with **MarginPercent**.

Remember that a parameter name cannot include a space or special character.

9   Replace the default prompt with **Margin %**.

Because the prompt is just a string that is displayed to a user in the HTML viewer, the prompt can contain spaces and special characters.

10   Click Float in the Data Type list box.

Review the other data type options that are available in the Data Type list box. The default data type is *String*, but you'll need to select a different data type if the expression in which you are using the parameter value requires a different data type. In this case, the value will be used to compare to a percentage value calculated in the report and must, therefore, be typed as **Float**.

11   Keep the Available Values option set to Non-Queried.

If you don't create a list of available values, the user must type in a report parameter value. You'll learn how to provide available values later in this chapter.

12   Click the Non-Queried option in the Default Values pane.

A default value is required to enable report rendering before the user makes a selection. If you opt to omit a default value, by selecting None, the report will not be rendered until the user enters a value.

13 Enter a default value: .15.

The dialog box looks like this:

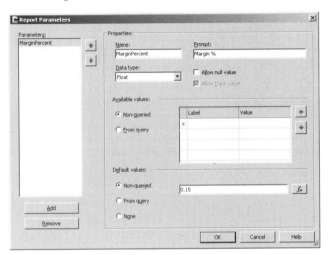

Notice the Expression button to the right of the Default Value input box. You can click this button to build an expression that calculates the default value rather than use a fixed value.

14 Click the OK button.

If you preview the report at this time, you see the report parameter, but because the report definition hasn't been changed yet to use its value, nothing happens if you try to change the value.

Using the Parameters Collection

A report parameter is an object in the *Parameters* collection that you can access using either its *Value* or *Label* property. The *Value* property retrieves the current value of the parameter, whereas the *Label* property retrieves the user-friendly name for the parameter that is defined in the list of available values. Using Microsoft Visual Basic collection syntax, you can refer to a report parameter in any expression.

In this procedure, you will modify the expressions that conditionally format the margin percentage so that they use the report parameter value instead of a fixed value.

Change conditional formatting with a report parameter

1 Click the Margin % cell, which is the cell in the sixth column of the third row (the details row).

2   In the Properties window, click Expression in the *Color* property for the Margin % cell.

3   Position the cursor after the greater than symbol (<), and then, while pressing SHIFT, use the Right Arrow button to select 0.15.

4   Expand the *Parameters* collection in the Fields list.

Each time you add a report parameter to the report, a new member is added to the *Parameters* collection for you to use in an expression.

5   Click *MarginPercent*, and then click the Insert button.

The Edit Expression dialog box looks like this:

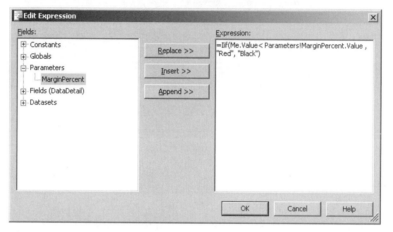

The *MarginPercent* parameter value, which can be changed at run time by the user, replaces the fixed value of 0.15. Now the conditional formatting will depend on the value of the parameter supplied by the user to determine whether the margin percentage value in the report is displayed in red or black.

6   Copy the expression to the Clipboard so that you can easily update the footer rows, and then click the OK button.

7   Click the Margin % cell in the table1_SubCategory footer, and then while pressing the CTRL key, click the same cell in the table1_Category footer and in the table footer to select all three cells. Paste the expression from the Clipboard into the *Color* property.

8   Select only the Margin % cell in the table footer, click Expression in the *Color* property list box, and then edit the expression to replace Black with **White**, as shown here:

```
=IIf(Me.Value<Parameters!MarginPercent.Value, "Red", "White")
```

In the table footer, the background is black. If the text color is also black, the margin percentage will not be visible to users when its value is greater than the value supplied for the report parameter.

Instead, use white to be consistent with the text color of other cells in this row.

9 Click the OK button to close the Edit Expressions dialog box.

10 Save your report, and then check the results by clicking the Preview tab. The report parameter is displayed above the HTML Viewer toolbar:

You didn't provide a list of available values for this parameter, so a parameter input box is displayed above the report, preceded by its prompt string (Margin %). Because the report parameter has a default value, the report is rendered on demand and the default value is displayed in the parameter's input box.

11 Enter **0.35** for Margin %, and then click the View Report button.

Clicking the View Report button renders the report using the new report parameter value, and now you can see the Full-Finger Gloves, L and the category footer rendered with a red font.

▶ **Tip** Allowing a null value for the report parameter is perfectly fine if the expression will evaluate correctly. If you want to allow the user to render this report without any conditional formatting, you can select the report parameter option Allow Null Value. Then, when the report renders, a NULL check box appears next to the Margin % parameter. If the user were to select the NULL check box, the expression would return false for all rows because none of the rows has a margin percentage that is less than null. The false result for the expression would cause all rows to display the margin percentage in black, except the table footer which would display in white, which effectively removes conditional formatting from the report.

How to Use Query Parameters

To use a query parameter, you must add a parameter name to the WHERE clause of the SQL query string. When Report Designer detects a new query parameter, it automatically creates a corresponding report parameter. Then you complete the report parameter definition by specifying a list of available values and an optional default value.

Adding a Query Parameter

You can make a query more flexible by adding a query parameter to the WHERE clause as a placeholder for a value that will be used to filter the data at the source. Always precede the parameter name with the @ symbol. If you have several datasets in the report, you can use the same query parameter in each dataset.

▶ **Important**   Some data sources do not support query parameters. For these data sources, you will need to use a report filter instead (which you'll learn how to use later in this chapter).

In this procedure, you will replace the fixed values in the WHERE clause of the dataset query with query parameters.

Add query parameters to the dataset

1   Click the Data tab to view the current query, as shown here:

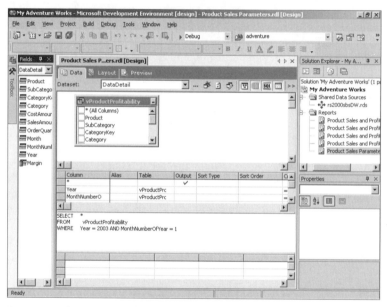

As currently written, this query will create data for a single month only, so a user of the report cannot change the month and year to view results for a different time period.

2   Replace the WHERE clause of the query with the following:

```
WHERE Year = @Year AND MonthNumberOfYear = @Month
```

▶ **Important**   If you're using an Oracle data source with a named query parameter as in this example, you must select the Oracle data provider instead of the generic ODBC data provider in the Data Link Properties of your data source.

3   Click the Verify SQL button to verify that the query is valid, and then click the OK button.

You might need to widen the Document window to see the Verify SQL button on the Dataset toolbar.

4   Click the Edit Selected Dataset button, which is the ellipsis button next to the Dataset list box, to view the Dataset dialog box:

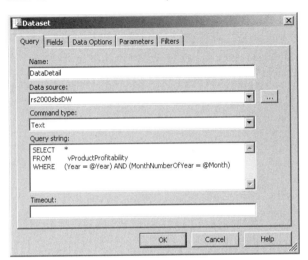

Notice that you can change the dataset name, the data source, and the query, as well as other properties related to the dataset using this dialog box.

5   Click the Parameters tab to view the parameter mapping:

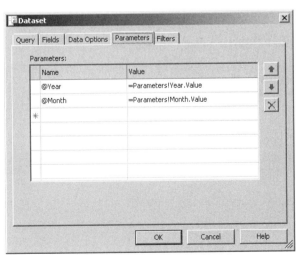

Report Designer automatically creates parameter expressions to which the query parameters, *@Year* and *@Month*, are mapped.

6   Click the Cancel button to close the Dataset dialog box.

Supplying Values for a Query Parameter

Before the query executes, Reporting Services replaces the query parameter with the current value of the corresponding report parameter. Even though you could let the user type in a value for a report parameter, a better approach is to create a list of available values for the report parameter to ensure that the user uses a valid value. You can maintain a fixed list of available values for the report parameter, which you'll learn how to do in this procedure, and you can also use a query to generate a list of available values, which you'll learn how to do later in this chapter.

A list of available values, regardless of how it is built, always contains labels and values. The label is added to the list of items that the user sees in the report parameter's list box. The value is the corresponding result passed to the report parameter for use in an expression or as a query parameter.

In this procedure, you will manually enter a list of available values for the *Year* and *Month* report parameters.

Define a list of available values for a report parameter

1   Click the Layout tab, and then click Report Parameters on the Report menu.

Notice the two new report parameters, *Year* and *Month*.

2   Click *Year* in the Parameters list.

By default, the name of the parameter is also used as the prompt, the options to allow a null or blank value are cleared, the Available Values option is set to non-queried, and the Default Values option is set to None.

3   In the Available Values table, type the following values:

Label	Value
2001	2001
2002	2002
2003	2003
2004	2004

In this table, the labels and the values are the same because the value in the database is a label that will be understood by the user when choosing a value from the report parameter's list box.

▶ **Note**   Instead of typing in a label or a value for the list, you can use an expression to generate the label or value at run-time. Just click the list box in the applicable field to access the Expression Editor. Alternatively, you can use a query to supply the values for the parameter, which you'll learn how to do later in this chapter.

4   Click the Non-Queried option in the Default Values pane.

5   Enter a default value: **2003**.

The dialog box looks like this:

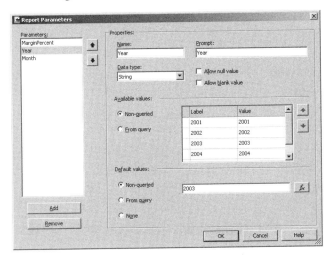

▶ **Tip**   Often, users want to view the most current data in a report. Instead of hard-coding the year, use an expression to calculate the year: =Year(Now). You must make sure that the result is in the parameter's table of Available Values and that the dataset will contain data for the current year; otherwise, the report will be empty.

6   In the Parameters pane, click the *Month* parameter.

7   In the Available Values table, type in the following values:

Label	Value
Jan	1
Feb	2
Mar	3

▶ **Note**   In an actual report, you would supply all months and month values. This example is abbreviated to reduce the amount of typing you need to do for this procedure.

In this example, the labels and values differ because *Month* is stored as a numeric value in the database and needs to be passed to the query as such. Although using a number to represent the month probably wouldn't confuse users, in other situations, a numerical value for the label might be meaningless to the user. For such cases, use a user-friendly label.

8   Click the Non-Queried option in the Default Values pane.

9   Enter a default value: **1**.

▶ **Tip**   As with the *Year* parameter, you can use an expression to use the current month as the default value for the *Month* parameter. In this case, use the following expression: =Month(Now).

10   Click the OK button.

11   Save the report, and then preview the results.

12   Click Mar in the Month list box, and then click the View Report button.

13   Click 75% in the Zoom list box to shrink the report so that you can see the full width.

The Document window looks like this:

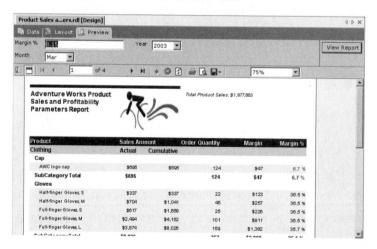

Now you have three report parameters in your report. The first, *Margin %*, is used in an expression in the report to change the report formatting. The other two, *Month* and *Year*, are used to define the query that executes to retrieve data for the report. Since default values were supplied for all the report parameters, the report was executed and rendered using those values. Notice that the report parameters are placed left to right, wrapping to the next row when space is limited, in the same order in which they appear in the Report Parameters dialog box.

Using Input Parameters with a Stored Procedure

Reporting Services supports the use of stored procedures to create a dataset as long as the stored procedure returns a single result set. Creating a dataset that uses a stored procedure is similar to creating a query-based dataset. In the Dataset dialog box, you must name the dataset, set the command type to *StoredProcedure*, and set the query string to the name of the stored procedure.

You can even use the value of report parameters as input parameters for the stored procedure. The Parameters tab of the Dataset dialog box allows you to map report parameters to the input parameters of the stored procedure. Type the name of the input parameter in the *Name* field, and then click the corresponding report parameter from the Values list box on the same row.

How to Use Parameters in Filters

A filter can be added to a dataset, a data region, or a grouping level. In all cases, the process is very similar. A filter is most commonly based on a report parameter's value, which might be selected from a list that is created from another dataset in the report. It can also be based on any valid expression. Before defining a filter using a report parameter, you must first add the report parameter to the report. Then you add a filter definition to the applicable object, such as the report's main dataset, using the object's properties dialog box. It's good practice to display the report parameter's label in the report in case the user decides to save or print the report for future reference.

Creating a Report Parameter for a Filter

A filter is similar to a query parameter in that both result in fewer detail rows for the report. However, a query parameter filters data at the data source when the query is executed and returns a filtered row set to the dataset. A filter, by contrast, prevents some rows in the dataset from being displayed in a report, but it does not eliminate them from the dataset. Using a filter can improve report performance when the user changes report parameters, because data is available for rendering without necessitating another query to the database.

▶ **Note**   A query parameter can also improve report performance by returning fewer rows in the dataset. Whether to use a query parameter or a filter parameter depends on the volume of rows that are being returned from the data source versus the volume of rows that are being filtered out of the dataset for rendering.

As with query parameters, you should make sure that the report parameter value used in a filter is valid. The best way to do this is to use a query to build a list of available values for the report parameter. This query should contain columns only for labels and values. By using a query, you can keep the list of available values up to date with actual values contained in the source database.

In this procedure, you will add a dataset to the report to retrieve valid values for a report parameter.

Add a dataset for report parameter values

1   Click the Data tab, and then click <New Dataset.> in the Dataset list box.

2   Type **Category** as the dataset name, and then click OK.

3   Click the Generic Query Designer button to toggle from the Generic Query Designer to the Query Builder.

4   Right-click in the Diagram pane (the top pane), and then click Add Table.

5   Click DimProductCategory in the list of tables, click the Add button, and then click the Close button.

    The DimProductCategory table is displayed in the Diagram pane. You can build a SQL query by using the table diagram to select columns from the table.

6   Select the ProductCategoryKey and ProductCategoryName check boxes in the DimProductCategory table diagram.

    The DimProductCategory table contains only five records that represent the distinct names of all product categories that Adventure Works sells, whereas the vProductProfitability view contains many records for sales transactions that also include category names. You get the same results whether you query the table or the view, but querying DimProductCategory to get values for a report parameter is potentially much faster because fewer records must be scanned.

7   Enter **AS CategoryKey** after ProductCategoryKey in the SQL pane, and then enter **AS Category** after ProductCategoryName so that the SQL statement looks like this:

```
SELECT ProductCategoryKey AS CategoryKey, ProductCategoryName AS
Category FROM DimProductCategory
```

The AS expression creates an alias to replace the actual column name, often to make shorter column names in the result set or to make the original column names more user-friendly in the result set. For example, CategoryName is the alias for ProductCategory-Name. You don't have to use an alias for ProductCategoryName, but sometimes doing so can make expressions in the report easier to read.

8 Click the Verify SQL button to check the query syntax.

9 Click the OK button.

Now that you have successfully added another dataset to the report, you'll need to update any report item using an aggregate in the report body to associate it with the correct dataset.

10 Click the Layout tab, right-click the textbox in the upper right corner of the report that contains the *Sum* aggregate function, and then click Expression.

11 Add "**DataDetail**" as a *Scope* argument to the expression so that it looks like this:

```
="Total Product Sales:
"+Format(Sum(Fields!SalesAmount.Value,"DataDetail"),"c0")
```

▶ **Tip** The *Scope* argument is required here because your report now contains two datasets. Without the *Scope* argument in aggregate expressions, the report will fail to process. For this reason, it's a good habit to always use a *Scope* argument in a report that contains only one dataset so that you can avoid having to fix the expression later if you need to add another dataset.

12 Click the OK button.

In this procedure, you will add a new report parameter that will use the Category dataset to build a list of available values.

Add a report parameter with a query for available values

1 Click the Layout tab, and then click Report Parameters on the Report menu.

2 Click the Add button.

3 Enter a name: **Category**.

4 Enter a prompt: **Category**.

5 Click Integer in the Data Type list box.

Because you will be using the value returned from the CategoryKey column as the report parameter, you must change the data type of the report parameter to match the data type of the database value.

6 Click the From Query option for Available Values.

7 Click Category in the Dataset list box.

All datasets in the report are available for selection. The field names created from the query, which in this case is just a single field name, are displayed in the Value and Label fields. They serve the same purpose as the Value and Label fields for which you added values earlier in this chapter. The query that you use to supply values for a report parameter should include only two columns, one for the value passed to the report and one for the value displayed to the user.

▶ **Tip**   You can build cascading parameters by using the value of one report parameter as a query parameter in a query used to populate the list of values for another report parameter. This is useful for reducing the size of a list of available values, thereby making it easier for a user to find a desired value.

8 Click *CategoryKey* in the Value Field list box.

9 Click *Category* in the Label Field list box.

10 Click the Non-Queried option for Default Values.

11 Enter 4 as a default value so that the Report Parameters dialog box now looks like this:

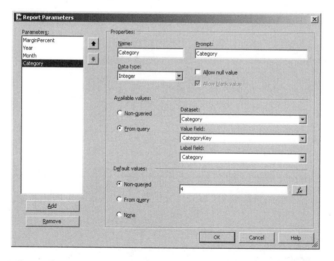

The value 4 corresponds to the Component category. The report parameter list box will display Component by default when the report is rendered. If you decide instead to use a query to set a default value, you must select the dataset and a value field.

Notice that the option to Allow Blank Value is not available. This option is not permitted when the data type is set to Integer. A blank value is possible only when using the string data type.

12 Click the OK button.

If you preview the report at this point, nothing is changed (other than the addition of the parameter to the Report toolbar) because you have not yet used the report parameter value in an expression.

Adding a Filter

You can apply a dataset filter by editing the properties of a dataset. Reporting Services will filter all data regions that use the filtered dataset in the report. The effect in a rendered report looks the same as it does when using a query parameter in the WHERE clause of a query, but it is different because the full dataset is retrieved from the data source.

You can also filter a single data region in a report and keep the full dataset for other data regions. Say, for example, you have a matrix that shows annual sales for multiple years, but you want to chart sales only for the most recent year. Instead of placing the filter on the dataset, right-click the data region that you want to filter so that you can access the data region's Properties dialog box. The Filters tab in this dialog box is similar to the dataset's Filters tab, but affects only the selected region. Similarly, a grouping level of a data region can be filtered by editing its properties.

In this procedure, you will apply a filter to the DataDetail dataset based on the value of the *Category* report parameter.

Add a filter to a dataset

1 Click the Data tab.

2 Click DataDetail in the Dataset list box.

3 Click the Edit Selected Dataset button.

4 Click the Filters tab.

5 Click `=Fields!CategoryKey.Value` in the Expression list box.

You must select this expression because it corresponds to the value returned by the report parameter, *CategoryKey*, and not the label, Category.

6 Click Expression in the Value list box.

7   Expand Parameters, click Category, and then click the Replace button.

8   Click the OK button.

The Dataset dialog box should look like this:

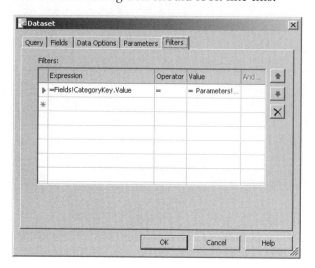

9   Click the OK button.

Using UNION to Expand a Dataset for a Report Parameter

In the previous procedure, you were able to use the *Category* parameter to select a specific category to display, but you had no way to view all categories because you cannot select multiple values in a report parameter list box. (However, you can write a custom application to allow the selection of multiple values, which you'll learn how to do in Chapter 16, "Building Custom Reporting Tools." Chapter 16 can be found on the companion CD.)

To provide All Categories as a value for the report parameter, you can modify your query using UNION to combine two queries. Simply add another query to the end of the SQL statement that creates the main list of available values, using a UNION operator and a query like this: `UNION SELECT -1, 'All Categories'`. When working in the Query Builder, a warning message will be displayed, but that's okay. Just click the Yes button to keep the modified query.

You'll also need to modify the dataset used to load values into the data regions by adding a query parameter to the WHERE clause like this: (CategoryKey = @Category OR @Category = -1). If the user selects All Categories as the *Category* report parameter, this part of the WHERE clause is ignored and all rows in the view are returned, which is the equivalent of All Categories. Otherwise, the value corresponding to the label selected will be passed to the query to filter the data at the source by *CategoryKey*. Be sure to use the Generic Query Designer when modifying this query to avoid an automatic restructuring of your query.

If you use this technique, remove the filter on the dataset based on *Category*, or the report will be empty when using All Categories. If left in place, the datset filter tries to display rows with the category All Categories, which doesn't exist.

Adding a Parameter Value to a Report

To ensure that users of a report clearly understand that a report has been filtered, include a textbox that displays the current value of the filter. To do this, display the *Label* property of the report parameter that is used as the filter in a textbox.

In this procedure, you will add a textbox to the top of the report to identify the current filter when the report is rendered.

Display a parameter value in a textbox

1   Click the Layout tab, click the Total Product Sales textbox while pressing CTRL, and then drag below the Total Product Sales textbox to make a copy of it.

2   Right-click the new textbox, and then click Expression.

3   Expand Parameters in the Fields pane, click Category, and then click the Replace button.

4   Change the expression so that it looks like this:

```
="Filtered by: "+Parameters!Category.Label
```

Even though the value passed to the report parameter is an integer, you have access to the label of the report parameter for display in a textbox.

5   Click the OK button.

6   Save, and then preview the report.

The top of your report should now look like this:

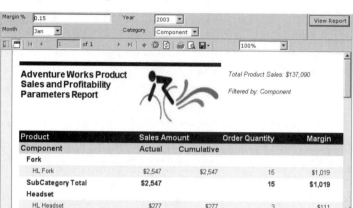

Notice that the *Category* default value, Component, is now displayed at the top of the report.

Linking Information with Interactive Features

Report parameters are a useful interactive feature of Reporting Services that allow a user to manipulate what is seen within a report. Other features are also available—actions, visibility properties, and subreports—to help users interactively navigate reports. Since these features are dependent on interaction with a user, the reports must be rendered on a device that not only supports HTML, but also maintains a connection to the Report Server during the reporting session.

As with many of the features of Reporting Services, the full range of potential applications is impossible to enumerate. One way to think about using these features is to consider how a user generally begins exploring information. A user often starts by examining summary information to determine which detailed data needs to be examined. Like the index at the back of this book, summary information can be used as a pointer to more specific information. Similarly, you can implement actions to allow a user to jump from summary data to detail data, whether or not all of the data is included in the same dataset or report. Alternatively, when the summary and detail data can be retrieved from the same data set, you can build a data region that includes all the data, and then use visibility properties to hide the details until the user chooses to view them. However, there are times when the details come from a different data set that precludes the use of a single data region, but you can easily solve this problem by nesting a subreport inside a data region.

How to Implement Actions

An action triggers a change in a report when a user clicks a report item. By using a bookmark, you can enable a user to jump to other sections of the same report using the simplest type of action. You can also use an action to jump from a report to a Web page or to jump to another report.

Choosing the Right Action

An *action* is used to link a report item to information located elsewhere. The type of action that you create determines where that information is located and what it looks like. When a user clicks a bookmark action, the report switches to another area of the report, which might be another data region or another page in the same report. Implementing a bookmark action is a two-step process. You have to add the bookmark to a report item (which is not limited to a textbox or an image) that is the destination of the bookmark action, and then add the bookmark action to the report item that serves as the origination point.

A hyperlink, or URL, action launches a Web page when a user clicks a report item. You can define a static URL, or you can use an expression to generate a URL dynamically at run-time. You might even consider storing URLs in a relational table that you can query and reference using a field expression. This would allow you to select an appropriate target destination based on current conditions in the source report, or to maintain destinations in a database table to avoid editing the report if a destination changes later.

An action that jumps to another report can simply open another report, or it can pass a value to a report parameter in the target report to control what happens when the report executes or is rendered. For this type of action, you identify the target report, and then, if you're taking advantage of a report parameter, you associate a value in the source report to a specific report parameter in the target report.

Adding Actions

You can add an action either by using the Navigation tab of a report item's Properties dialog box or by accessing the *Action* property of the report item in the Properties window. Although you have a lot of freedom to choose the direction an action will take a user, you can add an action only to a textbox or an image in a report.

In this procedure, you will add an action to the Product textbox in the Orders Detail report to jump to the Products Detail report and display information for the selected product.

Add an action to jump to a report

1 In Solution Explorer, right-click the Reports folder in the project My Adventure Works, point to Add, and then click Add Existing Item to add the Orders Detail.rdl saved in the C:\rs2000sbs\chap07 folder.

2 Right-click the Shared Data Sources folder, point to Add, and then click Add Existing Item to add the rs2000sbs.rds data source saved in the C:\rs2000sbs\chap07 folder.

3 In Solution Explorer, double-click Order Detail.rdl to open the report in the Document window, and then click the Preview tab to confirm that the top of the report looks like this:

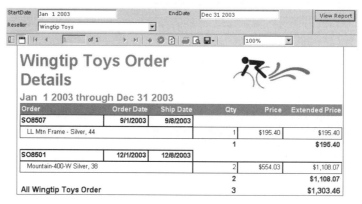

This report uses a table data region to display order detail information used by customer service representatives at Adventure Works to verify order status, troubleshoot order complaints, and answer questions from resellers.

4 Right-click the Reports folder in the project My Adventure Works, point to Add, and then click Add Existing Item to add the Product Detail.rdl saved in the C:\rs2000sbs\chap07 folder.

5 In Solution Explorer, double-click Product Detail.rdl to open it, and
then click the Preview tab, scrolling down to view the product information, which should look like this:

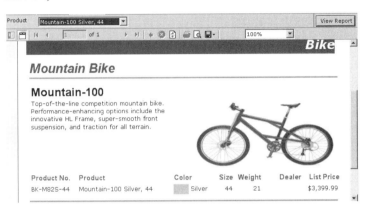

This report is used in conjunction with the Order Detail report to aid
in responding to resellers' questions. Notice the report parameter to
select a product.

6 Close the Product Detail report by clicking the Close button in the
upper right corner of the Document window.

7 Click the Layout tab of the Order Detail report, and then click the
Product cell in the first column of the detail row.

8 In the Properties window, click the ellipsis button for the *Action*
property, which is near the bottom of the properties list in the Misc
section, to display the Action dialog box:

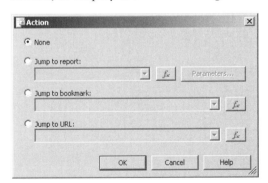

9 In the Action dialog box, click Jump To Report.

10 Click Product Detail in the Jump To Report list box.

Notice that the only reports available in the list are those located in
the same project. Also, notice the Expression button, which you can
use to build an expression to assign a report name.

▶ **Note**   You aren't required to use a report from the same project. The list box is just a convenience feature. You can type in the name of a report that is (or will be) on the Report Server. If the target report will not be in the same folder as the source report, you'll need to precede the report name with the absolute or relative folder path on the server.

If you select Jump To Bookmark, you can enter the bookmark identifier, or you can click the Expression button to build your own expression that evaluates to a bookmark identifier. This feature won't work until the bookmark identifier is added to a report item.

11 Click the Parameters button.

The Parameters dialog box is displayed. This dialog box allows you to provide a value to pass to the report parameter so that the target report can be executed and rendered. The value you supply here overrides the default value, if any, assigned to the report parameter.

12 Click Product in the Parameter Name list box.

The Parameter Name list box displays all report parameters in the target report. In this case, there is only one report parameter, *Product*.

13 Click =Fields!Product.Value in the Parameter Value list box so that the Parameters dialog box now looks like this:

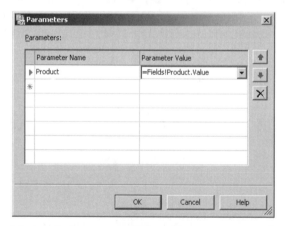

Notice that you can click <Expression.> in the Parameter Value list box to build an expression to return a value to be passed to the target report's report parameter.

14 Click the OK button twice to return to the Properties window, where the *Action* property contains a value, as shown here:

The three dots indicate that an action has been defined for the current report item. You'll have to click the Ellipsis button to access the Action dialog box to see what kind of action has been defined.

15 With the Product cell selected in the detail row, click the Underline button on the Report Formatting toolbar.

▶ **Tip** If the user points to a report item that has an action defined, the cursor changes to a pointing hand to indicate that clicking the item will launch an action. To provide a visual cue to users that an action exists, it's a good idea to underline the text (if the report item is a textbox) to simulate a hyperlink, which most users recognize as a navigation tool.

16 Save the report, and then preview it to test out the action.

17 Click the LL Mtn Frame – Silver, 44 product in the report to view the Product Detail report, which looks like this:

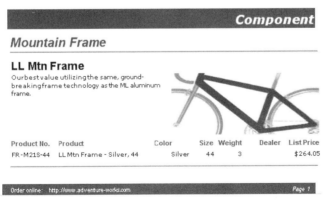

If the report does not refresh, click the action again.

18 On the Preview toolbar, click the Back button to return to the Order Detail preview.

How to Add Dynamic Visibility

Dynamic visibility in Reporting Services allows you to create a drilldown report. *Drilldown* is a term typically used to describe the ability to click a summary value, which then displays the detail values that contribute to the selected summary value. To implement dynamic visibility, you select the report items to be hidden when the report opens and set the *Hidden* property for these items to True. Then, for these same items, you use the *ToggleItem* property to specify the report item that the user must click to make the hidden report items visible, or to return the visible items to a hidden state.

Using the *Hidden* Property

The *Hidden* property, which appears in the Visibility category in the Properties window, controls the visibility of a report item using the fixed values True or False, or a conditional expression that evaluates as True or False. Although a drilldown report often has all detail rows hidden when the report is initially rendered, you can use an expression to display the Detail Rows for specific grouping levels while hiding other detail rows for other grouping levels.

In this procedure, you will hide the Detail Rows of the table in the Order Detail report.

Hide detail rows in a table

1   Click the Layout tab, click the table to display handles, and then click the detail row row handle to select the entire row.

2   In the Properties window, expand the Visibility category, and then click True in the *Hidden* property list box.

The *Hidden* property, when set to True, prevents a report item from appearing in a report. However, the value can still be referenced by an expression associated with another report item.

3   Click the table1_Order footer row handle.

4   In the Properties window, expand the Visibility category, and then click True in the *Hidden* property list box.

5   Save, and then preview the report.

The report should look like this:

Wingtip Toys Order Details

Jan 1 2003 through Dec 31 2003

Order	Order Date	Ship Date	Qty	Price	Extended Price
SO8507	9/1/2003	9/8/2003			
SO8501	12/1/2003	12/8/2003			
All Wingtip Toys Order			3		$1,303.46

The order detail rows and the order footers (which had the subtotals) are now hidden from view. The table footer still displays and calculates correctly.

Using the *ToggleItem* Property

ToggleItem is another property that is assigned to the Visibility category in the Properties window. The value of this property must be a textbox in the report. When the report is rendered, the specified textbox will be displayed with a plus sign. When a user clicks the plus sign, the visibility of the report item is reversed. So, for example, if a detail row is hidden when the report is rendered and its toggle item is a textbox in a header row, when a user clicks that textbox, the detail row is displayed. Conversely, if the detail row is visible, when the user clicks the toggle item, the detail row is hidden.

If group footer totals are in the rows that you are hiding when the report initially opens, you might want to include these totals in a visible group header temporarily. You can then use the *ToggleItem* property for individual cells to hide the totals in the group header when the group footer is visible.

In this procedure, you will assign the SalesOrderNumber textbox to the *ToggleItem* property of both the detail row and table1_Order footer in the table of the Order Detail report.

Toggle the hidden state of an item

1   Click the Layout tab, and then click the detail row row handle to select the entire row.

2   In the Properties window, expand the Visibility category, and then click SalesOrderNumber in the *ToggleItem* property list box.

SalesOrderNumber is the name of the textbox containing the order number in the table1_Order header. By selecting this item as a *ToggleItem*, the SalesOrderNumber textbox will be the item that the user clicks to display the underlying detail rows.

3   Click the table1_Order footer handle to select the entire row.

4   In the Properties window, expand the Visibility category, and then click SalesOrderNumber in the *ToggleItem* property list box.

5   Save and then preview the report to check the results.

6 Click the plus sign next to SO8501 to confirm that your report looks like this:

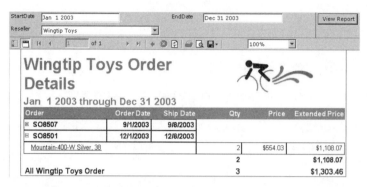

Now when you click a SalesOrderNumber, the detail rows and the order footer are displayed.

In this procedure, you will use the *ToggleItem* property to display the group footer totals in the group header when detail rows are hidden, and hide the group header totals when detail rows are visible.

Show group footer totals in the group header when detail rows are hidden

1 Click the Layout tab to return to the design grid.

2 In the table1_Order footer, click the Qty cell. While pressing SHIFT, click the Extended Price cell, and then copy the contents to the Clipboard.

3 Click the Qty cell in the table1_Order header, and then paste the contents of the Clipboard to the corresponding cells of the table1_Order header so that the table now looks like this:

When you copy these textbox formulas, the Visibility settings are not copied because the settings, in this case, are associated with the table rows and not the textboxes.

4 With the three cells still selected, expand the Visibility category in the Properties window, and then click SalesOrderNumber in the *ToggleItem* property list box.

▶ **Note** Don't change the *Hidden* property. It should still be False.

When the item is toggled, the values set for the property are hidden. In this case, the totals will be displayed in the group header when the detail rows are hidden. When toggled, the totals will be hidden in the group header.

5 Keep the three cells selected, click Solid in the list box for the *Borders* property.

6 Save the report and then preview it to confirm that your report looks like this:

Wingtip Toys Order Details

Jan 1 2003 through Dec 31 2003

Order	Order Date	Ship Date	Qty	Price	Extended Price
⊞ SO8507	9/1/2003	9/8/2003	1		$195.40
⊞ SO8501	12/1/2003	12/8/2003	2		$1,108.07
All Wingtip Toys Order			3		$1,303.46

Notice that the sales order totals are now visible in the order header row.

7 Click the plus sign next to SO8501 to view the details, which look like this:

Wingtip Toys Order Details

Jan 1 2003 through Dec 31 2003

Order	Order Date	Ship Date	Qty	Price	Extended Price
⊞ SO8507	9/1/2003	9/8/2003	1		$195.40
⊟ SO8501	12/1/2003	12/8/2003			
Mountain-400-W Silver, 38			2	$554.03	$1,108.07
			2		$1,108.07
All Wingtip Toys Order			3		$1,303.46

Now the totals in the header are hidden, and the detail rows and footer are displayed.

How to Use Subreports

A *subreport* is a report item that you can use to display another report inside the current report. To filter data in the subreport, you can pass a value from the main report to a report parameter in the subreport.

Deciding When to Use a Subreport

When you want to represent data from the same dataset in different ways in the same report, use separate data regions for the best performance. Even though the subreport behaves like another data region, it's really a different report and is treated as such by the Report Server, which must process each subreport separately from the main report. By comparison, the Report Server can process a report containing multiple data regions in one pass. When processing the subreport, the Report Server ignores report items and properties in the subreport that are not a part of the report body, such as page size, or the page header and footer.

Keeping these trade-offs in mind, in a couple of situations, you might find using a subreport useful. For example, even though you cannot nest data regions that use different datasets, you *can* nest a subreport regardless of its dataset. This technique is useful when you need to combine data from disparate data sources. Another reason for using a subreport is to minimize the re-creation of detailed data that is frequently used in many different reports. You can organize this data once, and then reuse it over and over.

Adding a Subreport

Adding a subreport to your report is much like adding a data region. You use the Toolbox window to add a subreport, and then position the subreport in the report body. A subreport can be freestanding in the report, or it can be nested inside a data region. Nesting a subreport allows you to display data from a dataset that is not associated with the data region, and thus is an especially useful feature when you want to provide supporting details that are stored in a separate data source from the summary information. You can even pass a value to the subreport to control the subreport's behavior when it executes or is rendered.

In this procedure, you will nest the Product Detail report as a subreport in the Order Detail report, and then pass the current Product value to a report parameter in Product Detail.

Nest a subreport in a table

1   In Solution Explorer, right-click the Product Sales and Profitability .rdl report, and click Copy.

2   Click the Reports folder in the Customer Sales folder, and then press CTRL+V to paste a copy of the report into that folder.

Because none of the reports are deployed at this point, both reports must be in the same folder to preview the reports.

3 Right-click the new report, click Rename, and then type a new name for the report: **Product Sales and Profitability Subreport.rdl**.

4 Double-click the Product Sales and Profitability Subreport.rdl report in Solution Explorer to display the report in the Document window.

5 Click the table, right-click the Details Row, and then click Insert Row Below to add a new row.

6 Clear the expression from the *Color* property of the last cell in the new row.

When you insert a row, the style properties are copied from the row from which you initiated the insert action. Since there is no string text or expression in this cell, the expression in the *Color* property won't do anything. Removing the expression will incrementally improve performance, because there will be one less expression evaluated when the report is processed.

7 In the Toolbox window, click Subreport and then click the first cell of the empty detail row.

8 Right-click the subreport, and then click Properties.

9 Click Product Detail in the Subreport list box, which should now look like this:

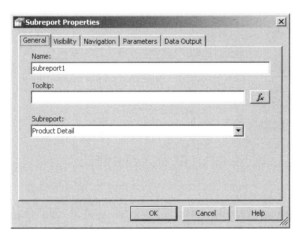

▶ **Note** As with actions, you aren't required to use a report from the same project. You can type the absolute or relative folder path to the report on the Report Server and the name of the report.

10 Click the Parameters tab.

11 Click Product in the Parameter Name list box.

12 Click =Fields!Product.Value in the Parameter Value list box, and then click the OK button.

▶ **Note** You must supply a value for each report parameter in the subreport to display the subreport correctly.

13 Click the second detail row, which contains the subreport, to select the entire row.

14 In the Properties window, expand the Visibility category, and then click True in the *Hidden* property.

15 Click Product in the *ToggleItem* property list box.

16 Save and then preview the report at a zoom factor of 75 percent to check the results.

17 Click to the left of the plus sign next to AWC logo cap, and then scroll to see the details, which should look like this:

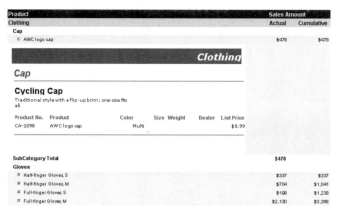

Now when you click a product in the detail rows, the subreport for the selected product displays. In this case, the subreport allows access to details from a completely different dataset. This access would not be possible within a table using nested data regions.

Working with Hierarchical Data

In addition to providing interactive features to help you build more sophisticated reports, Reporting Services helps you tackle the challenge of working with hierarchical data in reports. Specifically, Reporting Services supports the identification of levels in a recursive hierarchy and the aggregation of information across levels within a particular branch of the hierarchy. One type of recursive hierarchy that is encountered in data warehousing is a parent-child dimension.

Another hierarchical structure that Reporting Services can access is an Analysis Services online analytical processing (OLAP) database. Analysis Services, like Reporting Services, is bundled with SQL Server. Analysis Services is a server-based OLAP engine that structures data to facilitate fast and powerful queries that would be challenging to reproduce with traditional relational queries. Creating an OLAP database has three main benefits:

- Its hierarchical structure simplifies user navigation.

- An OLAP database can respond to queries faster than a relational database because it uses this hierarchical structure to store precalculated aggregations.

- An OLAP database uses sophisticated analytical formulas on the server, particularly time series analysis such as year-over-year comparisons.

Many commercial software companies have developed client tools that allow a user to perform interactive analysis directly with the OLAP database. Still, using Reporting Services to access OLAP data using an MDX query has two main advantages. First, you can provide a simple implementation of a thin-client solution when the majority of users don't need flexible analysis but do want access to the results of server-based calculations. Second, you can reduce the execution time of a report compared with retrieving the same data from a relational source.

How to Use Recursive Hierarchies

Reporting Services includes several features that support recursive hierarchies. The first feature allows you to group records in a recursive hierarchy so that data can be organized appropriately in a data region. The second feature is the *Level* function for expressions. Once you've established a recursive hierarchy through grouping, you can use the *Level* function to expose how far the current record is from the top of the hierarchy. This feature is handy for formatting data according to its position within the hierarchy. The third feature is the *Recursive* keyword, which you can use with functions to aggregate members of a hierarchy by group.

Displaying a Recursive Hierarchy in a Data Region

To add a recursive hierarchy to a data region, you need to modify the data region's grouping properties. The group expression must be the field expression that identifies the unique records in the hierarchy. Then, you specify a parent group expression that identifies the parent records. For example, in a table that describes the organizational relationship between employees and managers, each employee record has a key column to uniquely identify the employee and a parent key column that points to the parent record—the employee's manager—in the same table. You can group employees by manager using these key columns and perform aggregations of values within these groupings, such as counting employees by manager or totaling the employees' salaries.

In this procedure, you will add a grouping level to a table for a recursive hierarchy that has employees as unique records and supervisors as parent records.

Define a parent group for a recursive hierarchy

1   In Solution Explorer, right-click the Reports folder in the project My Adventure Works, point to Add, and then click Add Existing Item to add the Employee Salaries.rdl saved in the C:\rs2000sbs\chap07 folder.

2   Double-click the Employee Salaries.rdl report to open it in the Document window, and then click the Preview tab to confirm the top of the report looks like this:

Employee Salaries

Employee Name	Title	Level	Employee Count	Individual Salary	Total Salary
Terri Lee Duffy	VP Engineering			$129,461	
Jian Shuo Wang	Engineering Manager			$88,269	
John Wood	Marketing Specialist			$29,423	
Sheela Word	Purchasing Manager			$61,200	
Annette Hill	Purchasing Assistant			$26,010	
Reinout Hillmann	Purchasing Assistant			$26,010	
Gordon L Hee	Buyer			$37,269	
Erin M Hagens	Buyer			$37,269	
Eric S Kurjan	Buyer			$37,269	
Ben Miller	Buyer			$37,269	
Linda Meisner	Buyer			$37,269	
Fukiko Ogisu	Buyer			$37,269	
Frank Pellow	Buyer			$37,269	
Mikael Sandberg	Buyer			$37,269	
Arvind B Rao	Buyer			$37,269	
Dylan Miller	Research & Development Manager			$102,981	
Diane Margheim	Research & Development Engineer			$83,365	
Gigi Matthew	Research & Development Engineer			$83,365	
James R Hamilton	VP Production			$171,635	
Andrew R Hill	Production Supervisor- WC10			$51,000	

You'll be changing this report to group employees by supervisor.

3   Click the Layout tab, click the table, and then click the detail row to select the row.

4   In the Properties window, click the Ellipsis button for the *Grouping* property.

5   In the Details Grouping dialog box, type **RecursiveGroup** as the name.

6   Click =Fields!EmployeeKey.Value from the Expression list.

7 Click =Fields!ParentEmployeeKey.Value from the Parent group so that the Details Grouping dialog box now looks like this:

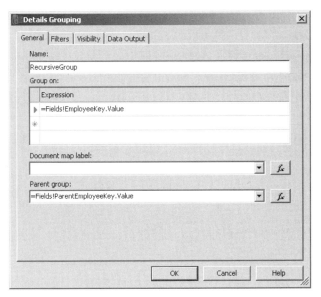

8 Click the OK button.

9 Click the table, right-click the table handle in the top left corner, and then click Properties.

10 Click the Sorting tab.

11 Click =Fields!Salary.Value in the Expression list box, click Descending in the Direction list box, and then click the OK button.

12 Save, and then preview the report at a zoom factor of 75 percent to check the results.

Now employees are sorted in groups by supervisor, and sorted within the group by salary in descending order. However, the layout still doesn't clearly distinguish supervisors from employees.

Using the *Level* Function

The *Level* function is used with recursive hierarchies to identify the relationship of the current row to the top of the hierarchy. The syntax of this function is *Level(Scope)* where *Scope* is the name of a grouping, data region, or dataset. If you omit *Scope*, the current scope of the expression is used. The function returns an integer value that starts at 0 for the top of the hierarchy and increments by 1 for each subsequent level. The most common use of this function is to change style properties for different levels of a hierarchy.

In this procedure, you will use the *Level* function to display the current level of the hierarchy and to format cells by level.

Use the *Level* function in an expression

1   Click the Layout tab, right-click the Level cell in the detail row, and then click Expression.

2   Type the following expression:

```
=Level("RecursiveGroup")
```

The scope of the function is *RecursiveGroup*, which is the employee grouping you created in the previous procedure.

3   Click the OK button.

4   Save, and then preview the report, which should now look like this:

Employee Salaries

Employee Name	Title	Level	Employee Count	Individual Salary	Total Salary
James R Hamilton	VP Production	0		$171,835	
Shai Bassli	Facilities Manager	1		$49,039	
Christian Kleineman	Maintenance Supervisor	2		$41,683	
Pat Coleman	Janitor	3		$18,870	
Jo Berry	Janitor	3		$18,870	
Magnus Hedlund	Facilities Assistant	2		$19,800	
Bob Gage	VP Sales	0		$147,115	
Stephen Yuan Jiang	North American Sales Manager	1		$98,126	
Tete Mensa-Annan	Sales Representative	2		$47,077	
David Campbell	Sales Representative	2		$47,077	
Fernando Caro	Sales Representative	2		$47,077	
Shu Ito	Sales Representative	2		$47,077	
Linda Mitchell	Sales Representative	2		$47,077	
Tsvi Reiter	Sales Representative	2		$47,077	
Garrett R Vargas	Sales Representative	2		$47,077	
Jae B Pak	Sales Representative	2		$47,077	
Michael Greg Blythe	Sales Representative	2		$47,077	
Syed E Abbas	Pacific Sales Manager	1		$98,126	
Lynn Tsoflias	Sales Representative	2		$47,077	
Amy E Alberts	European Sales Manager	1		$98,126	

Now you can see the employee groupings more easily, but formatting would make the groups stand out even better.

5   Click the Layout tab, and then click the first cell in the detail row.

6   In the Properties window, expand the *Padding* category, and then click <Expression.> in the *Left* property list box.

7   Replace the default expression with the following:

```
=2 + (Level("RecursiveGroup") * 20) & "pt"
```

This expression increases the padding used to indent the detail row as the level number increases.

8   Click the OK button.

9   Click the detail row handle in the table.

10   In the Properties window, expand the *Font* property, and then click <Expression.> in the *FontWeight* property list box.

11   Replace the default expression with the following:

```
=IIf(Level ("RecursiveGroup")=0, "Bold", "Normal")
```

This expression uses boldface text when rendering the highest level employees in the report.

12 Click the OK button.

13 Save, and then preview the report, which should now look like this:

Employee Salaries

Employee Name	Title	Level	Employee Count	Individual Salary	Total Salary
James R Hamilton	VP Production	0		$171,635	
Shai Bassli	Facilities Manager	1		$49,039	
Christian Kleineman	Maintenance Supervisor	2		$41,583	
Pat Coleman	Janitor	3		$18,870	
Jo Berry	Janitor	3		$18,870	
Magnus Hedlund	Facilities Assistant	2		$19,890	
Bob Gage	VP Sales	0		$147,115	
Stephen Yuan Jiang	North American Sales Manager	1		$98,126	
Tete Mensa-Annan	Sales Representative	2		$47,077	
David Campbell	Sales Representative	2		$47,077	
Fernando Caro	Sales Representative	2		$47,077	
Shu Ito	Sales Representative	2		$47,077	
Linda Mitchell	Sales Representative	2		$47,077	
Tsvi Reiter	Sales Representative	2		$47,077	
Garrett R Vargas	Sales Representative	2		$47,077	
Jae B Pak	Sales Representative	2		$47,077	
Michael Greg Blythe	Sales Representative	2		$47,077	
Syed E Abbas	Pacific Sales Manager	1		$98,126	
Lynn Tsoflias	Sales Representative	2		$47,077	
Amy E Alberts	European Sales Manager	1		$98,126	

Using the *Recursive* Keyword

The *Recursive* keyword acts as a modifier to any aggregate function with the purpose of returning a value that includes not only the detail rows, but also the value of the parent row in a group. The keyword must be placed after the *Scope* argument in an aggregate function.

In this procedure, you will use the *Recursive* keyword with the aggregate functions *Count* and *Sum*.

Use *Recursive* aggregate functions

1 Click the Layout tab, right-click the Employee Count cell in the detail row, and then click Expression.

2 Enter the following expression:

```
=Count(Fields!EmployeeKey.Value,"RecursiveGroup",Recursive)
```

3 Click the OK button.

4 Right-click the Total Salary cell in the detail row, and then click Expression.

5 Modify the expression so that it looks like this:

```
=Sum(Fields!Salary.Value,"RecursiveGroup",Recursive)
```

This expression calculates the total salaries for the employees in levels below the current row *and* includes the salary for the current row.

6 Right-click the Salary of Reports cell in the detail row, and then click Expression.

7 Change the expression so that it looks like this:

```
=Sum(Fields!Salary.Value,"RecursiveGroup",Recursive)-
Sum(Fields!Salary.Value)
```

This expression subtracts the salary of the current employee from the recursive aggregation so that only the value of the employees underneath the current employee is returned.

8 Click the OK button.

9 Save, and then preview the report using a zoom factor of 75 percent to confirm that the top of the report now looks like this:

Employee Salaries

Employee Name	Title	Level	Employee Count	Individual Salary	Total Salary	Salary of Reports
James R Hamilton	VP Production	0	6	$171,635	$319,986	$148,351
Shai Bassli	Facilities Manager	1	5	$49,039	$148,351	$99,313
Christian Kleinerman	Maintenance Supervisor	2	3	$41,683	$79,423	$37,740
Pat Coleman	Janitor	3	1	$18,870	$18,870	$0
Jo Berry	Janitor	3	1	$18,870	$18,870	$0
Magnus Hedlund	Facilities Assistant	2	1	$19,890	$19,890	$0
Bob Gage	VP Sales	0	17	$147,115	$1,053,493	$906,378
Stephen Yuan Jiang	North American Sales Manager	1	10	$98,126	$521,818	$423,692
Tete Mensa-Annan	Sales Representative	2	1	$47,077	$47,077	$0
David Campbell	Sales Representative	2	1	$47,077	$47,077	$0
Fernando Caro	Sales Representative	2	1	$47,077	$47,077	$0
Shu Ito	Sales Representative	2	1	$47,077	$47,077	$0
Linda Mitchell	Sales Representative	2	1	$47,077	$47,077	$0
Tsvi Reiter	Sales Representative	2	1	$47,077	$47,077	$0
Garrett R Vargas	Sales Representative	2	1	$47,077	$47,077	$0
Jae B Pak	Sales Representative	2	1	$47,077	$47,077	$0
Michael Greg Blythe	Sales Representative	2	1	$47,077	$47,077	$0
Syed E Abbas	Pacific Sales Manager	1	2	$98,126	$145,203	$47,077
Lynn Tsoflias	Sales Representative	2	1	$47,077	$47,077	$0
Amy E Alberts	European Sales Manager	1	4	$98,126	$239,357	$141,231

Compare the difference in the results of the Total Salary column and the Salary of Reports column. If you want a parent row's value aggregated with the lower levels, simply use an aggregation with the *Recursive* keyword to get a result like the Total Salary column. If you don't want the parent row's value included, you'll need to subtract out the current row to get results as shown in the Salary of Reports column.

How to Use Analysis Services Data in a Report

Using Analysis Services data in a report is very similar to using relational data. You still need to define a data source, create a dataset, and add fields to the report. However, when creating a dataset, you write a query using Multidimensional Expressions (MDX) instead of SQL. The procedures in this section will lead you through an examination of an existing report to illustrate these concepts.

> ▶ **Important** To perform the procedures in this section, you must have Analysis Services installed on your computer, and you must have restored the Analysis Services database by following the instructions in "Installing and Using the Practice Files" in the Introduction to this book.

Creating an Analysis Services Data Source

You must create the Analysis Services data source using the Microsoft OLE DB Provider for OLAP Services data provider.

In this procedure, you will review an Analysis Services data source that has been created for a report.

Examine an Analysis Services data source

1 In Solution Explorer, right-click the Shared Data Sources folder, point to Add, and then click Add Existing Item to add the rs2000sbsOLAP.rds data source saved in the C:\rs2000sbs\chap07 folder.

2 Right-click the Reports folder in the project My Adventure Works, point to Add, and then click Add Existing Item to add the Year over Year Sales.rdl saved in the C:\rs2000sbs\chap07 folder.

3 Double-click the Year over Year Sales.rdl to open the report, click the Preview tab, and then click the Date parameter list box to view its contents, which look like this:

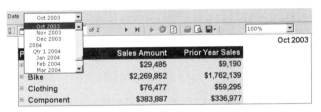

Unlike the Product Sales and Profitability Parameters report created earlier in this chapter, which had separate report parameters for month and year, the report parameter list box here has values for all levels in the time dimension: year, quarter, and month.

Notice also the comparison of the selected time period to the parallel period of the prior year, whether the period is year, quarter, or month. Constructing a SQL query to produce the same result would be challenging, but using an MDX query makes it very easy, because the previous period can be defined as a calculation in the database.

4 In Solution Explorer, double-click the Shared Data Sources folder, and then double-click the rs2000sbsOLAP.rds data source to view the Shared Data Source dialog box:

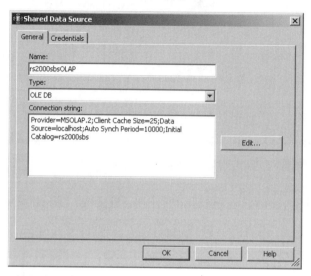

5 Click the Edit tab, and then click the Provider tab in the Data Link Properties dialog box to view the data provider.

To use Analysis Services data, you must use the Microsoft OLE DB Provider for Olap Services 8.0.

6 Click the Next button to view the connection information.

When working with an Analysis Services data source, you must use Microsoft Windows Integrated Security. Then, you select the applicable Analysis Services database as the initial catalog.

7 Click the Cancel button twice to close the data source without changes.

Creating an Analysis Services Dataset

Analysis Services uses Multidimensional Expressions (MDX) to query its OLAP database. An MDX query is similar to a SQL query in that it has a SELECT, FROM, and WHERE clause. However, where SQL is designed to deal with only a two-dimensional structure of rows and columns, MDX is designed to deal with the multidimensional OLAP structure. Because of its structural differences from SQL, you can add an MDX query to a dataset using only the Generic Query Designer.

If you're new to OLAP, MDX queries can seem pretty daunting to construct, but with lots of practice, you'll be rewarded with access to a rich and powerful source of data for reporting. A more complete explanation of MDX is beyond the scope of this book, but you can start learning more about this subject using SQL Server Books Online. (If you don't have SQL Server Books Online installed on your SQL Server, you can find information in the MSDN Library at *http://msdn.microsoft.com/library/default.asp?url=/library/en-us/startsql /getstart_4fht.asp*.) This section of Chapter 7 assumes that you already have some experience using MDX.

In this procedure, you will review an MDX query in a report's dataset.

Review an MDX query in a dataset

1 Click the Data tab to view the Generic Query Designer, as shown here:

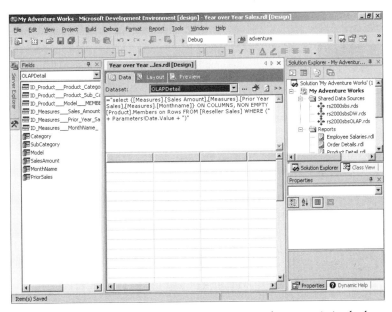

Here, the MDX query is a string expression because it includes a parameter expression in the WHERE clause. The WHERE clause filters the data at the source, which is also known as *slicing*. If the parameter expression were eliminated, the MDX query could be entered directly like a SQL query. The use of [Product].Members on ROWS in the SELECT clause will return a set of product categories, subcategories, and model names that come from different levels of the hierarchy known as the Product dimension.

2 Look at the fields in the Fields window.

Report Designer assigns each level of the Product dimension to a separate field so that you can create groupings by level in a data region. Notice also the addition of calculated fields that assign more user-friendly names to the default field names created by Report Designer.

3   Click DateList in the Dataset list box to view the MDX query used for the list of available values for the report parameter.

The DateList query looks like this:

```
With
  MEMBER Measures.DateKey as '[Order Date].CurrentMember.UniqueName'
  MEMBER Measures.DateName as 'Space([Order Date].CurrentMember.Level
.Ordinal*2) + [Order Date].CurrentMember.Name'
Select {Measures.DateKey, Measures.DateName} on Columns,
[Order Date].Members on Rows
FROM [Reseller Sales]
```

Here, the SELECT clause includes a calculated member *Measures .DateName* that is defined in the WITH clause as `Space([Order Date] .CurrentMember.Level.Ordinal*2) + [Order Date].CurrentMember .Name`. In this example, the *Ordinal* function, used to identify the level of the current row within the hierarchy, is combined with a multiplier to pad the name of the member for use as a label in the report parameter list box. As the level number increases, the amount of padding increases so that members on different levels are clearly differentiated in the list of available values for a report parameter.

Using an Analysis Services Dataset

Once the Analysis Services dataset is created, you can use field expressions in a data region or report item to organize data in your report. When the MDX query executes, the result is a flattened rowset that can be used almost like the results from a SQL query. You need to use the *First* aggregate function to use the pre-calculated aggregates for each level; if you used the *Sum* function, some values would get double counted. You can also use the *Hidden* and *ToggleItem* properties on group rows to create a drilldown report similar to the one you developed earlier in this chapter.

In this procedure, you will take a look at the use of aggregate functions and report filters with Analysis Services data.

Examine the use of Analysis Services data in a table

1   Click the Layout tab, click the table, and then click the table1_Category header to select the entire row so that the table looks like this:

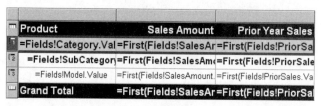

Notice the use of the *First* function in each row. Also, notice there are no detail rows in this table.

2   In the Properties window, click the Ellipsis button for the *Grouping/
   Sorting* property, and then click the Filters tab so that the Details
   Grouping dialog box looks like this:

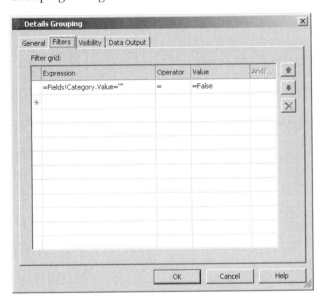

Each grouping level contains a similar expression to eliminate rows
that have an empty value for the key for the current level. Put
another way, the filter will allow the display of only those rows that
have a value in the field used for grouping.

3   Click Cancel to close the dialog box.

4   Save, and then close the solution.

Chapter 7 Quick Reference

To	Do this
Use a report parameter value as a variable	Click Report Parameters on the Report menu while a report is in Layout mode, click the Add button, and then provide a name and data type for a report parameter. Optionally, provide a list of available values or a default value. Use the report parameter value in an expression using the following syntax: *Parameters!ObjectName.Value*.
Display the label of a report parameter	Add the following expression to a textbox in a report: **Parameters!ObjectName.Label**.

To	Do this
Use a query parameter	Add a parameter to the WHERE clause of a dataset query, such as: WHERE Year = @Year. Update the corresponding report parameter, such as *Year*, to specify the appropriate data type, and optionally the list of available values or a default value.
Use a report parameter as a filter	To filter all data regions in a report, click the Data tab, click the dataset in the Dataset list box, and then click the Edit Selected Dataset button. Click the Filters tab, and then select the expression that corresponds to the report parameter's value. *or* To filter a data region, right-click the data region in the design grid, and then click Properties. Click the Filters tab, and then select the expression that corresponds to the report parameter's value. *or* To filter a grouping level, right-click the group row in the design grid, and then click Properties. In the Properties window, click the Ellipsis button for the Grouping property, click the Filters tab, and then select the expression that corresponds to the report parameter's value.
Add an action	Right-click a textbox or an image, click the Ellipsis button for the *Action* property in the Properties window, and then click the option for the type of action to add. Enter the bookmark identifier, report name, or URL to which the action will direct the user. If a target report has a report parameter, click the Parameters button, and then click a report parameter in the Parameter Name list box and an expression in the Parameter Value list box.
Create a drilldown report	Click the row handle of the detail row, and change its *Hidden* property to True in the Properties window. In the *ToggleItem* property for the same row, click the name of the textbox to use as a toggle for the visibility of the detail row.
Add a subreport	Open the Toolbox window, click Subreport, point to the target destination, and click to place the subreport. Right-click the subreport, and then enter the name of the subreport if it's not in the same project folder as the host report, or click to select a report from the Subreport list box if it is in the same project folder.
Group relational data in a recursive hierarchy	In the Properties window, click the Ellipsis button in the *Grouping* property for a data region or in the *Grouping /Sorting* property for the group row in a data region. Click the field expression in the Group On list box to identify a unique row, and click the field expression in the Parent Group list box to identify a parent row.

To	Do this
Identify levels in a recursive hierarchy	Use the *Level* function in an expression, using the group name as scope. For example, for the group Recursive-Group, use the following expression: `=Level("RecursiveGroup")`.
Aggregate data in a recursive hierarchy	Add the *Recursive* keyword to the aggregate function, *=Function(Expression,Scope,Recursive)*. For example, to count employee rows in a recursive group and the parent row, use the following expression: `=Count(Fields!EmployeeKey.Value, "RecursiveGroup", Recursive)`.
Query an Analysis Services database	Create a dataset using the Microsoft OLE DB Provider for OLAP Services 8.0, and then, using the Generic Query Designer, enter an MDX query.
Calculate a group total for an Analysis Services dataset	Delete the detail row from the data region, and use the *First* function instead of *Sum* to prevent overcounting rows in the total.
Filter Analysis Services data rows with an empty value for the current level	In the Properties window, click the Ellipsis button for the *Grouping/Sorting* property of a group row, and then click the Filters tab. Enter an expression that compares the group field to an empty value, such as **=Fields!Category .Value=""**, and then enter the Value expression **=False**.

Part

3

Managing the Report Server

Managing Content

In this chapter, you will learn how to:

■ Publish report definitions and other resources to the Report Server.

■ Arrange content on the Report Server.

■ Create a linked report.

■ Use report properties to manage report content.

■ Control report execution with report properties.

By completing Part 2, "Authoring Reports," you learned not only the basics of authoring reports, but also advanced techniques that you can use to produce a wide variety of useful reports for your organization. The three chapters of Part 3 provide you with the skills to properly manage and secure the reports you create as well as perform administrative tasks on the Report Server. These activities are all part of the managing stage of the reporting life cycle.

In this chapter, you learn how to manage the content on the Report Server. You start by publishing several reports. Then you reorganize content on the Report Server by adding folders, moving content into the new folders, and creating linked reports. You also work with report properties to control both how reports interact with data sources to retrieve data and how reports are processed and rendered.

Your ability to publish and manage reports is determined by the permissions assigned to you. This chapter assumes that you are a local system administrator on the Report Server, which allows you to perform all the tasks described here. Specific information about how to use security permissions to limit a user's actions on the Report Server is discussed in Chapter 9, "Managing Security."

Publishing Reports

When you publish a report, Reporting Services stores the report definition in a SQL Server database named ReportServer database (introduced in Chapter 2, "Installing Reporting Services"). You can also publish other items, such as images referenced by reports or other file types that need to be accessed by the reporting community. If you're a report author, you will generally use Microsoft Visual Studio to publish reports. If you're a report administrator, you can use either Report Manager or a small utility named rs.exe to move previously created reports to the ReportServer database. You can even use a custom application for publishing reports by using the Reporting Services Web Services API, which is covered in greater detail in Chapter 15, "Programming Report Server Management." (Chapter 15 can be found on the companion CD.)

How to Publish by Using Visual Studio

As a report author, you can use standard deployment procedures in Visual Studio to publish content to the Report Server. Before you start, you must define deployment properties for each project that contains objects to be deployed. Then you choose what you want to deploy and launch the process.

Defining Deployment Properties by Project

You cannot deploy content until you update a project's deployment properties with a target Report Server for each project that contains content to be deployed. The *TargetServerURL* property must contain a valid URL, which is not validated until you try to deploy. When you use the Report Wizard to create a report, you must supply a URL for the Report Server before you can complete the wizard, but when you start authoring with a blank report, you must add a value to the *TargetServerURL* property of the report's project.

You should also review the other project deployment properties to ensure you get the results that you want when content deploys. By default, the target folder will be the same as the project name. This folder will be created, if it does not exist, as a path on the root node of the Report Server, which is the Home page that you view by using Report Manager. For example, for the My Adventure Works project, a corresponding default folder will be added to the Home page of Report Manager. You can also create nested folders by adding a relative path folder structure, such as Adventure Works/My Adventure Works, to create a folder called My Adventure Works that is contained within the Adventure Works folder on the Home page.

Another project deployment property is *OverwriteDataSources*. This controls whether shared data sources in the project will be published to the server if the file already exists. The default value of False causes a shared data source to be written to the server only if the data source doesn't already exist. The *Overwrite-DataSources* property is discussed in the context of managing data sources later in this chapter.

Visual Studio Configuration Manager has additional options to control the behavior of deployment. First, you can decide whether the build process should detect and display errors in Visual Studio. Second, you can decide whether the deployment process should actually push the report to the Report Server or simply display the rendered report in the Preview mode in Visual Studio.

In this procedure, you will set the deployment properties for the My Adventure Works project.

Set project deployment properties

1   Start Visual Studio, and open the solution My Adventure Works that you saved in the C:\rs2000sbs\Workspace\My Adventure Works folder.

▶ **Note**   If you skipped Chapter 7, "Building Advanced Reports," open the solution My Adventure Works in the C:\rs2000sbs\Answers\chap07\My Adventure Works folder.

2   In Solution Explorer, right-click the My Adventure Works project, and then click Properties.

3   In the My Adventure Works Property Pages dialog box, type **http://localhost/ReportServer** as the *TargetServerURL* so that the dialog box looks like this:

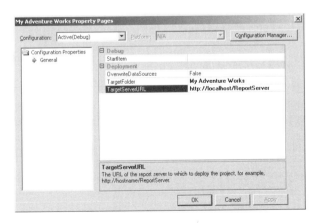

▶ **Important**   You must supply a valid URL for the *TargetServerURL* before a
report can deploy because no default URL is supplied automatically for you. If
you have multiple properties contained in a single solution, you must enter this
URL in each project's properties individually. The URL must be the virtual directory of the Report Server, which is *http://localhost/ReportServer* if you used the
default installation of Reporting Services on your computer.

In this procedure, you will set the project context properties for the My Adventure Works project.

Set project context properties

1   Click the Configuration Manager button.

2   Select the Build and Deploy check boxes for the Debug configuration
of the My Adventure Works project so that the Configuration Manager dialog box looks like this:

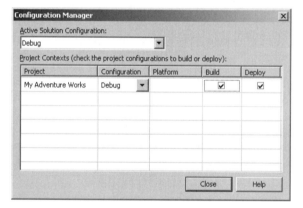

Now when you deploy this project, any detected errors will display
in the Task List window of Visual Studio, and the project's reports
will be published to the target Report Server.

If you clear the Build check box, errors can be detected only if you
try to preview the report in Visual Studio or, after deployment, try to
open the report on the Report Server. If you clear the Deploy check
box, the report will not be published to the server but rather will display in Visual Studio in Preview mode.

3   Click the Close button, and then click the OK button to close all dialog boxes.

Deploying Reports

You can choose to deploy a single object, such as a report or a shared data source, in a solution. You can also decide to deploy an entire solution or just some objects in a particular project.

In this procedure, you will deploy the My Adventure Works solution.

Deploy a solution

1   On the Build menu, click Deploy Solution. Alternatively, you can right-click the solution in Solution Explorer, and then click Deploy Solution.

▶ **Tip**   In a situation in which you have already deployed a solution to which you later add a report, you can deploy the report individually without deploying the entire solution again. Just right-click the report in Solution Explorer, and then click Deploy. You can also use this procedure to deploy a project or a data source.

2   Review the results of the deployment in the Output window, which should look like this:

If the deployment fails, you need to review all errors detailed in the Task List window and take the appropriate action to resolve the problems. However, errors will be listed only if you selected the Build option in the Configuration Manager for the property.

3   To confirm the successful deployment of your solution, start Report Manager by navigating to *http://localhost/Reports* in Microsoft Internet Explorer.

The Home page of Report Manager looks like this:

The My Adventure Works folder corresponds to the single project in the solution that you just deployed. If you have deployed other projects, you will see additional folders on this page. For example, if you completed Chapter 3, "Building Your First Report," you will see the Adventure Works folder.

4   Click the My Adventure Works folder link to see its contents in the list view, which looks like this:

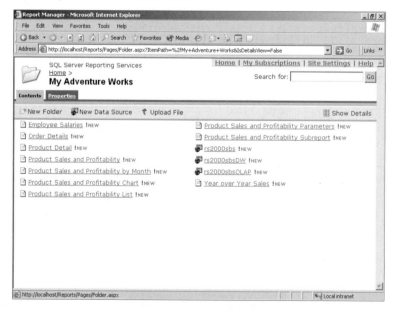

Report Manager queries the ReportServer database to retrieve a list of the resources, such as reports and shared data sources, that are associated with the current folder, My Adventure Works. Notice that the list view displays the folder contents as two columns, with items in alphabetical order.

5   Click the Product Sales And Profitability report link to view the report, which looks like this:

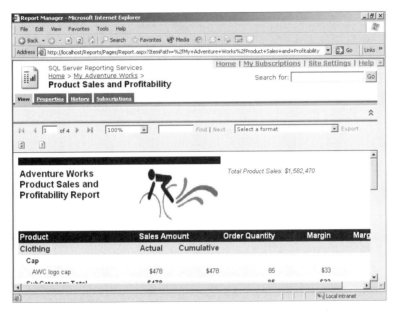

Report Manager passes the request for the report to the Report Server, which in turn manages the processes that result in a report that you can now view in your browser.

Republishing Reports

Sometimes a report needs to be modified, perhaps as a result of issues discovered during testing or because of the development of new business requirements. After making changes to the report, you can redeploy the modified report to the Report Server. When you redeploy a report, the original report definition stored in the ReportServer database is replaced with the new report definition.

Report properties (such as execution, parameters, history, security, and subscription properties) that you assign by using Report Manager will continue to apply after you redeploy a report. Redeployment updates only the report definition.

How to Publish by Using Report Manager

If you're a report administrator and not a report author, you might not have access to Visual Studio to deploy reports to the Report Server. One option that you can use is to upload files individually to the Report Server by using the Report Manager application. You can upload reports, data sources, and other resources that need to be made available to the reporting community.

Uploading Reports

You can use the Upload File feature in Report Manager to navigate to a file on your computer or on a network file share that you want to upload to the Report Server. Like deploying reports with Visual Studio, the upload process actually stores the file in the ReportServer database. You can upload only one file at a time using this method.

In this procedure, you will upload the definition of Product Sales YTD by using Report Manager.

Upload a report file to the My Adventure Works folder

1 Open Report Manager, and then click the My Adventure Works link in the top left corner of the browser window.

2 Click the Upload File button on the Report Manager toolbar, and then click the Browse button to navigate to the C:\rs2000sbs\chap08\ folder and open the file Product Sales YTD.rdl.

Your screen looks like this:

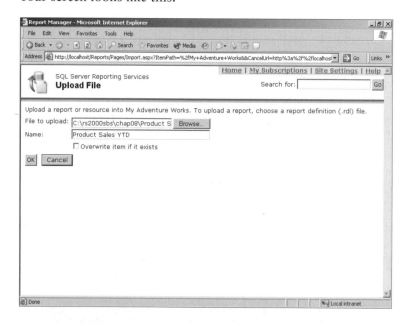

If you prefer, you can type the path and filename in the File To Upload box, and the name in the Name box.

If the file already exists in the current folder, an error message will be displayed when you click OK, unless you select the Overwrite Item If It Exists check box. If this check box is already selected, the overwrite of the file is performed without any warning.

3   Click the OK button.

Report Manager uploads the file and places it in the ReportServer database. The name of the report now displays in the Contents page of the My Adventure Works folder.

4   Click the Product Sales YTD report link to open the report, which looks like this:

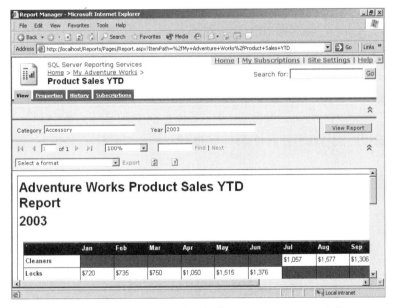

You should always test an uploaded report in Report Manager to confirm that the Report Server can connect properly to the data source, execute the report's query, and render the report.

Uploading Resources

You can also use Report Manager to upload additional items, known as resources, to the Report Server for storage in the ReportServer database. Resources are items such as images—for example, JPEG files—that might be referenced as a link in a report. However, you can also add resources that are not used in a report, such as Microsoft Word or Microsoft Excel files, or even text files. If a user opens a resource, Reporting Services does not process the resource but instead downloads the resource for saving or for viewing, if the client computer has the requisite application. After a resource is uploaded, it can be moved to another folder just like a report. You'll learn more about moving reports and resources later in this chapter.

How to Publish by Using the rs Utility

Another option for publishing reports is the rs utility, which is a command-line utility that you can use to run scripts that manage the Report Server. The rs utility uses a script file to execute commands on the Report Server. You'll learn more about other ways to use this utility in Chapter 15, which can be found on the companion CD. A script to publish reports to the server comes as a sample with Reporting Services. To publish reports with this utility, you need to have a script that provides the details about the reports to be published. Then you execute the rs utility, passing any arguments used to modify the behavior of the script at run time.

Creating a Script File

The rs utility requires an input file with an .rss file extension that is written in Microsoft Visual Basic .NET. Reporting Services ships with a sample Visual Basic .NET script file, PublishSampleReports.rss (located in the C:\Program Files\Microsoft SQL Server\MSSQL\Reporting Services\Samples\Scripts folder), that you can adapt to your needs. The script file used in the following procedure is a simplified version of the official sample script.

Using the rs Utility

When you want to use the rs utility to publish reports, you need to provide at least two arguments, the name of the script file, and the URL for the Report Server, using this syntax: `rs -i input_file -s ReportServerURL`. The current Windows credentials are used for authentication to the Report Server, unless you use arguments to pass a user name and password. To view a description of all available arguments, use the following syntax: `rs -?`. You'll learn more about the rs utility in Chapter 15, which can be found on the companion CD.

In this procedure, you will execute the rs utility using the PublishReports.rss script file as an input file.

Execute the rs utility

1 On the Start menu, click Run, type **cmd,** and then click OK to open a command prompt window.

2 Type **cd c:\rs2000sbs\chap08** at the command prompt to navigate to the folder that contains the script file.

3 Type **rs -?** to view the online help for this utility.

4 Run the rs utility by typing the following: **rs –i PublishReports.rss –s http://localhost/ReportServer.**

Your screen now looks like this:

5 To confirm that the reports were successfully published, open the Home page of Report Manager in Internet Explorer. If the Home page is already open, use the Refresh button on the Internet Explorer toolbar to update the page.

6 Click the Adventure Works Samples folder link.

There should be three reports in this folder: Actual Vs Quota.rdl, Employee Product Sales.rdl, and Product Catalog.rdl.

7 Click the each report link to confirm the reports execute successfully.

Organizing Content

You are not limited to using the folders created as part of the publishing process. In addition, you can add more folders to create a hierarchical organization much like the hierarchy you use in a file system on your computer. You can move reports and resources from their original folder to a new folder quite easily. As part of the content management process, you can also create linked reports to create custom versions of a report without physically reproducing the report definition.

How to Organize Content in Report Manager

Report Manager offers several features to help you organize and manage content on the Report Server. You can add, move, or delete folders to manage a logical grouping of items on the server. Once you have folders structured to your liking, you can move reports, resources, and shared data sources to folders other than the ones to which they were originally published. You can create linked reports to create alternate versions of a report so that you can use different parameter values or security settings for different groups of users. Finally, you can use folder properties and report general properties to modify names and descriptions to help users locate information more easily.

Working with Folders

Folders are an important tool for organizing reports and resources on the server. In addition, folders are used to apply security to groups of items, which you'll learn about in Chapter 9. The folders that you create and access in Report Manager do not physically exist as folders in a file system, but are recognized by the Report Server as containers to logically organize their content.

To create a folder, you must navigate to the folder that will become the parent folder, or navigate to the Home page if the folder will not be nested. You can move a folder after it has been created to nest it within another folder. If you want to rename a folder, add a description, or hide the folder name from the list view in Report Manager, you can make the necessary changes on the folder's Properties page. If you delete a folder, all of its contents will also be deleted, so be careful to check the contents of a folder beforehand.

Some folders are reserved and cannot be moved, renamed, or deleted. These reserved folders are Home, My Reports, and Users. These latter two folders exist only if you enable My Reports on the Report Server, which is discussed later in this chapter.

In this procedure, you will add a folder to contain shared data sources.

Add a folder

1   In Report Manager, click the Home page link, and then click the New Folder button on the Report Manager toolbar.

2 Replace the default name with **Data Sources** so that your screen looks like this:

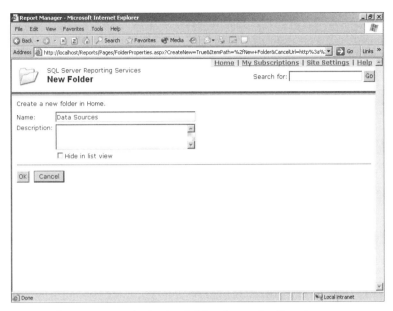

Notice the option to hide the folder from the list view.

3 Click the OK button.

The Home page of Report Manager now includes another folder, Data Sources. Now you're ready to move content into the new folder.

Using My Reports

My Reports is an optional feature of Report Manager and is disabled by default. It provides a personal workspace for each user to use for such things as private, personalized reports or perhaps reports that are being tested before deployment to the user community. Users cannot share the content of their folders with other users within the Report Manager interface. (However, a user can export a report to another file format and share the exported content through e-mail or placement on a network file share.)

To enable My Reports, click the Site Settings link, and then select the Enable My Reports check box. You can use roles to modify what a user can do with My Reports. You'll learn all about roles in Chapter 9.

Moving Content

As a report administrator, you can move reports, linked reports, resources, folders, and shared data sources from one folder to another. If you move a report, all its properties will remain the same in its new location, and its history will follow the report if it exists. Similarly, when you move a shared data source, its relationship to reports and subscriptions are maintained.

Reorganizing files and folders is particularly useful with data sources. You might refer to the same logical data source from several different projects. On the server, you can put one copy of the data source into a special folder and point to that one data source from all the reports and folders.

In this procedure, you will move shared data sources from the My Adventure Works folder to the Data Sources folder.

Move shared data sources

1 On the Report Manager Home page, click the My Adventure Works folder link.

2 Click the Show Details button on the Report Manager toolbar to see the details view, which looks like this:

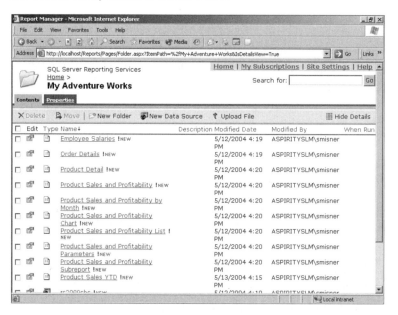

Report Manager now displays the contents of the folder as a single list with check boxes to the left of each item and the item details, such as modification date and author. Notice that the Delete and Move buttons are currently inactive. You must first select one or more items in the folder to activate these buttons.

3 To select all data sources in this folder, select the check boxes for rs2000sbs, rs2000sbsDW, and rs2000sbsOLAP, and then click the Move button on the Report Manager toolbar.

The folder hierarchy of the Report Server displays in the Move Multiple Items page. You can navigate this hierarchy to locate a target folder for the items selected from the previous page. Alternatively, you can enter the path of the folder in the Location box.

4 Click the Data Sources folder, as shown here, and then click the OK button:

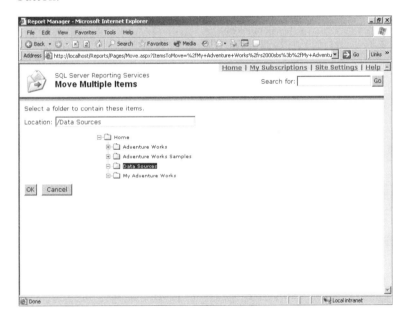

5   Click the Home page link, and then click the Data Sources folder link to confirm that the data sources have been moved, as shown here:

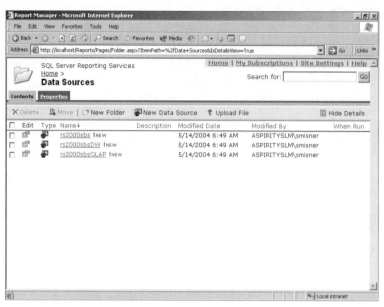

6   Click the rs2000sbsDW data source link, and then click the Reports tab to see the list of associated reports, which looks like this:

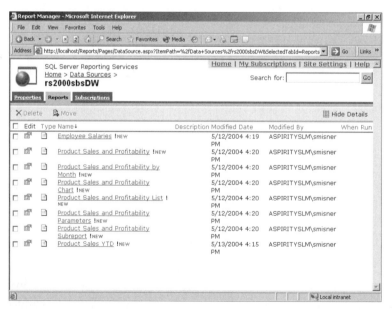

The reports that were associated with this data source during the authoring stage will continue to use the data source, even though it's been relocated to another folder.

▶ **Note** When you upload a shared data source to the server and then move that data source to a new folder, Visual Studio considers the data source as nonexistent and uploads a new copy to the server during deployment, even if *Overwrite-DataSources* is set to False. The data source is not used (because the report now points to the data source in the new folder), but it might be confusing to users. The simplest solution is to hide the new copy of the data source by using item-level security, which you'll learn in Chapter 9. The other alternative is to delete the unused data source following each deployment using Visual Studio.

Linking Reports

Creating a linked report is an easy way to customize report output for users. You can use one report as a base from which to create many representations of report data without physically duplicating reports. A linked report uses the same report definition and data source property as its base report, but can have its own execution, parameter, subscription, and security properties. For example, you can create a linked report that uses the Product Sales and Profitability Parameter report as a base, and then assign a different default value for the *Category* report parameter. If you place the linked report in a separate folder, you can limit access to the report to those users who need to see data related to a particular category. Be careful with linked reports, though. If you delete the base report, any reports linked to it won't work anymore!

In this procedure, you will create a linked report and store it in a new folder.

Add a linked report

1 Click the Home page link in the Report Manager, and then click the New Folder button on the Report Manager toolbar.

2 Replace the default name with **Adventure Works Bikes**, and then click the OK button.

3 Click the My Adventure Works folder link, click the Product Sales And Profitability Parameters report link, and then click the Properties tab.

   You don't need to wait for the report to display to click the tabbed pages of this report.

4 Click the Create Linked Report button.

5 Enter a name for the linked report: **Bike Sales and Profitability**.

   If you click the OK button now, the linked report will be added to the current folder, My Adventure Works. However, linked reports are often placed in separate folders to take advantage of the ability to manage permissions by folder.

6 Click the Change Location button, click Adventure Works Bikes in the folder hierarchy, and then click the OK button so that your screen now looks like this:

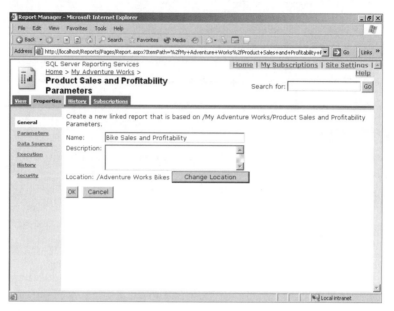

7 Click the OK button.

The linked report now displays in the browser window. This linked report is not a physical copy of the base report, but rather a version rendered online that uses the same report definition and data source as the base report. You'll need to change the report's properties to display only the Bike category, which you'll learn how to do later in this chapter.

Working with General Properties

In addition to creating a linked report, you can use the General Properties page of a report to change its name or description. When you create a name, you cannot use special characters, but you have more flexibility in the report's description. Only users who have access to a report can view its description. You can also use the General Properties page of a report to move a report from one folder to another on the Report Server or to delete the report from the server. If you delete a report, any linked reports will be broken and all history, report-specific schedules, and subscriptions associated with the report will also be deleted.

The General Properties page of a report also allows you to access and update the report definition. The Edit link allows you to only extract the report definition for read-only purposes. Any edits you make to the extracted file do not change the report definition used by the Report Server. However, you can save the file to a network share, and then use the Upload link to replace the server's report definition.

In this procedure, you will add a description to the Bike Sales And Profitablity report.

Change general properties

1 With the Bike Sales And Profitability report still open in Internet Explorer, click the Properties tab to view the report's general properties, which look like this:

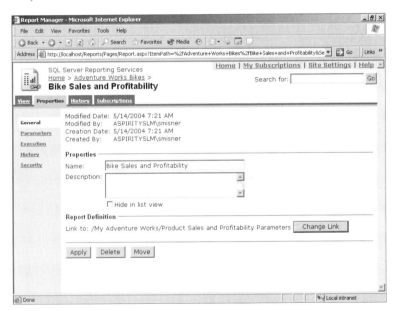

Notice that you can change the name of the report on this screen as well as add a description. This page also includes buttons that allow you to modify this report:

■ The Change Link button allows you to associate the current report with a different report definition. You might need to do this if the original base report changes or is deleted. Only the report definition for the linked report changes; the linked report's properties remain unchanged.

- ▣ The Delete button allows you to delete the linked report from the current folder and any subscriptions, schedules, or history associated with the linked report. Deleting the linked report does not have an impact on the base report.

- ▣ The Move button allows you to move the linked report from the current folder to another location in the Report Server's folder hierarchy.

2 Type the following description: **Bike sales amount, order quantity, margin amount, and margin percentage by month and year. Margin percentage exceptions at 15% or below, customizable.**

▶ **Tip**   A description should provide users with enough information to let them know what kind of data the report includes as well as any unique interactivity features.

3 Click the Apply button.

4 Click the Adventure Works Bikes link at the top of the browser window to view the report description.

5 Click the Hide Details button on the Report Manager toolbar so that your screen looks like this:

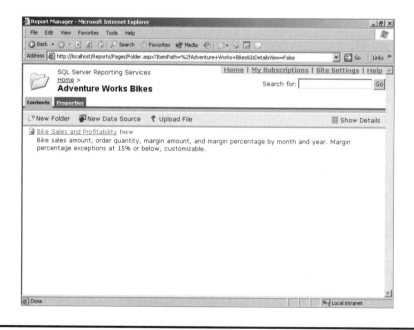

Using Properties to Manage Report Content

In addition to accessing a report's general properties as part of the management of the Report Server's content, you can use Report Manager to manage report properties that affect the content of reports. A data source is needed to connect to the database that is hosting the source data required for the report, and to authenticate the connection so that the report's query will execute. If the connection or authentication fails, data cannot be displayed in the report. You can override the data source associated with the report when it was published by changing its data source properties.

Report content can also be affected by changing parameter values. You can override a default parameter value provided in the report definition with a new value using parameter properties. Although you can still permit the user to select a different value, you can also hide the parameter altogether to prevent a change.

How to Manage Data Sources

You first add a data source definition to a report in the authoring stage, but you can change this definition by using Report Manager. You can update a report's data source properties to change the data processing extension, the connection string to locate the data, and the credentials needed to permit access to the data.

Working with Data Sources

Often you want to manage a report's data source on the Report Server independently of the data source in Visual Studio. For example, while developing a report, you might use a small sample database as the data source, but once the report is on the server, you want it to access the full production database. Likewise, in development, you might want to use integrated security for the data source, but in production store the user name and password in the report. You can use Report Manager to update the data source and overwrite the report's data source properties that are stored in the ReportServer database. The *OverwriteDataSources* property for the project in Visual Studio controls whether redeploying a report will overwrite changes you make on the Report Server. By leaving *OverwriteDataSources* with the default value of False, you keep the development and production data sources decoupled, which is convenient in most situations.

The selection of a shared data source or the creation of a custom data source, which requires a data processing extension and a connection string, is a pretty straightforward process. However, you need to give some careful thought to your selection of the way that credentials are used to connect to the data source.

Most of the time, storing the credentials securely with the report in the database is best. These are not the credentials used to access the report, but the credentials used by the report to access the source data. You most likely don't want to give report users even read access to the source database. In rare cases, you might want to use prompted credentials or Windows credentials, but these can be used only when the user accesses reports in real time. If your database does not require credentials to read the data, you can create a data source using no credentials, but this is an uncommon scenario because it's good practice to require credentials on all databases.

If reports will be executed as an unattended process, such as for scheduled snapshots and subscriptions, you must use stored credentials, because the Report Server executes a scheduled report without a user context. Stored credentials are stored in reversible encryption in the ReportServer database and are not stored in the report definition. The same credentials will be used each time the report is processed for all users of a report that is configured to use stored credentials.

In this procedure, you will modify the shared data source rs2000sbs to use prompted credentials.

Configure prompted credentials

1   In Report Manager, click the Home page link, click the Data Sources folder link, and then click the rs2000sbs shared data source link.

2   Under Connect Using, click The Credentials Supplied By The User Running The Report option so that your screen now looks like this:

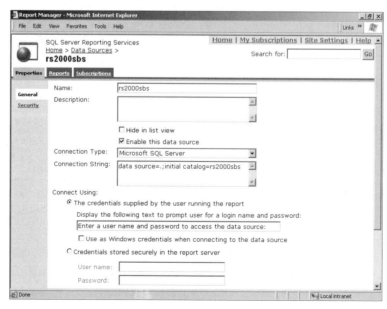

If the database to which the data source connects uses Windows authentication, you can click Use As Windows Credentials When Connecting To The Data Source, but for this example, you should leave this option cleared.

▶ **Important**   You should use prompted credentials or integrated security only when users will be accessing a report in real time. These types of authentication require a user to be physically connected (and possibly to have responded to the authentication prompt) before the report's query can execute.

3   Click the Apply button at the bottom of the page.

You'll test this data source later in this chapter when you execute a report on demand.

In this procedure, you will create a custom data source that uses stored credentials for the Product Sales and Profitability Parameters report.

Configure stored credentials

1   In Report Manager, click the Home page link, click the My Adventure Works folder link, and then click the Product Sales And Profitability Parameters report link.

2   Click the Properties tab, and then click the Data Sources link in the left frame of the page.

3   Click A Custom Data Source.

4   Enter the following connection string: **data source=localhost;initial catalog=rs2000sbsDW**.

▶ **Note**   Unlike Report Designer, Report Manager does not provide a dialog box to help you build a connection string. You will have to enter the connection string manually or copy it from another source.

5   Under Connect Using, click Credentials Stored Securely In The Report Server, and then enter **ReportExecution** as the user name and **ReportExecution** as the password.

▶ **Note**   The ReportExecution user is a special account created as a generic SQL Server account with read access to the rs2000sbs and rs2000sbsDW databases. This user was created with a script that executed during installation of the practice files. When you set up stored credentials for your production environment, you can use either a Windows logon or a database-specific login for stored credentials.

The data source section of the screen should look like this:

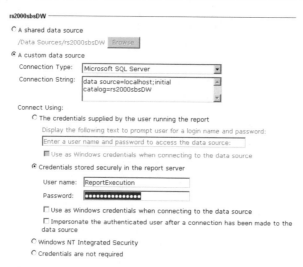

6   Click the Apply button.

The Product Sales and Profitability Parameters report now uses a custom data source and is no longer associated with the rs2000sbsDW shared data source. The shared data source continues to use the user's Windows authentication, while the custom data source uses a special SQL Server login account for authentication. This means that a preview of the report in Visual Studio will use a different data source from the production report (which might simply be different credentials but could also be a different database). You might or might not want that difference.

▶ **Tip**   If you have many reports that need to use a special account, you should instead set up a shared data source rather than a custom data source so that you have one place to manage the data source. It's okay to have several different data source definitions that connect to the same database, but use different authentication methods.

The linked report, Bike Sales and Profitability, is also affected by the change to the data source. The data source property is the only property of the base report that cannot be managed separately in the linked report.

How to Manage Parameters

By using Report Manager, you can control the content of a report by eliminating or adding a default report parameter value or by changing the default value to another value. You can also change the prompt text used with the report parameter or hide the parameter completely from view so that the user can't select a new value.

Specifying a Default Value

If a report parameter has been defined with a default value in the authoring stage, you can override this value by using Report Manager to update the report's parameter properties. This is a useful technique in combination with linked reports to generate separate reports by parameter value. For example, if product categories are managed by different departments, you can create a folder for each department, and then create a linked report that has the default parameter value changed to reflect the applicable category for the folder in which it's placed.

You can also disable a default value that has been provided in the report definition. When you disable the default value, the report will not execute until the user supplies a value for the report parameter.

In this procedure, you will set the default value for the Category report parameter to 2, which is the key value for the Bike category.

Change a parameter's default value

1. In Report Manager, click the Home page link, click the Adventure Works Bikes folder link, and then click the Bike Sales And Profitability report link.

2. Click the Properties tab, and then click the Parameters link in the left frame of the page.

3. Change the default value for Category from 4 to 2 so that your screen looks like this:

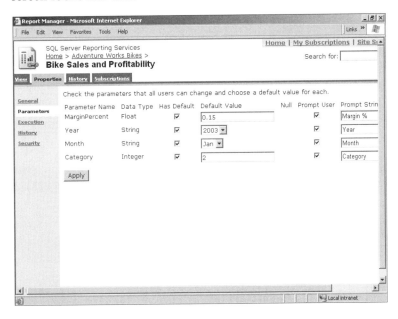

The value 2 is the CategoryKey value that corresponds to Bike.

4 Click the Apply button.

5 Click the View tab.

The report executes using the *Bike* category as a default. Notice that you can still select a different category. If you don't want the user to view another category, you must remove the prompt.

Disabling a Parameter Prompt

When you don't want a user to be able to change a report parameter value, you can remove the prompt so that a new value cannot be entered or selected from the list of available values. If you decide to use separate folders for linked reports using different parameter values, you can use this technique to prevent users from viewing another category. You can also remove a prompt from reports that run attended, as long as you make sure the report has a default value for the parameter; otherwise, the report will never execute.

In this procedure, you will disable the prompt for the *Category* report parameter.

Hide a parameter prompt

1 Click the Properties tab for the Bike Sales And Profitability report and then, if necessary, click the Parameters link.

2 Clear the Prompt User check box for the Category parameter.

▶ **Important** Don't disable the prompt without providing a default value. Otherwise, the report cannot execute and the user has no way to provide a value for the report parameter. The result is an empty report.

3 Click the Apply button.

4 Test the removal of the Category prompt by clicking the View tab to confirm that your report looks like this:

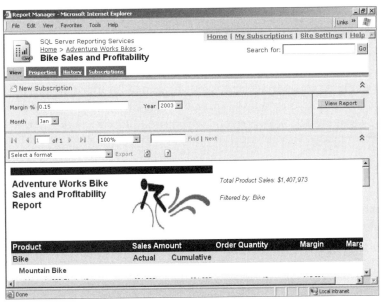

Notice that the Category prompt is no longer displayed. The textbox in the upper right corner of the report properly indicates that the report is filtered by the Bike category, and the table contains only data for the Bike category.

Managing Report Execution

Report execution is the process of turning a published report into a rendered report. More specifically, Reporting Services retrieves the data defined by the query in the dataset, and then combines the report's layout definition with the resulting data to produce an intermediate version of the report. Reporting Services then uses a rendering extension with this intermediate report to produce the report in its final format, which is in turn delivered to users. You can optimize report execution by controlling whether the processing steps occur when the user is accessing a report online or before the user opens the report.

When deciding how to manage report execution, you'll need to balance the users' needs for timely data and fast response with the Report Server's ability to process reports. If the user needs access to real-time data or data that is relatively recent *and* the report query can execute and return results in a reasonable amount of time, you can consider the On Demand execution options. When using On Demand execution, you need to decide whether to cache a report. If users need access to historical data *or* a report takes a long time to process, consider using Scheduled execution options to maintain a snapshot or to build a history of reports on a manual or scheduled basis. The On Demand and Scheduled execution options are compared in the following table. The remainder of this chapter reviews each option in detail.

| | On Demand | | Scheduled | |
	Non-cached	Cached instance	Snapshot	Report history
Stored Credentials	No	Yes	Yes	Yes.
Storage Format	Each time report is opened	First time report is opened	In advance	In advance.
Limits (per report)	None	One per combination of parameter values	One	Multiple.
Persistence	Temporary	Expires	Is replaced	Limited or unlimited number. Specific history deletion.

How to Manage On Demand Reports

You can use the default execution properties for reports that query frequently changing source data or when there is no particular advantage to having a report ready in advance of browsing. If the data in a frequently accessed report needs to be relatively fresh but does not have to be as current as the data source, you can configure the report's execution properties to use a cached instance.

Executing Reports with Current Data

When a report is configured to use the default execution properties, Reporting Services processes a report on demand each time a user requests the same report, which results in a new query for each request. The overhead of all these queries might have negative performance consequences on the source database as well as on the Report Server, so you must weigh this against the benefits of providing users with access to up-to-date data.

To improve the experience of report viewing and navigation with Report Manager, Reporting Services uses session management. A session begins when a user opens a report for viewing in a browser or client application. After the intermediate format of the report is created, a copy is placed in the session cache, which is maintained in the SQL Server database ReportServerTempDB. The session ends when the user closes the browser or client application. If a report's definition changes while a user is viewing it in an active session, the user will not see the updated version of the report until manually refreshing the report, which retrieves the current version from the ReportServer database.

In this procedure, you will execute a report on demand and respond to prompted credentials.

Execute a report on demand with prompted credentials

1   In Report Manager, click the Home page link, click the My Adventure Works folder link, and then click the Order Details report link to see this report:

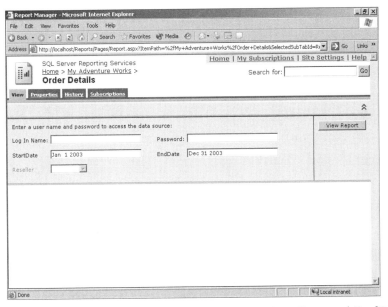

The default values for the report parameters *StartDate* and *EndDate* are non-queried, so these values are available to the report prior to execution. However, the Reseller report parameter is dependent on a query that uses the rs2000sbs data source that you converted to prompted credentials earlier in this chapter. Even though a default value has been defined for this report parameter, the query must execute to build the list of available values for Reseller. Accordingly, the user must enter a login name and a password.

2   Enter **ReportExecution** as the login name and **ReportExecution** as the password.

3   Click the View Report button to confirm that the top of your screen looks like this:

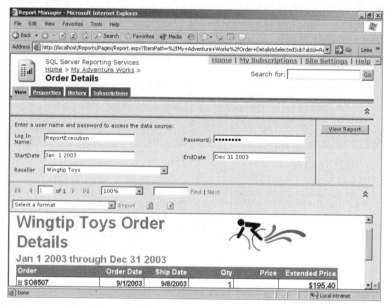

The query for the *Reseller* report parameter executes, and because the report parameter includes a default value, the report query also executes. Now the report is visible and you can change any report parameter value to update the report. The credentials are retained in the report for use in the next query, which is triggered when you click the View Report button.

▶   **Note**   Technically, the report is not executed on demand each time you view it. The report is stored in the session (in ReportServerTempDB) and subsequent refreshes of the page in the same session retrieve the same report. In effect, the session is a private cache of the report. To force the report to retrieve new data, you must click the Refresh Report button on the toolbar.

Implementing Cached Instances

A cached instance of a report is like a session report, except that the same intermediate report can be shared between multiple users. Using a cached instance of a report reduces the number of queries to the source database and potentially improves the performance of report execution. In this case, Reporting Services starts the process with the intermediate format of the report, which is stored temporarily in the ReportServerTempDB database. This intermediate report is flagged as a cached instance and is used for rendering in response to subsequent requests for the same report until the cached instance expires.

If a report uses query parameters, the query parameters are applied when the cached instance is created. This means that, if the user selects a different parameter value that changes the value of a query parameter, a new cached instance is placed in the ReportServerTempDB database, but only if a cached instance with that parameter value doesn't already exist. Consequently, it's possible to have a cached instance for every combination of parameter values in a report.

Whereas a change in a query parameter triggers a new cached instance, a filter based on a report parameter value is applied each time to the existing cache instance. In this case, each change in a filter value renders the report again without the advantage of storing the results as a cached instance.

When you change a report's execution properties to use a cached instance, you limit the amount of time that it persists in the ReportServerTempDB database by establishing an expiration rule for caching. You can expire a cached instance in regular intervals or according to a report-specific schedule or shared schedule. Regardless of how you choose to expire a cached instance, the report must use a data source that uses stored credentials.

In this procedure, you will configure a report as a cached instance that expires on a report-specific schedule.

Configure a cached instance

1   In Report Manager, click the Home page link, click the Adventure Works Bikes folder link, and then click the Bike Sales And Profitability report link.

2   Click the Properties tab, and then click the Execution link.

3   Click the third rendering option, Cache A Temporary Copy Of The Report. Expire Copy Of Report On The Following Schedule, so that your screen looks like this:

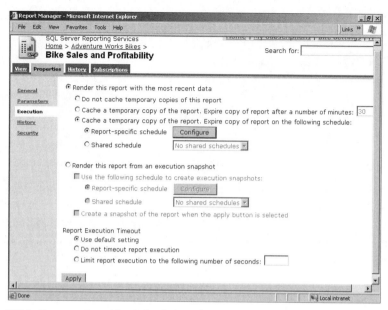

4   With Report-Specific Schedule selected, click the Configure button.

▶   **Tip**   If you want the cache instance of several reports to expire at the same time, consider using a shared schedule.

5   Keep the default values, which indicate a daily schedule that executes on every day of the week.

6   Type **11** for Start Time so that your screen now looks like this:

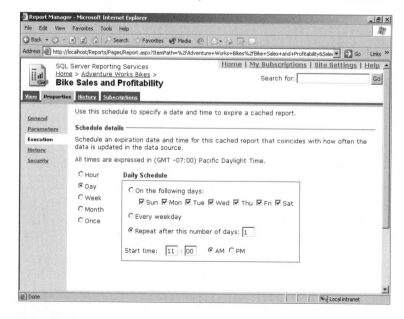

Notice at the bottom of the screen that you can optionally specify a start date or an end date for the schedule, or both.

7 Click the OK button, and then click the Apply button to complete the configuration.

▶ **Important** The SQL Server Agent must be running to define a schedule for cache expiration. If it's not running, you will receive an error when you click the Apply button to set the cache rendering option.

8 Click the View tab to browse the report.

A cached instance of the report was just created and will expire at 11 PM this evening. If another user opens this report, Reporting Services does not execute the report query, but instead retrieves the cached instance from the ReportServerTempDB and renders the report for viewing.

How to Manage Scheduled Reports

Before you can begin scheduling reports, you must define a schedule. Then you can use the schedule to create a snapshot of a report that can be accessed later by users, or to build a history of a report to capture information at fixed intervals of time.

Working with Shared Schedules

Although you can define a unique schedule for each report, a more efficient approach is to create a shared schedule that can trigger several activities according to the same time intervals. You can use a shared schedule to manage snapshot creation, cache expiration, and subscription delivery for multiple reports.

In this procedure, you will create a shared schedule to execute tasks on the first day of every month.

Create a shared schedule

1 In Report Manager, click the Site Settings link.

2 Scroll to the bottom of the page to find the section titled Other, and then click the Managed Shared Schedules link.

3 Click the New Schedule button on the Report Manager toolbar.

4 The Scheduling page is nearly identical to the page you used to create a report-specific schedule earlier in this chapter.

5 In the Schedule Name textbox, type **Beginning of Month**.

6 Under Schedule Details, click Month.

7 Under Monthly Schedule, click On Calendar Days, and then replace the default values with **1** to execute this schedule on the first day of the month.

8 In the Start Time hours box, type **05** so that your screen now looks like this:

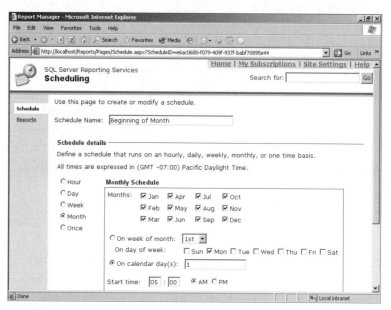

9 Click the OK button to see the schedule display on the Shared Schedules page, as shown here:

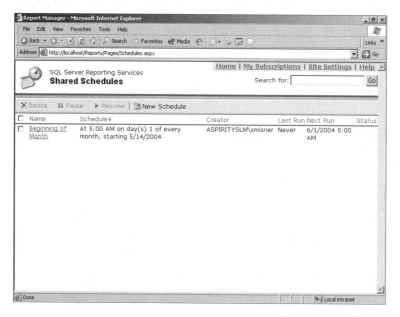

▶ **Important**   To add a Shared Schedule, SQL Server Agent must be running. Otherwise, you will receive an error when you click the OK button to create the shared schedule.

You can select schedules on this page to which you want to apply an action. After you select one or more schedules by selecting the check box to the left of the schedule name, you can use the Delete button to permanently remove a selected schedule, the Pause button to temporarily disable a selected schedule, or the Resume button to enable a selected schedule that had been previously paused.

Managing Snapshots

If a report is configured to render from a snapshot, Reporting Services performs the data retrieval and processing before a user opens the report. This can be useful when you need to capture data in a report as of a particular point in time, such as a financial statement at month-end, or when queries take a long time to execute, such as year-to-date queries in a large transactional database. You can create a snapshot manually, but typically a snapshot is created on a scheduled basis to update a report with more current data. Either way, Reporting Services uses the query results and the report layout to create an intermediate report that is stored as a snapshot in the ReportServer database. When a user requests the report, Reporting Services retrieves the intermediate report for rendering and delivery to the user.

As with a cached instance, query parameters are applied when the snapshot is created. A snapshot is not an interactive report, so parameter values cannot be changed once it has been created. However, report parameter values used as filters are applied against the snapshot during browsing, which can be an alternative approach to filtering data with query parameters.

You can create a snapshot manually or on a regular basis by using either a report-specific schedule or a shared schedule. However, only one snapshot at a time can exist. Each subsequent snapshot replaces the previous one. To configure a report to execute as a snapshot, you must select a data source that uses stored credentials for the report.

In this procedure, you will use a shared schedule to regularly create a snapshot for the Product Sales and Profitability Parameters report.

Schedule a snapshot

1   Click the Home page link, click the My Adventure Works, click the Product Sales YTD report, and then click the Properties tab.

2   Click the Data Sources link and create a Custom Data Source.
As the connection string, use **data source=localhost;initial catalog=rs2000sbsDW**.

3   Select the option, Credentials Stored Securely In The Report Server.
Use **ReportExecution** as the user name and **ReportExecution** as the password.

4   Click the Apply button.

▶ **Note**   When you plan to schedule snapshots for a report, the report's data source must use stored credentials. It doesn't matter whether you use a shared or custom data source. You can skip this step when your report is already using a data source with stored credentials.

5   Click the Execution link.

6   Click Render This Report From An Execution Snapshot, select the Use The Following Schedule To Create Execution Snapshots check box, and then click Shared Schedule.

Notice that Beginning Of Month is available in the Shared Schedule list box. Because it is the only shared schedule, it is automatically selected. The schedule details appear below the selected schedule.

7   To prevent a snapshot from being created now, clear the Create A Snapshot Of The Report When The Apply Button Is Selected check box so that your screen now looks like this:

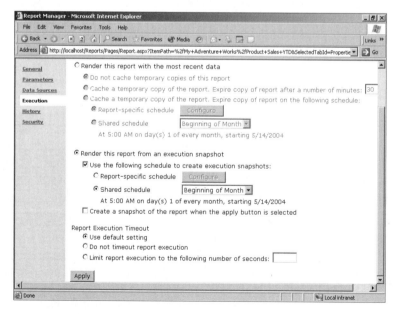

8   Click the Apply button.

▶   **Note**   If the data source you are using for the current report is not using stored credentials, you will get the following error message when you click the Apply button: "Credentials used to run this report are not stored." You must change the data source to use stored credentials before you try to assign a snapshot schedule to the report.

9   Click the View tab to view the error message that is displayed when a snapshot is not yet ready:

The report will not be available until it executes for the first time, which will be the first day of the next month.

Using Report History

If you want to save snapshots for future reference, you can enable a report's history properties. Then you can add a snapshot to report history manually or automatically each time a snapshot is created. Alternatively, you can use a schedule to update report history with the current snapshot, which Reporting Services creates if a current snapshot doesn't already exist. Because the report is executed as a snapshot, the report must use a data source that uses stored credentials.

Although you can keep an unlimited number of snapshots in report history, you might want to establish a maximum limit to keep the number of accumulating snapshots under control. You can set a global limit to apply to all reports that use report history, but you can override this number for any report. You can change the global or report-specific limit any time, but be careful when lowering the number of snapshots in history. The oldest snapshots will be eliminated immediately, and users might not appreciate losing access to these reports without some forewarning. You can also delete individual snapshots in report history manually, but there is no utility for deleting report history in bulk apart from deleting the report itself.

In this procedure, you will configure report history to store all report snapshots.

Store snapshots in history

1   Click the Properties tab of the Product Sales YTD report, and then click the History link.

2   Click Store All Report Execution Snapshots In History.

3   Under Select The Number Of Snapshots To Keep, click Limit The Copies Of Report History, and then type **12** in the box so that your screen looks like this:

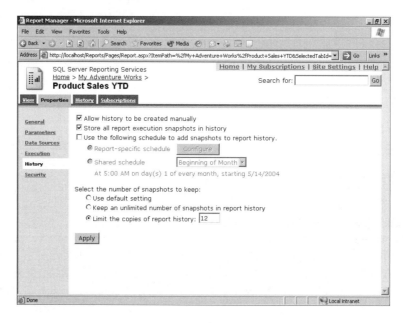

4   Click the Apply button, and then click the OK button to confirm the message that warns you about changing the report history.

5   Click the Execution link.

6   Click Create A Snapshot Of The Report When The Apply Button Is Selected, and then click the Apply button.

7   Click the View tab.

You can view the report now that a snapshot is created ahead of schedule. Notice that you cannot change the report parameter values.

8   Click the History tab to confirm that your screen looks similar to this:

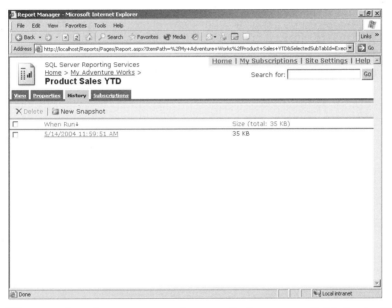

The snapshot that you created manually is now available in the History list and is listed by date and time of creation. The list will grow as the Beginning of Month shared schedule executes each month. When the thirteenth snapshot is added to the list, the oldest snapshot will be deleted from the list so that only 12 snapshots are in the list, as defined in the History properties.

▶   **Note**   You can use the New Snapshot button on the History tab of the current report to add snapshots manually to the list. This button is enabled only when the report uses a data source with stored credentials *and* the option to Allow History To Be Created Manually is enabled on the History Properties page.

Chapter 8 Quick Reference

To	Do this
Set project deployment properties	In the Solution Explorer window of Visual Studio, right-click the project name and then click Properties. At a minimum, enter a TargetServerURL. For example: **http://localhost/ ReportServer**.
Set the project context properties for deployment	In the Properties dialog box for the project, click the Configuration Manager button and set Build and Deploy to control deployment behavior.
Publish a report by using Visual Studio	In Solution Explorer, right-click the object or objects to deploy. If the object is a solution, click Deploy Solution. For all other objects, click Deploy.
Open Report Manager	In Internet Explorer, type Report Manager's URL. For example: **http://localhost/Reports**.
Upload resources by using Report Manager	In Internet Explorer, open Report Manager, click the folder links to navigate to the parent folder for the resource, and then click the Upload File button on the Report Manager toolbar. Enter the resource filename, or use the Browse button to navigate to the resource by using the file system.
Publish reports with the rs utility	Prepare a script file that uses the Web Service proxy object *rs* and the methods *CreateFolder* and *CreateReport*. Then use this file as an input argument to the rs utility by using the following syntax: rs -i *input_file* -s *ReportServerURL*.
Add a folder	In Report Manager, navigate to the parent folder, and then click the New Folder button on the Report Manager toolbar.
Move a resource	In Report Manager, navigate to the resource's parent folder, and then click the Show Details button on the Report Manager toolbar. Select the check box preceding the resource, and then click the Move button on the toolbar.
Link a report	In Report Manager, open the base report, and then click the Properties tab. On the General Properties page, click the Create Linked Report button and name the linked report. Click the Change Location button to select a different folder.
Change a report's name or description	In Report Manager, open the base report, and then click the Properties tab. Enter a revised name or description.
Configure credentials for a data source	In Report Manager, navigate to the shared data source or open a report, click the Properties tab, and then click the Data Sources link. Select the applicable Connect Using option to apply one of the following: prompted credentials, stored credentials (and supply the login name and password), Windows NT credentials, or no credentials.

To	Do this
Change a report parameter's default value or prompt	In Report Manager, open the report, click the Properties tab, and then click the Parameters link.
Change a report's execution properties	In Report Manager, open the report, click the Properties tab, and then click the Execution link.
Enable report history	In Report Manager, open the report, click the Properties tab, and then click the History link to select a method for adding snapshots to report history. You can also specify a limit to the number of snapshots kept in history.

Managing Security

In this chapter, you will learn how to:

■ Use item-level role assignments to secure items in groups or individually.

■ Define administrative permissions with system-level role assignments.

■ Combine roles with parameters to secure data in linked reports.

■ Use a permissions table to restrict access to data in reports.

After publishing content on the Report Server, which you learned how to do in Chapter 8, "Managing Content," it's important to implement security. At a minimum, you need to grant users access to the Report Server and its contents. In this chapter, you learn how to use role-based security to control not only what users can see on the Report Server, but also what they can do. You also learn three different techniques to restrict data within a report based on the user currently accessing the report. This chapter assumes that you are a local system administrator on the Report Server so that you have appropriate permissions to perform all the tasks described here.

Using Report Server Security

Reporting Services uses role-based security to allow individual users or groups of users to perform specific activities. In a role-based security system, *roles* are used to establish groups of activities based on the functional needs of users. For example, some users of Reporting Services need to only view reports, so all activities that relate to viewing items on the Report Server are organized into a predefined role. Similarly, other users need to be able to publish reports, so activities related to viewing, publishing, and managing reports are organized into another predefined role.

Reporting Services has 13 predefined user activities, or *tasks*, and 8 predefined system tasks. These tasks include everything that a user or administrator can do in Reporting Services. You cannot create or delete tasks. A specific list of tasks that can be associated with a role is known as a *role definition*. Reporting Services provides four item role definitions and two system role definitions. You can use the role definitions as provided, modify them, or create your own.

An *item role assignment* associates a Microsoft Windows user or group, an item role, and a single *item*, such as a report or a folder. Item role assignments are used to apply security at the item level to manage what users can do with each item. A *system role assignment* associates a Windows user or group with a system role. System role assignments determine who can perform certain server-wide administrative tasks, such as managing schedules.

How to Use Role-Based Security

You implement security on the Report Server and its contents by using Report Manager. You might need to edit the existing roles or add your own roles to organize tasks into functional groupings that are appropriate for your environment. To grant access to the Report Server to other users, you must assign each user, either individually or as part of a group, to an existing role for the items on the server with which they can interact. You might also want to create system role assignments for other administrators and for users who need to perform administrative tasks on the server.

Adding Role Assignments

In the standard security model, Reporting Services requires users to be authenticated by the Windows operating system. It is possible to create a custom security extension when you need to use a different method to authenticate users. (Creating custom extensions is discussed in Chapter 16, "Building Custom Reporting Tools," which can be found on the companion CD.) Using the standard security model, you must use existing local or domain user accounts or groups in order to create a new role assignment.

For any one item, a user or group can have only one role assignment. You can, however, establish a role assignment for a user who is also a member of a group with a role assignment for the same item. Reporting Services grants that user permissions for all the tasks in the role definitions of both the user and group role assignments.

In theory, you could create a unique role assignment for a single user for every report on the server, but a much simpler approach is to place role assignments on folders. The items contained in a secured folder, as well the contents of the folders that it contains, inherit the parent folder's security settings. You can break the chain of inheritance at any level, either for a branch of the folder tree, or for an individual report, resource, or data source.

The four default roles provided with Reporting Services will likely meet most of your security requirements. Browser is the most restrictive role, and limits users to navigating through the folder hierarchy and opening reports. My Reports, which assumes that you enabled the My Reports feature on the server, allows users to manage their own reports separately from the main folder hierarchy. Publisher allows users to add content to the server. Content Manager, the broadest role, allows a user to take ownership of the item, including the ability to manage security. Incidentally, as a member of the local system administrators on the Report Server computer, you are automatically granted the permissions of the Content Manager role, which gives you the ability to set security.

The following table shows a check mark for tasks enabled by default for each role. In general, the term *manage* in a task means the ability to add, change, or delete the item.

Default task	Browser	My Reports	Publisher	Content Manager
Create linked reports		✓	✓	✓
Manage all subscriptions				✓
Manage data sources		✓	✓	✓
Manage folders		✓	✓	✓
Manage individual subscriptions	✓	✓		✓
Manage report history		✓		✓
Manage reports		✓	✓	✓
Manage resources		✓	✓	✓
Set security for individual items				✓
View data sources		✓		✓
View folders	✓	✓		✓
View reports	✓	✓		✓
View resources	✓	✓		✓

In this procedure, you will add a role assignment to the Home folder for the group AWSalesAnalyst.

Add a Browser role assignment

1 Open Report Manager in Microsoft Internet Explorer at *http://localhost/Reports*.

2 Click the Properties tab.

The Security Properties page for the Home folder is displayed:

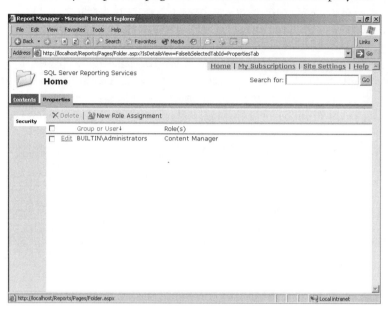

The default role assignment for the Home folder is Content Manager, to which the local system administrators group, BUILTIN \Administrators, is assigned.

3   Click the New Role Assignment button on the Report Manager toolbar. The New Role Assignment page is displayed:

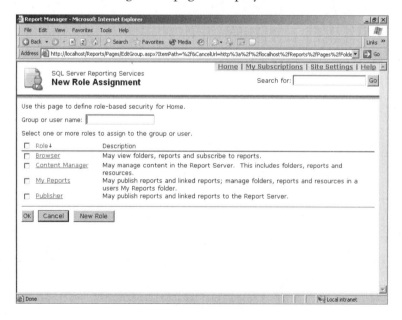

4   Click the Browser link to view the tasks in the role definition, as shown here:

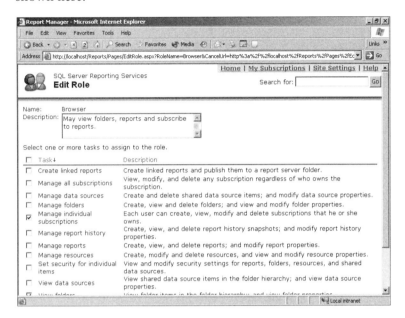

▶ **Note**   You can also reach this page to add a new role or edit an existing role at any time by using the Site Settings link at the top of any Report Manager page. Follow the Configure Item-Level Role Definitions link to access the Item-Level Role page.

Here you can see a full description of each task to help you decide the task assignments for the current role.

▶ **Important**   Be careful when adding or removing tasks from the role definition. The impact can be far-reaching, because every role assignment with the modified role will be immediately changed across the Report Server. If an item does not currently have an explicit role assignment, remember that its security is inherited from its parent folder (which might, in turn, inherit from a higher-level parent folder).

5   Click the Cancel button.

6   In the Group Or User Name box, type **AWSalesAnalyst**.

▶ **Note**   The AWSalesAnalyst is a Windows group that you should have added to the local groups on your computer as part of the installation of the practice files. If you skipped this step, please refer to this book's Introduction for instructions.

7   Select the Browser check box to select this role.

You can assign a user or group to multiple roles. If you click the Role check box above the list of roles, you can select all roles with a single click.

Notice that you can add another role by clicking the New Role button. You can also edit the existing roles, or even just take a look at the current settings, by clicking the link for the role you want to review.

8   Click the OK button.

The Security Properties page of the Home folder is displayed:

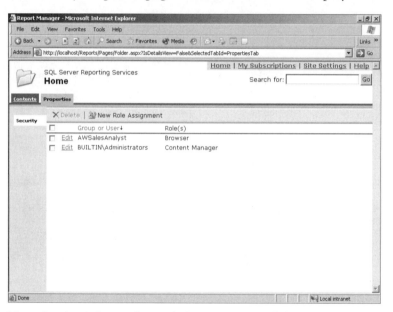

Now the AWSalesAnalyst role has access to all folders and reports, because each folder nested under the Home folder inherits the security properties of the Home folder.

In this procedure, you will add a role assignment to the Home folder for the group AWSalesDirector.

Add a Content Manager role assignment

1   On the Properties page of the Home folder, click the New Role Assignment button on the Report Manager toolbar.

2   In the Group Or User Name box, type **AWSalesDirector**.

▶ **Note**   The AWSalesDirector is a Windows group that you should have added to the local groups on your computer as part of the installation of the practice files. If you skipped this step, please refer to this book's Introduction for instructions.

3   Select the Content Manager check box to select this role.

4   Click the OK button.

The Security Properties page of the Home folder is displayed:

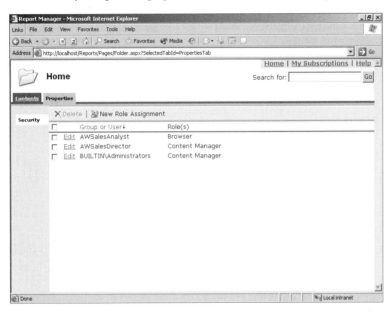

Now the AWSalesDirector role can perform any task assigned to the Content Manager role for any folder and its contents on the Report Server.

Applying Item Security

When you apply security to a folder, the items within that folder and its nested folders inherit the same security settings. If you take away the ability to view a report or other item, the user will not even see that item on the Contents page. Whenever possible, organize content by folder so that you can take advantage of this functionality and also minimize the administrative overhead of managing security for individual items. To handle exceptions to the rule, you can override security on individual items by adding role assignments to reports, resources, or data sources. After choosing to override security on an item, you will have the option to restore the parent folder's security settings when needed.

In this procedure, you will restrict access to the Adventure Works Bikes folder by removing a role assignment for the group AWSalesAnalyst to this folder.

Edit report security

1   On the Security Properties page of the Home folder in Report Manager, click the Contents tab.

▶   **Note**   If you skipped Chapter 8, to follow the procedures in this chapter, run publishChap09.cmd in the C:\rs2000sbs\chap09 folder so that you can publish the reports that you need. You will need to refresh the Home page after publishing the reports.

2   Click the Adventure Works Bikes folder, click the Properties tab, and then click the Security link.

The Security Properties page of the Adventure Works Bikes folder is displayed:

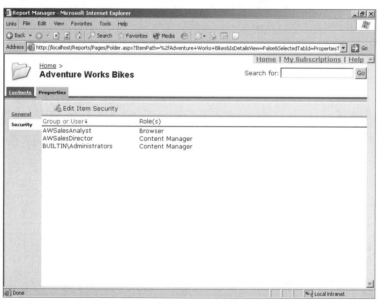

The same role assignments appear in this folder because they were inherited from the Home folder.

3   Click the Edit Item Security button.

A warning message is displayed:

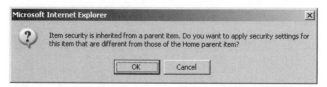

This message is a reminder that, if you proceed, the Adventure Works Bikes folder will no longer inherit security settings from the Home folder.

4 Click the OK button.

The Security Properties page of the Adventure Works Bikes folder is displayed:

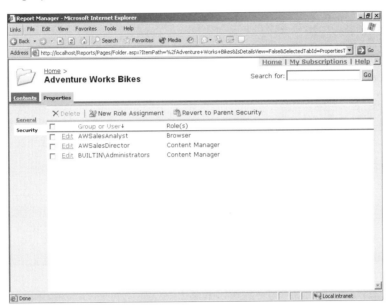

Notice that a new button, Revert To Parent Security, appears on the Report Manager toolbar. If you change your mind about security settings for the Adventure Works Bikes folder, this button provides an easy way to reset the security settings to match the parent folder, Home.

5 Select the AWSalesAnalyst check box, and then click the Delete button on the Report Manager toolbar.

6 Click the OK button to confirm the deletion.

The AWSalesAnalyst role no longer has access to the Adventure Works Bikes folder, but continues to have access to all other folders.

7 Close Internet Explorer.

8 Click Start, point to All Programs, right-click Internet Explorer, and then click Run As.

9 Click The Following User, and then type **SalesAnalyst** as the user and **SalesAnalyst** as the password.

10 Open Report Manager at *http://localhost/Reports*.

The Home page is displayed:

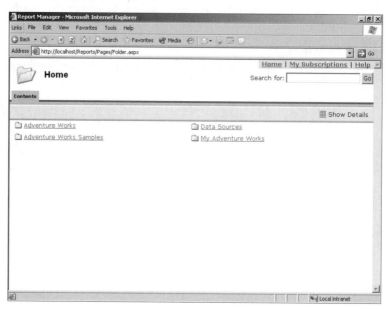

Notice that the Adventure Works Bikes folder is not visible to the SalesAnalyst user. Also, notice that the Properties tab is not available for the Home folder. Members of the AWSalesAnalyst group do not have access to the Site Settings link either because the Browser role is limited to folder and report links.

11 Close Internet Explorer.

Applying System Security

System role assignments allow selected users or groups to perform system administration tasks that are independent of content managed on the server. System roles provide access only to server activities. If a user is assigned to a system role, but is not assigned to an item-level role and is not a local system administrator, that user cannot view any content on the Report Server.

As a protective measure, local system administrators can always access a Report Server to change site settings. This way, if someone inadvertently creates role assignments that lock out all the users, a local administrator can still reset security. However, in case you need to restrict a local system administrator from opening confidential reports, you will have to implement security at the data level, which is discussed later in this chapter.

Reporting Services has two default system roles that you can use unchanged or extend to better meet your needs. The System User role, by default, allows access to the Site Settings page so that role members can view the server properties and shared schedules. Any user who needs to use a shared schedule for executing scheduled reports or creating subscriptions must be assigned to this role. The default tasks for the System Administrator role include not only managing server properties and shared schedules (which can be viewed *and* edited), but also managing running jobs, system role assignments, and role definitions.

The following table shows a check mark for tasks enabled by default for each system role.

Default task	System User	System Administrator
Generate events		
Manage jobs		✓
Manager Report Server properties		✓
Manage Report Server security		✓
Manage roles		✓
Manage shared schedules		✓
View Report Server properties	✓	
View shared schedules	✓	

In this procedure, you will assign the AWSalesAnalyst group to a new role based on the System User role with permission to view shared schedules only.

Add a system role assignment

1 Open Report Manager in Internet Explorer at *http://localhost /Reports.*

2 Click the Site Settings link at the top right corner of the Home page.

Anyone with system role assignment that includes View Report Server Properties or Manage Report Server Properties will have the Site Settings link on any page in Report Manager.

3 Click the Configure Site-Wide Security link.

The System Role Assignments page is displayed:

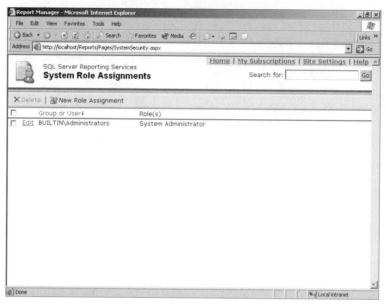

Notice the default system role assignment of the local system administrators group, BUILTIN\Administrators, as System Administrator. You will always need at least one System Administrator role assignment.

4   Click the New Role Assignment button on the Report Manager toolbar. The New System Role Assignment page is displayed:

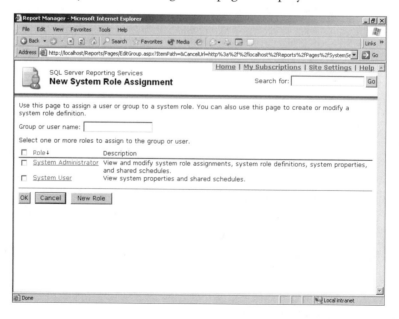

As with item-level role assignments, you can assign a user or group to multiple roles. If you click the Role check box above the list of roles, you can select all roles.

You can also add another role by clicking the New Role button, or edit the existing roles by clicking the role link.

5 Click the System User link.

6 Click the Copy button.

A new role is created with the same tasks that are assigned to the System User role.

7 Type a name for the new role: **Shared Schedule User**.

8 Add a description that details the assigned tasks: **View shared schedules**.

▶ **Tip** By listing the tasks in the description, a System Administrator won't have to open the role definition to see the task assignments in the New System Role Assignment page.

9 Clear the View Report Server Properties check box.

Your screen should look like this:

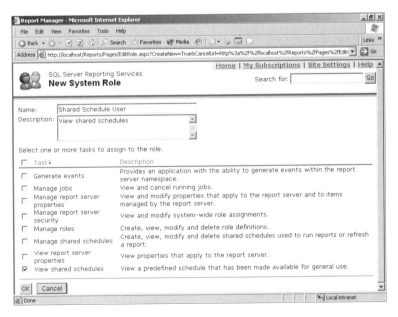

▶ **Tip** You can also add a new system role or edit an existing system role whenever necessary by using the Site Settings link at the top of any Report Manager page. Click the Configure System-Level Role Definitions link to access the System Roles page.

10 Click the OK button.

11 In the Group Or User Name box, type **AWSalesAnalyst**.

12 Select the Shared Schedule User link check box.

Your screen looks like this:

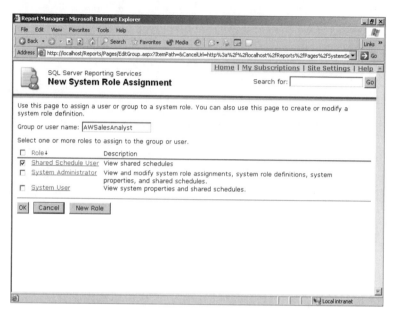

13 Click the OK button.

The System Role Assignments page is displayed:

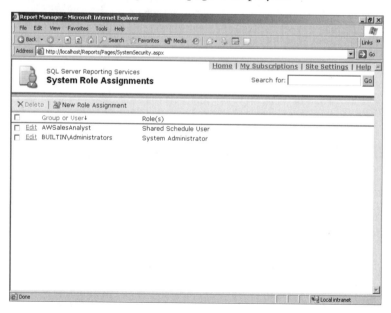

Now the AWSalesAnalyst role can use shared schedules with the reports that it can access as defined by item-level role assignments.

Applying Data Security

Sometimes different users need access to the same report, but each user is allowed to see only some of the data. For example, a sales territory manager might be allowed to view only data that pertains to his or her sales territory. In this case, using item-level security works only if you create a separate report using a different query in each report to restrict the data to a single sales territory. If many reports require a similar separation for different groups of users, the administrative overhead of maintaining and securing all the variations can quickly become overwhelming. Instead, you can choose a technique that leverages the use of one report, yet still satisfies the requirement to restrict data by user.

How to Secure Data in Reports

The simplest way to restrict the data that a user can see in a report is to use linked reports with parameters. Using this approach, you can easily control which data is displayed in the report, and then use item-level security to control access to each linked report. Alternatively, you can design a report that takes advantage of the *User* function from the global parameters collection to identify the current user. You can pass the user identification either to a query parameter or to a filter to restrict the data in the report.

Using Roles and Parameters to Restrict Data

As you learned in Chapter 7, "Building Advanced Reports," you can use a report parameter to filter data at the source with query parameters or to filter the report data after the full dataset has been retrieved. You can then set a different parameter value in each linked report, which you learned how to do in Chapter 8. By removing the parameter prompt, you prevent users from changing the parameter value and thereby restrict the report to the data defined by the parameter value. You can store each linked report in a separate folder to which you add role assignments to secure access, or you can add role assignments to each linked report to manage security at the report level.

In this procedure, you will create a linked report from the Actual Vs Quota report, using a parameter and item-level security to restrict access to user EuropeDirector and local system administrators.

Use a query parameter in linked reports to restrict data

1   If it's not already open, launch Report Manager in Internet Explorer at *http://localhost/Reports*.

2   Click the Home link at the top of the page, click the Adventure Works Samples folder link, click the Actual Vs Quota report link, and then click the Properties tab.

3   Click the Security link.

4   Click the Edit Item Security button, and then click the OK button to confirm the folder setting changed from its parent's setting.

5   Select the AWSalesAnalyst and the AWSalesDirector check boxes, and then click the Delete button.

6   Click OK to confirm the deletion.

7   Click the General link.

8   Click the Create Linked Report button.

9   Type a name for the report, **Actual Vs Quota Europe**, and then click the OK button.

▶   **Note**   Remember that it's easier to maintain security on a report by folder. In a production environment, create a separate folder for the linked report if one is not already available, and then create the linked report with that folder's location specified. Item-level security can then be set on the folder rather than on its contents separately. These steps are omitted here to focus you on using parameters as part of your security solution.

Notice that the *Group* parameter defaults to North America. For this linked report, you need to change this value to Europe, and then hide the parameter prompt.

10 Click the Properties tab, and then click the Parameters link.

11 Type **Europe** in the Group parameter's Default Value box.

12 Clear the Prompt User check box.

The Parameters Properties page looks like this:

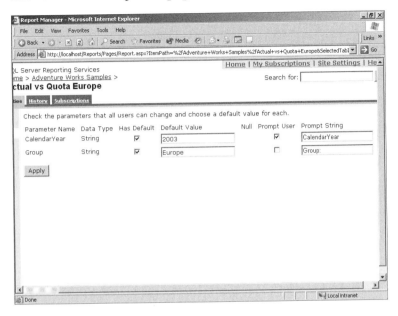

13 Click the Apply button.

14 Click the Security link.

15 Click the Edit Item Security button, and then click the OK button to confirm the folder setting change from its parent's setting.

16 Select the AWSalesAnalyst check box and the AWSalesDirector check box, and then click the Delete button.

17 Click OK to confirm the deletion.

18 Click the New Role Assignment button.

19 Type **EuropeDirector** in the Group Or User Name box.

▶ **Note** The EuropeDirector is a Windows user that you should have added to the local users on your computer as part of the installation of the practice files.

20 Select the Browser check box.

21 Click the OK button.

The Security Properties page of the Actual Vs Quota Europe report looks like this:

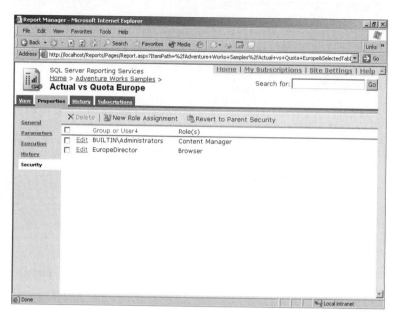

22 Close Internet Explorer.

23 Click Start, point to All Programs, right-click Internet Explorer, and then click Run As.

24 Click The Following User, and then type **EuropeDirector** as the user and **EuropeDirector** as the password.

▶ **Note**   The EuropeDirector is another Windows user that you should have added to the local users on your computer as part of the installation of the practice files.

25 Open Report Manager at *http://localhost/Reports*.

26 Click the Adventure Works Samples folder link, and then click the Actual Vs Quota Europe report.

Notice that the Actual Vs Quota report is no longer visible.

27 Click the View tab, click the Full Screen button to expand the view, and then scroll down to view the whole table.

The report page looks like this:

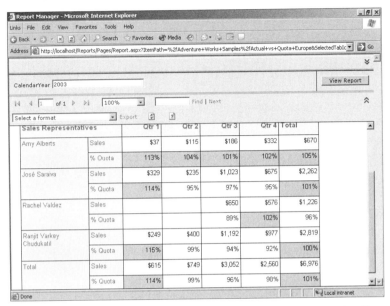

You should see only the following Sales Representatives for Europe: Amy Alberts, José Saraiva, Rachel Valdez, and Ranjit Varkey Chudukatil.

28 Close Internet Explorer.

29 Click Start, point to All Programs, right-click Internet Explorer, and then click Run As.

30 Click The Following User, and then type **NADirector** as the user and **NADirector** as the password.

31 Open Report Manager at *http://localhost/Reports*.

32 Click the Adventure Works Samples folder link.

Neither the Actual Vs Quota nor the Actual Vs Quota Europe is available to the NADirector since the item-level security doesn't include a role assignment for this user.

33 Close Internet Explorer.

Restricting the Source Query by User

Using parameters and linked reports to restrict access is a good approach when you're not concerned about local system administrators opening these reports. Even if a Content Manager removes the BUILTIN\Administrators role assignment from a report, a local system administrator still has the ability to reset security and the potential to open restricted reports. To protect confidential data, you can design a report that uses a query parameter to filter the dataset at the source based on the current user (which should be a domain user account rather than a local user account to further tighten security).

This technique requires you to create and maintain a permissions table that maps a Windows user account with a value used to restrict the data. For example, you can map the user account EuropeDirector to value Europe. The permissions table includes a column for the user account and a column for the value filter. Then you add the permissions table to the dataset query in the confidential report and join the value filter column in the permissions table to the corresponding column in an existing table in the query. You also add a query parameter to the WHERE clause of the query that compares the user account column in the permissions table to a query parameter. This query parameter will be used differently from the way you learned to use a query parameter in Chapter 7, because its value comes not from a report parameter, but from the operating system. To get the value from the operating system, you use the expression =User!UserID.

When you use the *@UserID* query parameter in a dataset, the report must always run on demand to set the proper user context. Therefore, you will have many more queries against the source database than would result if you instead filtered the dataset, which you'll learn how to do later in this chapter. Because the query returns fewer rows than it would without the *@UserID* query parameter, the query might run faster, but you will need to weigh performance against the impact of more database queries when designing restricted reports for your organization.

In this procedure, you will add a query parameter to a report's dataset to pass the current user as a filter in the source query.

▶ **Important**   For this procedure to work correctly, you cannot be logged in to your computer with the Administrator account or the accounts installed by the practice file installation—SalesAnalyst, PacificDirector, NADirector, or Europe-Director. You can log in with any other Windows user account.

Add a query parameter to a report

1 Open Enterprise Manager.

2 Expand the (local) server (or the instance to which you installed Reporting Services and the practice files) and navigate to the Tables folder of database rs2000sbsDW.

3 Right-click PermissionsSalesTerritory table, point to Open Table, and then click Return All Rows.

The data in this table is displayed:

UserId	SalesTerritoryGroup
ASPIRITYSLM\Administrator	Europe
ASPIRITYSLM\EuropeDirector	Europe
ASPIRITYSLM\NADirector	North America
ASPIRITYSLM\Administrator	North America
ASPIRITYSLM\PacificDirector	Pacific
ASPIRITYSLM\Administrator	Pacific

▶ **Note** This table is populated when you install the practice files. The domain name of the users in the UserId column should match your computer name.

This table maps users to sales territory groups so that you can customize the SecuringSourceQuery report for each territory group director. You must create a similar table to use with your data sources when you need to restrict data by user. You can certainly include other columns in your own permissions table, but at minimum you need a column for the full name of the Windows account and a column to hold the value to filter the data at the source.

4 Close Enterprise Manager.

5 Start Microsoft Visual Studio, and open the solution DataSecurity in the C:\rs2000sbs\chap09\DataSecurity folder.

6 In Solution Explorer, double-click SecuringSourceQuery.rdl to open the report.

7 Click the Data tab.

8 Click the Show/Hide Grid Pane button on the Query Designer toolbar, and then click the Show/Hide Result Pane button to make some room for the Diagram and SQL Panes.

9 With Detail dataset selected, click the Add table button in Query Designer toolbar.

10 Double-click the PermissionsSalesTerritory table, and then click the Close button.

11 Click the *SalesTerritoryGroup* field in the DimSalesTerritory table, and then drag and drop this field onto the *SalesTerritoryGroup* field in the PermissionsSalesTerritory table.

Your Diagram pane, when fully visible, should look similar to this:

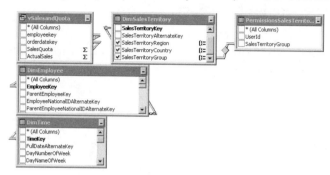

The PermissionsSalesTerritory table is now joined to the DimSales-Territory table on the SalesTerritoryGroup column. However, the query still needs to be modified to use this join to filter the dataset by user.

12 Add the following to the end of the WHERE clause:

```
and PermissionsSalesTerritory.UserId = @UserID
```

13 Click the Verify SQL button to check the query syntax and then click OK.

14 Click the Edit Selected Dataset button to the right of the Dataset list box.

15 Click the Parameters tab in the Dataset dialog box.

16 In the Parameters list, change the value for the *@UserID* query parameter to =User!UserID.

The Dataset dialog box looks like this:

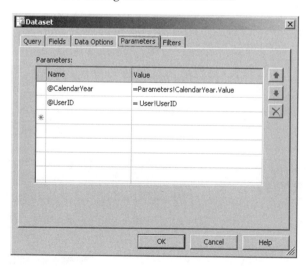

The expression =User!UserID returns the Windows account for the user running the report, a value that is contained in the User globals collection.

17 Click the OK button.

18 Click the Layout tab, and then click Report Parameters on the Report menu.

19 Click UserID in the Parameters list, click the Remove button, and then click the OK button.

When you add a query parameter, a corresponding report parameter is added to the report. However, in this case, the value for the query parameter is provided from an expression, so the report parameter should be removed.

20 Save the solution, and then click the Preview tab to test the report. Your screen should look similar to this:

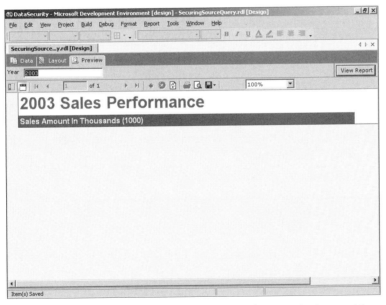

Because your Windows account is not in the permissions table, you cannot see any data in the report.

▶ **Tip**   When developing reports for your organization, add your Windows account to the permissions table to properly test reports before deployment.

21 In Solution Explorer, right-click the SecuringSourceQuery.rdl report, and then click Deploy.

22 Click Start, point to All Programs, right-click Internet Explorer, and then click Run As.

23 Click The Following User, and then type **EuropeDirector** as the user and **EuropeDirector** as the password.

24 Open Report Manager at *http://localhost/Reports*.

25 Click the DataSecurity folder link, and then click the SecuringSource-Query report link.

The top of the report looks like this:

2003 Sales Performance

Sales Amount in Thousands (1000)

Sales Reps			Qtr 1	Qtr 2	Qtr 3	Qtr 4	Total
United Kingdom	José Saraiva	Sales	$329	$235	$1,023	$675	$2,262
		% Quota	114%	95%	97%	95%	101%
	Total	Sales	$329	$235	$1,023	$675	$2,262
		% Quota	114%	95%	97%	95%	101%
Germany	Rachel Valdez	Sales			$650	$576	$1,226
		% Quota			89%	102%	96%
	Total	Sales			$650	$576	$1,226

If you scroll through the report, you can see that the data in the report includes only United Kingdom, Germany, and France. If a user who is not listed in the permissions table tries to open this report, no data will be displayed, as you experienced when previewing the report in Visual Studio.

26 Close Internet Explorer.

Filtering the Report Data by User

Another way to protect confidential data is to design a report to use the expression =User!UserID to filter the dataset after the query executes. As with the query parameter approach, this approach requires a table of users that can be joined to the dataset. Using this scenario, you still join the permissions table to an existing table in the query. However, instead of using the WHERE clause of the query to filter the data by user, you add the UserId column from the permissions table to the SELECT clause so that it becomes a field in the dataset. Then you add a filter to the dataset that compares the field value with the value returned by the expression =User!UserID.

When you filter the dataset by user, the full query runs against the source database each time the report executes. However, the filter is applied only when the user is browsing the report. As a result, this method allows you to execute the report on a schedule to minimize the potential impact on the underlying database of running the full query.

In this procedure, you will add a filter to a report's dataset to limit the display of data in the report during browsing based on the current user.

▶   **Important**   For this procedure to work correctly, you cannot be logged in to your computer with the Administrator account or the accounts installed by the practice file installation—SalesAnalyst, PacificDirector, NADirector, or Europe-Director. You can log in with any other Windows user account.

Add a filter to a report

1   In Solution Explorer in Visual Studio, double-click SecuringReport-Data.rdl to open the report.

2   Click the Data tab.

3   With Detail dataset selected, click the Add table button on the Query Designer toolbar.

4   Double-click the PermissionsSalesTerritory table, and then click the Close button.

5   Click the *SalesTerritoryGroup* field in the DimSalesTerritory table, and then drag and drop this field onto the *SalesTerritoryGroup* field in the PermissionsSalesTerrritory table.

6   In the PermissionSalesTerritory table, click UserId to add the column to the query's SELECT clause.

7   Click the Verify SQL button to check the query syntax.

8   Click the Edit Selected Dataset button to the right of the Dataset list box.

9   Click the Filters tab in the Dataset dialog box.

10   Click =Fields@UserId.Value in the Expression list box.

11   Click <Expression.> in the Value list box.

12   Expand Globals in the Fields list, click UserID, and then click the Replace button. Alternatively, you can type **=User!UserID** in the Expression box.

13   Click the OK button.

The Dataset dialog box looks like this:

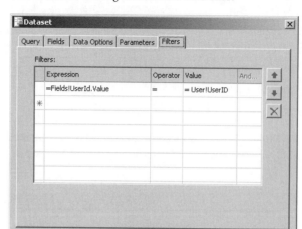

14 Click the OK button.

15 Click the Layout tab.

16 Save the solution, and then click the Preview tab.

As with the SecuringSourceQuery report, you cannot see any data in the report because your user account is not in the permissions table.

17 Right-click the SecuringReportData.rdl report in Solution Explorer, and then click Deploy.

18 Click Start, point to All Programs, right-click Internet Explorer, and then click Run As.

19 Click The Following User, and then type **NADirector** as the user and **NADirector** as the password.

20 Open Report Manager at *http://localhost/Reports*.

21 Click the DataSecurity folder link, and click the SecuringReportData report.

The top of the report looks like this:

2003 Sales Performance

Sales Amount In Thousands (1000)

Sales Reps			Qtr 1	Qtr 2	Qtr 3	Qtr 4	Total
United States	David Campbell	Sales	$379	$417	$1,124	$860	$2,779
		% Quota	111%	88%	103%	103%	101%
	Fernando Caro	Sales	$918	$1,279	$1,252	$953	$4,402
		% Quota	109%	93%	107%	98%	102%
	Linda Mitchell	Sales	$926	$1,164	$1,623	$1,284	$4,996
		% Quota	108%	114%	106%	101%	107%
	Michael Blythe	Sales	$821	$1,227	$1,498	$1,200	$4,746

If you scroll through the report, you can see that the data in the report includes only North America territories—the United States and Canada.

22 Close Internet Explorer.

Chapter 9 Quick Reference

To	Do this
Add an item-level role assignment to a folder	Navigate to the folder in Report Manager, and then click the Properties tab. Click the New Role Assignment button, type a Windows user or group account, and then select one or more roles to assign.
Add an item-level role assignment to a report, resource, or data source	Open the item in Report Manager, click the Properties tab if necessary, and then click the Security link. Click the Edit Item Security button, and click the OK button to confirm the change from the folder's security settings. Click the New Role Assignment button, type a Windows user or group account, and then select one or more roles to assign.
Add an item-level role	Click the Site Settings link in Report Manager, click the Configure Item-Level Role Definitions link, and then click the New Role button. Type a name and a description for the new role, and then click the tasks to be assigned to the role.
Add a system role assignment	Click the Site Settings link in Report Manager, and then click the Configure Site-Wide Security link. Click the New Role Assignment button, type a Windows user or group account, and then select one or more roles to assign.
Add a system role	Click the Site Settings link in Report Manager, click the Configure System-Level Role Definitions link, and then click the New Role button. Type a name and description for the new role, and then click the tasks to be assigned to the role.
Restrict data using linked reports with a query parameter and item-level security	In Report Manager, open the base report, and then click the Properties tab. On the General Properties page, click the Create Linked Report button and name the linked report. Click the Properties tab, and then click the Parameters link. Enter a default value for the parameter, and clear the Prompt User check box, if necessary. Then click the Apply button. Click the Security link, and then click the Edit Item Security button to make role assignments as needed.

To	Do this

Restrict data using a query parameter and permissions table	Create a permissions table that contains user accounts and filter values. Join the permissions table to a table in the dataset query on columns containing the filter value, and then add a query parameter to the WHERE clause of the query that references the permission table's user account column. For example:
	
	`and PermissionsSalesTerritory.`
	`UserId = @UserID`
	
	Click the Edit Selected Dataset button, click the Parameters tab, and then change the Value for the query parameter to =User!UserID. Click the Layout tab, click Report Parameters on the Report menu, click UserID in the Parameters list, and click the Remove button.

Restrict data using a dataset filter and permissions table	Create a permissions table that contains user accounts and filter values. Join the permissions table to a table in the dataset query on columns containing the filter value, and then add the permission table's user account column to the SELECT clause of the query. Click the Edit Selected Dataset button, and then click the Filters tab. Click =Fields!UserID in the Expression list box. Click <Expression.≿ in the Value list box, and then type =User!UserID as an expression.

Chapter

10

Managing Server Components

In this chapter, you will learn how to:

- Use configuration files to modify Reporting Services components.
- Monitor Reporting Services performance with execution logging.
- Terminate or suspend jobs.
- Manage the Reporting Services databases.

In the previous two chapters, you learned how to publish and secure content on the Report Server as part of the management stage of the report life cycle. Another aspect of management concerns the maintenance of the components that support the reporting life cycle. In this chapter, you learn how to configure these Reporting Services components. You also learn several ways to monitor activity on the Report Server so that you can tune the design of reports or the configuration of server components for optimal performance. In addition, you see the options for limiting or temporarily suspending the execution of reports so that you can proactively manage activity on the server. Management of the server also includes monitoring database growth and protecting the data in the case of disaster, so this chapter closes by showing you which tables require the most attention (and why) and by recommending a backup strategy for your databases.

Configuring Reporting Services

Settings that you can change to control the behavior of Reporting Services components are contained in four configuration files. Some of the settings in these configuration files are supplied by you during installation; the remaining settings have default values that you can change as needed. Each configuration file is associated with a separate component, which is shown in the following table:

Component	Configuration file	Default installation folder
Report Server engine	RSReportServer.config	Program Files\Microsoft SQL Server\MSSQL\Reporting Services\ReportServer
Report Server service	ReportingServices-Service.exe.config	Program Files\Microsoft SQL Server\MSSQL\Reporting Services\ReportServer\bin
Report Manager	RSWebApplication.config	Program Files\Microsoft SQL Server\MSSQL\Reporting Services\ReportManager
Report Designer	RSReportDesigner.config	Program Files\Microsoft SQL Server\80\Tools\ReportDesigner

Notice that Report Server has two configuration files. One—ReportingServices-Service.exe.config—controls only the trace logs, which will be covered later in the chapter. The other—RSReportServer.config—controls everything else. Of all the configuration files, RSReportServer.config is the most important.

Report Manager and Report Designer are applications that are separate from the core report server engine. If you don't use these applications because you instead use a custom or third-party application, you don't need to concern yourself with their configurations. However, if you do use either of these applications and need to make a configuration change, such as add a rendering extension, you modify the corresponding configuration files.

In addition to the four main configuration files just described, the two Web services—Report Manager and the Report Server—each have a Web.config file, like many ASP.NET Web applications. You might want to modify these configuration files to control trace logs or to add configuration settings for your own custom applications that use the Reporting Services platform.

Reporting Services also includes some configuration files that are internally managed and that should not be modified. For example, Rspreviewpolicy.config (for Report Designer), Rsmgrpolicy.config (for Report Manager), and Rssvrpolicy.config (for the Report Server Service) all manage encrypted keys for critical trusted services. There are also some .ini configuration files that are used for internal purposes and should not be modified.

How to Configure Reporting Services

If you need to change the default behavior of Reporting Services, you can use an XML editor to modify the RSReportServer.config file. Connection information stored in RSReportServer.config is encrypted, so naturally you cannot simply edit the XML file. You must use a connection utility that is installed with Reporting Services to make changes to the encrypted data.

Editing the RSReportServer.config File

The RSReportServer.config file contains all the settings that apply to the report server engine (except the trace log settings). These settings include the connection string for the ReportServer database, thread and memory management settings, timeout values, SMTP server settings, and an open connection limit setting for a single user. (For a complete list of settings in this and other configuration files, refer to Reporting Services Books Online, which you can find in the MSDN Library at *http://msdn.microsoft.com/library/default.asp?url= /library/en-us/RSPORTAL/HTM/rs_gts_portal_3vqd.asp* if you don't have it installed on your computer.) This file also contains configuration information about delivery, rendering, data, and security extensions, so if you create a custom extension (as discussed in Chapter 16, "Building Custom Reporting Tools," which can be found on the companion CD), you will need to modify this file.

▶ **Note** The RSWebApplication.config file contains settings needed by the Report Manager application. Report Manager needs to know the URL for the Report Server Web service, so if you change the location of the Report Server service, you need to change the URL stored in the RSWebApplication.config file.

In this procedure, you will edit the RSReportServer.config file in Microsoft Visual Studio to change the number of active sessions permitted per user.

Change unencrypted information in the RSReportServer.config file

1   Using Microsoft Windows Explorer, make a backup copy of the RSReportServer.config file in the Program Files\Microsoft SQL Server\MSSQL\Reporting Services\ReportServer folder (assuming you used the default installation location for Reporting Services).

▶ **Important** Before making changes to configuration files, you should always make a copy of the file to restore settings in case a change you make causes a problem.

2   Using Visual Studio, open the RSReportServer.config file. You can alternatively use any XML editor, or even Microsoft Notepad, to open a configuration file and make modifications.

Your screen should look similar to this:

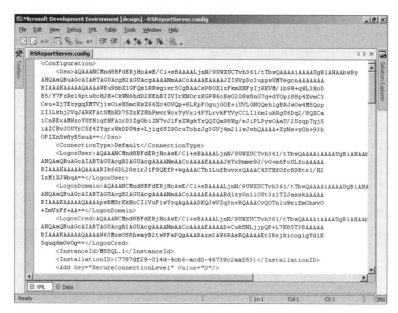

Notice the encrypted data in the *<Dsn>*, *<LogonUser>*, *<Logon-Domain>*, and *<LogonCred>* elements. You need to use a utility to change this data, and you'll learn about how to use this utility later in this chapter.

3   Scroll through the file (or press CTRL+F to use the Find feature) to find the *<UnattendedExecutionAccount>* element.

This section of the configuration file looks like this:

```
<UnattendedExecutionAccount>
   <UserName></UserName>
   <Password></Password>
   <Domain></Domain>
</UnattendedExecutionAccount>
```

The elements nested in the *<UnattendedExecutionAccount>* element currently have no values (assuming you're never used the rsconfig utility to add credentials for unattended reports). Because the data stored here must be encrypted, you can't provide credentials using the XML editor now, but you'll learn in the next procedure how to update these values.

4   Scroll up from the *<UnattendedExecutionAccount>* element to find the setting *MaxActiveReqForOneUser*, and then change its value from 20 to **10**.

This section of the configuration file looks like this:

```
<Add Key="MaxActiveReqForOneUser" Value="10"/>
```

▶ **Important**   Before making any changes to a configuration file, take the time to review the description of the configuration settings in Reporting Services Books Online to be sure you understand the purpose of a setting and the type of values that are appropriate for each setting.

By changing this setting, you are limiting each user to a maximum number of 10 active requests on the Report Server.

5   Save and close the file, but keep Visual Studio open for the next procedure.

Configuration changes are seamlessly integrated into the running application, so you will not have to stop and restart the service.

Changing Encrypted Configuration Information by Using the rsconfig Utility

As you have just seen, to keep the connection information that Reporting Services uses to connect to the ReportServer database properly secured, the values for the connection information elements in the RSReportServer.config file are encrypted. When you need to change the name of the ReportServer database, the server instance where the database is located, or the credentials used to connect to the database, you must use the rsconfig utility supplied with Reporting Services.

You must have administrator privileges on the Report Server to use the rsconfig utility. Here is the syntax for using this utility on the Report Server using Windows authentication:

```
rsconfig -c -m computername -s SQLServername -d ReportServerDatabaseName
-a windows -u [domain\]username -p password
```

You can omit the *–m* argument if you are running the utility on the Report Server. The *–s* argument isn't needed if the ReportServer database is located in a local default SQL Server instance. If the database is located in a named instance, use *servername\instancename* for the *–s* argument. For the *–a* argument, you will need to instead use *sql* rather than *windows* if you are using a SQL login to connect to the server. You can add a *-t* argument (with no value) to add trace information to error messages.

▶ **Note**   When you use the *–c* argument with the rsconfig utility, the values in the *<Dsn>*, *<LogonUser>*, *<LogonDomain>*, and *<LogonCred>* elements are updated with encrypted values. One common scenario that requires using this utility is a change in the credentials used to connect to the ReportServer database. Another common situation is the movement of the ReportServer database to a remote SQL Server instance (such as during deployment), which requires a change to the connection information that can only be made using the rsconfig utility.

If you have reports that run unattended (scheduled reports and subscriptions) and use a data source that does not require credentials, the Report Server still needs credentials to connect to the computer hosting a remote data source. You use the rsconfig utility to store the credentials to connect to the remote computer as encrypted data in the Report Server's configuration file.

▶ **Note**   This situation should be pretty rare because all your data sources should be secured. However, you might have a circumstance in which a database that contains general reference information doesn't require security. If an unattended report using such a database tries to run when Report Server has no credentials to use to connect to the host computer, the execution will fail.

The syntax to use to add credentials for unattended report processing is shown here:

```
rsconfig -e -m computername -s SQLServername -u [domain\]username -p password
```

Again, you can omit the *–m* and *–s* arguments if you're running on a Report-Server database with a local SQL Server instance. The *–t* argument can also be used to add trace information to error messages when configuring the unattended report execution credentials.

In this procedure, you will add credentials for the Report Server to use when running unattended reports.

Encrypt credentials for unattended reports

1   On the Start menu, click Run, type **cmd**, and then click OK to open a command prompt window.

2   Type **rsconfig -?** to view the online help for this utility.

3   Run the rsconfig utility by typing the following: **rsconfig –e –u** *YourUserName* **–p** *YourPassword* (replacing *YourUserName* and *YourPassword* with a valid user name and password).

▶ **Note**   The syntax used in this step assumes that you have all components installed on your local computer. If you later want to use your local installation of Reporting Services in a production environment, use the rsconfig utility to assign the appropriate credentials. If you don't want to assign any credentials for unattended reports, you can edit the XML file to clear the values for the elements nested in the *<UnattendedExecutionAccount>* element—but don't remove the element tags.

4   Using Visual Studio, open the RSReportServer.config file in the Program Files\Microsoft SQL Server\MSSQL\Reporting Services\Report-Server folder (assuming you used the default installation location for Reporting Services).

10

Managing Server Components

5 Scroll through the file to find the *<UnattendedExecutionAccount>* element.

This section of the configuration file looks similar to this:

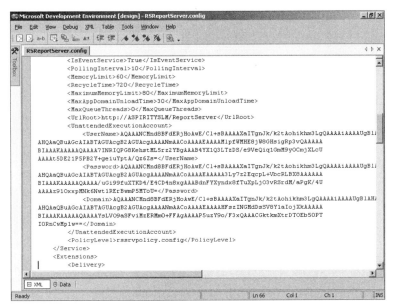

The elements nested in the *<UnattendedExecutionAccount>* element now have values, each of which is encrypted.

6 Close the file, but keep Visual Studio open for the next procedure.

Configuring Tracing on the Report Server

Reporting Services records information about server operations in trace logs that are located in the Program Files\Microsoft SQL Server*<SQL Server Instance>*\Reporting Services\LogFiles folder. Each day, beginning with the first traceable activity that occurs after midnight (local time for the Report Server) or again if Reporting Services is restarted, new trace logs are created. There are four types of trace log files:

■ *ReportServerService_main_<timestamp>.log*   Logs operations of the Report Server Windows and Web services, such as server resource allocation and initialization of settings defined in the configuration files.

■ *ReportServerService_<timestamp>.log*   Records details about operations such as the initialization of certain service settings as well as the status of polling activities related to schedules, subscriptions, and delivery notifications.

■ *ReportServerWebApp_<timestamp>.log*   Captures information about Report Manager operations, such as HTTP headers and stack trace information, as well as SOAP envelopes and exceptions.

■ *ReportServer_<timestamp>.log*   Logs various information for the Report Server engine, such as exceptions and warnings generated by the Report Server or calls to perform actions like processing reports, creating folders, or deleting items.

These trace logs can be quite helpful when you are debugging a custom application that uses the Report Server, or if you need to troubleshoot a problem that appears in the event log or execution log. (You'll learn more about these other logs later in this chapter.) You can control the amount of detail that is recorded in the trace log files by changing the value of the *DefaultTraceSwitch* setting in the ReportingServicesService.exe.config file and the Web.config file (found in the Program Files\Microsoft SQL Server\MSSQL\Reporting Services\Report-Server). You can also disable tracing with this setting, but Microsoft recommends that you always trace at some level in case you ever need to troubleshoot an issue. The possible values for this setting are shown in the following table:

Value	Tracing level
0	Disables tracing
1	Exceptions and restarts
2	Exceptions, restarts, and warnings
3	Exceptions, restarts, warnings, and status messages (Default setting)
4	Verbose mode

You can also change settings in the ReportingServicesService.exe.config file to route tracing to a debug window instead of to a file. You can use another setting in this file to limit tracing to a single component. By default, trace logs are created for the Report Server, Report Server Web Application, and Report Server service. In addition, you can change the number of days for which trace logs are kept. As a reminder, before making any changes to a configuration file, first read the description of the configuration settings in Reporting Services Books Online.

In this procedure, you will change the ReportingServicesService.exe.config file to keep log files for 10 days only.

Edit the ReportingServicesService.exe.config file

1   Using Visual Studio, open the ReportingServicesService.exe.config file in the Program Files\Microsoft SQL Server\MSSQL\Reporting Services\ReportServer\bin folder (assuming you used the default installation location for Reporting Services).

The configuration file looks like this:

```
<configuration>
  <configSections>
      <section name="RStrace" type="Microsoft.ReportingServices.
          Diagnostics.RSTraceSectionHandler,
          Microsoft.ReportingServices.Diagnostics" />
  </configSections>
  <system.diagnostics>
      <switches>
          <add name="DefaultTraceSwitch" value="3" />
      </switches>
  </system.diagnostics>
  <RStrace>
      <add name="FileName" value="ReportServerService_" />
      <add name="FileSizeLimitMb" value="32" />
      <add name="KeepFilesForDays" value="14" />
      <add name="Prefix" value="tid, time" />
      <add name="TraceListeners" value="debugwindow, file" />
      <add name="TraceFileMode" value="unique" />
      <add name="Components" value="all" />
  </RStrace>
</configuration>
```

Notice the default value of 3 for the *DefaultTraceSwitch* setting that controls the level of tracing.

2   Change the setting *KeepFilesForDays* value to **10**.

You can raise or lower this number as desired to control the length of time that trace logs are kept. When the number of days is exceeded, the trace logs are deleted from the file system.

3   Save, and then close the file.

Managing the Report Server

In addition to using trace logs to capture details about Reporting Services operations, you can use an execution log to help you manage report execution. An execution log provides even more detail about the reports that are processed than you will find in the trace log. With an *execution log*, you can monitor the duration and success rate of report executions; identify bottlenecks by examining execution times; and optimize report executions by using request frequency, execution times, and user information to help you choose an appropriate execution method for each report.

Besides monitoring activity on the server, Reporting Services provides several methods that you can implement to proactively manage the resources on your server. You can use timeout settings to stop queries or report executions that take too long. In addition to this automatic approach to shutting down jobs, you can manually cancel a job whenever necessary. You can also temporarily suspend jobs, by disabling either a shared data source or a shared schedule.

Using Performance Counters

Reporting Services also includes ASP.NET performance counters to provide visibility into the performance of the services. Reviewing these performance counters can help you make decisions about how to best manage your server. Performance counters belong to two objects. The first object, *RS Windows Service*, includes counters for all activity that happens on the server, whether scheduled or interactive. The second object, *RS Web Service*, includes counters for activity initiated through a scheduled operation. Fourteen counters appear in both objects, nine others are specific to the *RS Web Service* object, and four are specific to the *RS Windows Service* object.

Some counters show current state (for example, Active Session), some show current rates (for example, Requests/Sec), and some show a cumulative total since the service was last started (for example, Total Requests). To find instructions for using the Windows Performance tool, search the help file for your operating system. Details about the performance counters themselves are in Reporting Services Books Online.

Here are some performance counters that you might monitor regularly:

- Active Sessions, to obtain the count of all active browser sessions
- Reports Executed/Sec, to determine the volume of successful report execution
- Requests/Sec, to compare with Reports Executed/Sec to evaluate the proportion of reports executed to reports returned from the cache
- Total Requests, to track the number of requests since the service started
- Total Processing Failures, to monitor failure rates since the service started as compared with Total Requests

How to Monitor Performance

You can monitor execution performance by using Report Manager to enable or disable logging and to limit the number of days for which logging is retained. Execution logs differ from trace logs because the latter are stored in a set of files, whereas execution logs are stored in the ReportServer database. Because execution logs are intended for continual analysis, the data is stored relationally. The information that is stored in the ExecutionLog table of the ReportServer database is not the best format for general reporting and analysis, but you can create your own logging database to which you can export logging records on a periodic basis. Reporting Services supplies you with the following tools to facilitate reporting on the logs:

- A script to create tables in your own database
- A Data Transformation Services (DTS) package to load logging records into this database
- Reports that allow you to review the execution information loaded into the new database

You will work with these tools later in this chapter. You can schedule the DTS package to perform periodic extracts from the ExecutionLog table to keep your logging database current and to allow you to delete rows from the log tables.

Managing Execution Logging

You can use the Site Settings page in Report Manager to start or stop execution logging at any time. You must be assigned to the System Administrator role in SQL Server to be able to change this setting. By default, execution logging is enabled, and log records will be kept only for 60 days. You can increase or decrease the number of days as desired to limit the amount of logging history that accumulates in the ExecutionLog table in the ReportServer database. Logging records that exceed the specified number are removed each day at 2:00 AM (local time for the Report Server). Alternatively, you can remove this limitation if you want to allow logging records to accumulate indefinitely. If you use the DTS package mentioned earlier to copy the logs to a reporting database, you can delete logs as soon as they are copied to the logging database by adding an additional package step.

In this procedure, you will open the Site Settings page in Report Manager to review the current execution logging settings.

Review current execution logging settings

1 Open Report Manager in Microsoft Internet Explorer at *http://localhost /Reports*.

2   Click the Site Settings link to review the settings shown here:

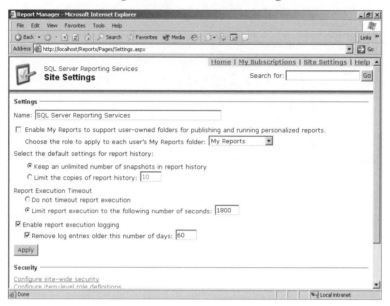

If you want to disable execution logging, you can clear the Enable Report Execution Logging check box. Notice that you can type a different number of days to change the frequency with which logging records are removed from the ExecutionLog table. To make the changes take effect, you need to click the Apply button.

Initializing an Execution Log Database

Reporting Services provides the tools you need to effectively report and analyze information related to report processing. To get started, you will need to create a SQL Server database, and then you can use a supplied script to build the necessary tables in your new database. After creating the tables, you can use the DTS package supplied by Reporting Services to load the new tables with data from the ExecutionLog table. You will need to make a small modification to this DTS package to reference the correct path to an .ini file needed by this DTS package.

In this procedure, you will create the RSExecutionLog database in which you will create tables using a script and then use a DTS package to load data into the tables.

Create and load the execution log database

1   Open Enterprise Manager.

2   Expand the (local) server (or the instance to which you installed Reporting Services and the practice files), right-click the Databases folder, and then click New Database.

3 Type a name for the database in the Database Properties dialog box, **RSExecutionLog**, and then click the OK button.

4 Expand the Databases folder, click the RSExecutionLog database, and then click SQL Query Analyzer on the Tools menu.

Opening SQL Query Analyzer this way ensures that the RSExecution-Log database is the current database context in SQL Query Analyzer.

5 In Query Analyzer, open the createtables.sql file in the C:\rs2000sbs\chap10 folder.

▶ **Note** The createtables.sql file is included for your convenience in the practice files. Reporting Services supplies this file on the installation CD in the \Extras \Execution Log DTS Package folder.

6 Click the Execute Query button (or press F5) to run the createtables .sql script.

▶ **Important** If you opened Query Analyzer using an approach other than the one described in this procedure, be sure to select the RSExecutionLog data-base in the Database list box before executing the script.

The results of the query execution are displayed in the Messages tab on the Results pane:

```
Dropping tables...
Creating ReportTypes...
Creating Reports...
Creating Users...
Creating Machines...
Creating RequestTypes...
Creating SourceTypes...
Creating FormatTypes...
Creating StatusCodes...
Creating ExecutionLogs...
Creating ExecutionParameters...
Creating RunLogs...
Script completed.
```

7 Close Query Analyzer.

8 In Enterprise Manager, right-click the Data Transformation Services folder, and then click Open Package.

9 Open the RSExecutionLog_Update.dts file in the C:\rs2000sbs\chap10 folder.

▶ **Note** As with the script file you just used, the RSExecutionLog_Update.dts file is also included for your convenience in the practice files. You can find the identical file on the Reporting Services installation CD in the \Setup \x86 \Reporting Services\Execution Log folder.

The Select Package dialog box is displayed:

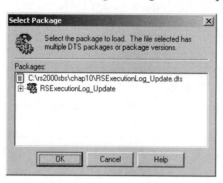

10 Double-click RSExecutionLog_Update to open the package.
The package is displayed in the DTS Designer:

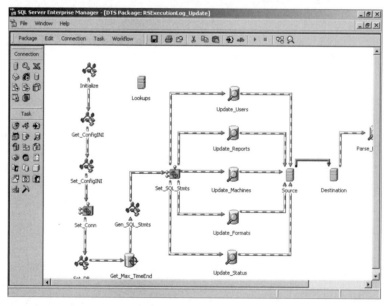

11 On the Package menu, click Properties, and then click the Global
Variables tab.

12 Click the Value column for the *sConfigINI* global variable, and then
type **c:\rs2000sbs\chap10\RSExecutionLog_Update.ini.**

The DTS Package Properties: RSExecutionLog_Update dialog box looks similar to this:

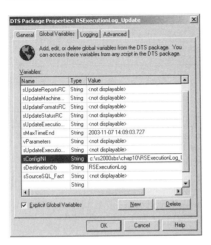

The *sConfigINI* global variable will now use this .ini file to identify the host server and database names for the ReportServer and the RSExecutionLog databases. Just below the *sConfigINI* global variable is the *sDestinationDb* global variable, which contains the value RSExecutionLog. You don't need to worry about changing this value because the .ini value for databases overrides values set in this package. This package was created so that you have to update the .ini file only once; you won't have to update the global variable and all the data-driven query tasks that require specification of a destination database.

▶ **Note** If you used different database names for these databases, or if you installed them on a remote server, you will need to edit the RSExecutionLog _Update.ini file in the C:\rs2000sbs\chap10 folder. If you later remove this file from your computer, the .ini file installed by Reporting Services (and used by the package if there is no global variable value specified for *sConfigINI*) can be found in the Program Files\Microsoft SQL Server \80\tools\Reporting Services \Execution Log folder. The files are identical.

13 Click the OK button.

14 On the Package menu, click Execute to run the DTS package.

▶   **Important**   If you opened the .ini file to review or edit its contents, you need
to close the file before executing the DTS package or else the package will
fail to execute.

When package execution is complete, your screen looks like this:

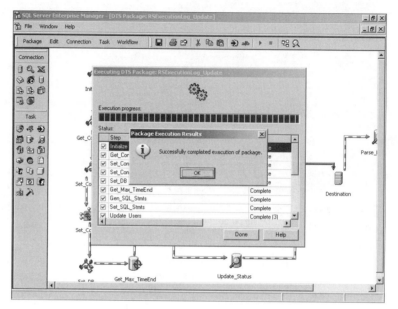

15 Click the OK button, and then click the Done button, but keep DTS
Designer open for another procedure in this chapter.

Using an Execution Log Report

To help you review the information extracted to the RSExecutionLog database,
Reporting Services supplies several execution logging reports. You can use the
reports with or without modification, or add your own reports to use the execution logging information in different ways.

In this procedure, you will deploy the execution logging reports, review the
Average Report Execution Times report, and then deploy reports for comparing
execution times.

Deploy execution logging reports

1 Using Visual Studio, open the ExecutionLog solution in the C:\rs2000sbs \chap10\Execution Log folder.

The Solution Explorer window looks like this:

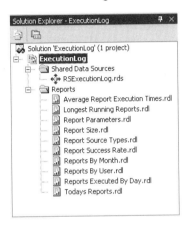

▶ **Note** The shared data source in this solution assumes that you have named the new database RSExecutionLog as described in the previous procedure, and that the database is on the local server. The reports in this solution are similar to the sample reports you can find on the Reporting Services installation CD in the \Extras\Execution Log Sample Reports folder. The following reports in the ExecutionLog solution (included in the practice files) have been enhanced with additional information or improved formatting: Longest Runnning Reports, Report Parameters, and Report Size. Additionally, this solution contains the following reports not included with Reporting Services: Average Report Execution Times and Report Source Types.

2 Right-click the ExecutionLog solution, and then click Deploy Solution.

3 When the solution successfully deploys, open the Home page in Report Manager.

4 Click the Example Reports folder link, click the Execution Log Reports folder link, and then click the Average Report Execution Times report link.

The top of the report looks similar to this:

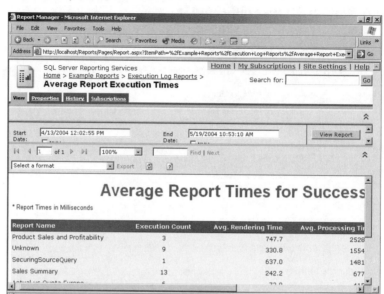

You will see report names and metrics in this report that correspond to your usage of Reporting Services, but the speed of your computer might result in different times than those shown in this report. You'll need to scroll horizontally to see all averages calculated for a report. Notice the report parameters to select a start and end date for the report. The default values for these report parameters are calculated from the earliest and latest dates in the RSExecutionLog database tables.

In the sample report shown here, the Product Sales and Profitability report has the longest rendering time. Your computer might render faster or slower. As you review the details of this report, you can see that the reports are listed in descending order of average total execution time. This execution time includes data retrieval, processing, and rendering time, which are displayed in separate columns for comparison.

5   Using Visual Studio, open the Filter vs parameter solution in the C:\rs2000sbs\chap10\Execution Log folder.

6   On the Build menu, click Deploy Solution.

The two reports in this solution use identical queries. You will execute these reports to compare the difference between the time to execute a report that uses a dataset filter, Product Profitability Filter, and the time to execute a report that uses a query parameter, Product Profitability Query Parameter.

7   When the solution is successfully deployed, switch from Visual Studio to Report Manager, and then click the the Execution Log Reports link.

8   Click the Product Profitability Filter report link to execute the report.

The execution time required for this report includes data retrieval, report processing, and rendering time, because this is the first time the report has been executed since deployment to the Report Server.

9   In the Category list box, click Accessory, and then click the View Report button.

Because this report uses a dataset filter, there is no execution time for data retrieval or report processing when you change the category value. Only rendering time will be required to display Accessory data in this report.

10   In the Category list box, click Bike, click the View Report button, and then repeat this step for the Clothing category.

11   Click the Execution Log Reports folder link.

12   Click the Product Profitability Query Parameter Report to execute the report.

13   In the Category list box, click Accessory, click the View Report button, and then repeat this step for the Bike category and then again for the Clothing category.

This report is created with query parameters, so each time you click the View Report button, execution time includes data retrieval, report processing, and rendering time.

14   Click the Execution Log Reports folder link.

15   Click the Average Report Execution Times report link.

Notice that neither the Product Profitability Filter report nor the Product Profitability Query Parameter report is displayed in this report. The execution log reports are dependent on the data that currently exists in the RSExecutionLog database, which was extracted *before* you executed the product reports. You need to update the RSExecutionLog database to append records for the execution logging for the product reports.

Adding Current Data to the Execution Log

The RSExecutionLog is not designed to stay synchronized with the execution logging data in the ReportServer database. You need to determine a reasonable frequency for updating the RSExecutionLog database with new execution logging records, and then schedule the DTS package to execute with this frequency. (Refer to SQL Server Books Online for more information about scheduling a DTS package.)

In this procedure, you will update the RSExecutionLog database by executing the RSExecutionLog_Update package.

Update the execution log database

1   Switch to SQL Server Enterprise Manager and then, in DTS Designer, click Execute on the Package menu.

2   Click the OK button, and then click the Done button.

The DTS package appended new records to the RSExecutionLog database.

▶ **Note**   Rather than append records to the logging database, you might want to remove records for older data. You can use the cleanup.sql script in the C:\rs2000sbs\chap10 folder. This file is also located in the \Extras\Execution Log DTS Package folder of the Reporting Services installation CD.

3   Close the DTS package, and click Yes to save the changes that you made.

In this procedure, you will use execution logging reports to compare the performance of the Product Profitability Filter and Product Profitability Query Parameter reports.

Compare execution performance

1   In Report Manager, return to the Execution Log Reports page, and then click the Average Report Execution Times report link.

2   If necessary, replace the values in the Start Date box with the current date and the values in the End Date box with the current date and time, and then click the View Report button. You might need to scroll through the report to find the product reports.

The averages for the product reports should look similar to this:

Average Report Times for Successful Reports

* Report Times in Milliseconds

Report Name	Execution Count	Avg. Rendering Time	Avg. Processing Time	Avg. Data Retrieval Time	Avg. Total Time
Product Profitability Filter	4	86.8	148.3	448.8	683.8
Product Profitability Query Parameter	4	73.3	83.0	245.8	402.0

▶ **Note**   The report shown in this example was exported to Microsoft Excel and reformatted to better display all data for these two reports. You might need to scroll horizontally to view the values in each column in Report Manager.

The averages shown in your report will differ because of variations in server configurations. Using the report illustrated here, you can see that the relative performance of the two reports is similar. The average rendering time of the two product reports in the previous illustration is nearly the same, because rendering was required when each report was opened and each time the View Report button was clicked. The processing time and data retrieval time is higher for the Product Profitability Filter report, even though the query executed only one time. However, the query retrieved data for all categories, which increased the data retrieval time as well as the processing time of the report. In the case of the Product Profitability Query Parameter report, the use of query parameters to retrieve a smaller dataset actually resulted in faster performance overall as compared with the other report.

As indicated in the Average Report Execution Times report, the times displayed in the report are milliseconds, so the user experience in executing these reports is not particularly noticeable. However, when you are working with reports with production data, you can use the information in the Average Report ExecutionTimes report to help you discover bottlenecks so that you can take appropriate action to resolve report problems. For example, if you see that data retrieval is consuming a considerable amount of the overall processing time, you might try to improve the performance of the SQL query. If, on the other hand, you see processing is taking a long time, you might look for ways to reduce the complexity of the report.

3   Click the Execution Log Reports folder link, and then click the Report Parameters report link.

4   Click the plus sign next to Product Profitability Filter, and then click the plus sign next to Product Profitability Query Parameter.

The top of the report looks similar to this:

Report Parameter Summary

* Report Times in Milliseconds

Report/Parameter Name	Execution Count	Avg Total Time
⊞ Bike Sales and Profitability	48	1168.5
⊞ Product Sales and Profitability Parameters	24	973.666666666667
⊞ Actual vs Quota Europe	14	1910.42857142857
⊞ Product Sales YTD	14	355
⊟ Product Profitability Filter	12	683.75
Year	4	683.75
2003	4	683.75
Month	4	683.75
1	4	683.75
Category	4	683.75
Component	1	904

This report lets you compare and contrast the average total execution time by report parameter. This average is computed by dividing the total execution time for the report by the number of report executions.

5 Click the Execution Log Reports folder link, and then click the Report Source Types report link.

6 Click the plus sign next to Product Profitability Filter, and then click the plus sign next to Product Profitability Query Parameter.

The top of the report looks similar to this:

Report Source Type Summary

* Report Times in Milliseconds

Report Name / Start Time	Source Type	Report Execution Time
⊞ Average Report Execution Times		1526
⊟ Product Profitability Query Parameter		1608
5/20/2004 12:57:54 PM	Live	313
5/20/2004 12:57:46 PM	Live	612
5/20/2004 12:57:40 PM	Live	239
5/20/2004 12:57:33 PM	Live	444

Here you can see execution times by source type. Possible source types are Snapshot, Live, Cache, and History. Because the source type can have an impact on execution times, you should review this report when evaluating the performance of a report.

How to Manage Server Resources

There are several proactive steps that you can take to manage performance on the Report Server. For instance, you can use timeout settings to force a query or report execution to end if either can't complete within a specified time frame. Instead of using timeouts to cancel a job automatically, you can use Report Manager to cancel a job manually. You can also prevent jobs from running by disabling a shared data source or by pausing a shared schedule.

Applying Timeouts to Source Queries

A source query timeout can be added to a report only during the authoring stage. When the report executes, if the query doesn't finish before the query timeout is exceeded, the execution of the report will fail. You can use a query timeout to protect the source database from the impact of unexpectedly long-running queries. Each dataset in a report has its own query timeout setting.

In this procedure, you will add a query timeout to the Product Profitability Query Parameter report.

Add a timeout to a source query

1 In Visual Studio, open the Product Profitability Query Parameter
report. If you closed the solution after completing the previous
procedure, open the Filter vs Parameter solution in the folder
C:\rs2000sbs\chap10\Execution Log, and then open this report.

2 Click the Data tab, click Category in the Dataset list box, and then
click the Edit Selected Dataset button.

3 Type **30** in the Timeout box.

The Dataset dialog box looks like this:

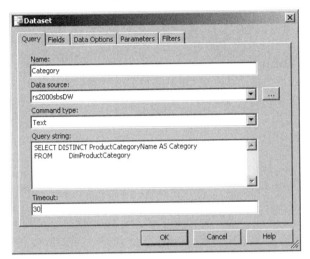

4 Click the OK button, and then save the solution.

If you were to deploy the report, the query timeout would be applied
each time the Category query executes.

Applying Timeouts to Report Execution

Another option for managing server resources is to use Report Manager to
establish timeouts for report execution. You can set a global timeout value that
applies to all reports on the Report Server, or you can override the global value
on individual reports. You also have the option of not using timeouts for report
execution.

In this procedure, you will review the global timeout value and apply a timeout
value to the Average Report Execution Times report.

Add a timeout to report execution

1   In Report Manager, click the Site Settings link.

The Site Settings page looks like this:

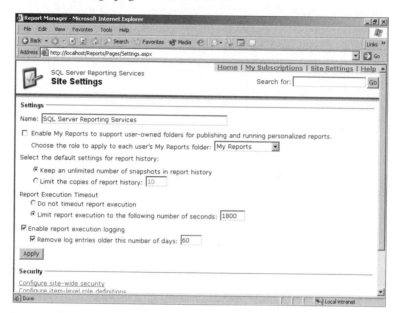

Notice that the current default setting for Report Execution Timeout is set to 1800 seconds. This setting will apply to all reports that execute on the Report Server, unless you override the setting for an individual report.

2   Click the Home link.

3   Click the Example Reports folder link, click the Execution Log Reports folder link, and then click the Average Report Execution Times report link.

4   Click the Properties tab, and then click the Execution link.

5   If necessary, scroll to the bottom of the page to find the Report Execution Timeout section.

6   Click Limit Report Execution To The Following Number Of Seconds, and type **60** in the box to the right.

The bottom of the screen looks like this:

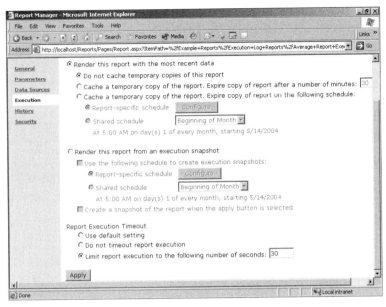

7 Click the Apply button.

Now this report will fail when execution takes longer than 60 seconds. Of course, you'll need to monitor reports in your own production environment to determine an appropriate timeout value globally or for individual reports.

Canceling Jobs

In addition to using timeouts to stop a report, you can manually cancel a report by using Report Manager. From the Site Settings page, you can access the Manage Jobs page to display jobs that are currently executing. You can select one or more jobs on this page to cancel. However, bear in mind that killing the job with Report Manager doesn't necessarily kill the corresponding process in the source database.

In this procedure, you will execute a report to see how jobs appear in the Manage Jobs page. To perform this procedure, you will need to have two instances of Internet Explorer running Report Manager.

Review the Manage Jobs page

1   In the first instance of Internet Explorer, use Report Manager to navigate to Site Settings.

2   At the bottom of the Site Settings page, click the Manage Jobs link. This page currently has no jobs to display.

3   In a second instance of Internet Explorer, use Report Manager to open the Reports Executed By Day report, which is found in the Execution Log Reports subfolder of the Example Reports folder.

4   Switch to the first instance of Internet Explorer, and then click the Refresh button on the Internet Explorer toolbar to update the page. You might need to click the Refresh button a few times in quick succession to see the job appear on this page.

▶   **Note**   If after a few seconds, you still don't see the job appear, you might not have switched between applications fast enough. In that case, click Execution Log Reports and open another report. Quickly switch to the Manage Jobs page, refreshing the page until the job appears. If you still can't see the job, it might be that your computer is too fast for the job to be displayed on this page. In a production environment, you will likely have an opportunity to monitor jobs on this page.

The Manage Jobs page looks like this:

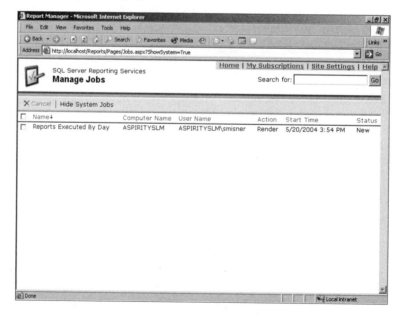

If you need to cancel one or more jobs, you can select the job's check box, and then click the Cancel button on the Report Manager toolbar.

Disabling a Shared Data Source

Sometimes you might want to temporarily prevent reports from executing altogether. You might need to suspend jobs while performing maintenance on a source database or when troubleshooting data issues. Any reports that had been assigned to the disabled shared data source can't execute until the shared data source is enabled or a new data source is assigned. Subscriptions using a disabled shared data source are also prevented from executing. Disabling a shared data source is an easy way to temporarily suspend many reports with one step. You should consider using shared data sources whenever possible so that you can take advantage of this feature, because you can't disable custom data sources.

In this procedure, you will suspend the rs2000sbsDW shared data source in the Execution Log Reports subfolder.

Suspend jobs by disabling a shared data source

1 In Report Manager, open the rs2000sbsDW shared data source in the in the Execution Log Reports subfolder of the Example Reports folder.

2 Click the Reports link.
   Your screen looks like this:

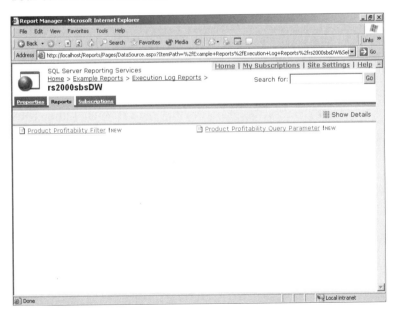

A list of reports that are associated with the current shared data source is always available. This feature gives you the opportunity to assess the impact of disabling the shared data source. Notice also the Subscriptions link, which serves the same purpose for subscriptions dependent on the current shared data source.

3   Click the Properties tab.

4   Clear the Enable This Data Source check box.

Your screen looks like this:

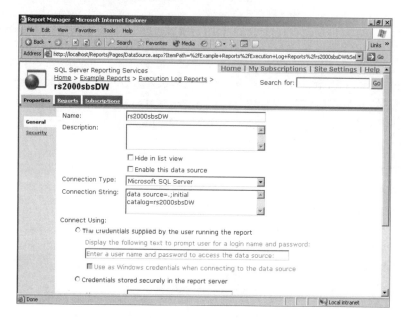

5   Click the Apply button.

Now any reports or subscriptions that use this shared data source will be suspended.

6   Click the Execution Log Reports link, and then click the Product Profitability Filter report link.

Your screen looks like this:

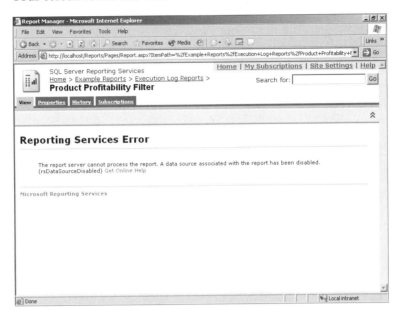

If a user attempts to execute an on-demand report that uses a disabled shared data source, an error message is displayed. However, a snapshot of the report can still be viewed.

Pausing a Shared Schedule

You can also pause a shared schedule to temporarily suspend jobs. In Chapter 8, "Managing Content," you learned how to create a shared schedule by accessing the Shared Schedules page from the Site Settings page. You were also introduced to the Report Manager toolbar buttons that allow you to pause or resume a schedule. By pausing a schedule, you are suspending related jobs, such as report executions and subscriptions. However, no list of reports or subscriptions is provided for you to examine before pausing the schedule. Also, like disabling a shared data source, pausing a shared schedule is an easy way to temporarily suspend many reports with one step, which isn't possible when using a custom schedule.

Administering Reporting Services Databases

You learned about the ReportServer and the ReportServerTempDB databases while learning how to deploy reports and manage report execution. Now it's time to take a closer look at these databases from an administrative perspective. To manage these databases, you need to understand the factors that affect their size so that you can manage your disk space resources appropriately. You also need to implement an appropriate disaster recovery strategy for these databases.

How to Manage the Reporting Services Databases

You use standard SQL Server tools to monitor the size of the tables in the ReportServer and ReportServerTempDB databases. You will need to understand how Reporting Services implementation decisions can increase or decrease their space requirements. To protect the data from disaster, you can use SQL Server backup utilities. However, because some information in the ReportServer database is encrypted, you'll also need to use the Reporting Services rskeymgmt utility to back up the encryption key.

Monitoring Database Storage Consumption

Reporting Services uses the ReportServer database as its primary storage component not only for reports but also for configuration information, security assignments, and schedules. As such, Reporting Services cannot operate without the ReportServer database. The ReportServerTempDB database is also a storage component, but only for temporary data such as session and caching information. The following table compares the contents of each database:

ReportServer	ReportServerTempDB
Folders, reports, resources	User session information
Shared data sources	Session caching
Snapshots and report history	Cached instances
Security	
Schedules	
Subscriptions and notifications	
Configuration	
Execution log	

Most tables in either database do not consume much space, with the exception of the ChunkData table. In the ReportServer database, the ChunkData table contains snapshots and report history. Because snapshots and report history are stored in the intermediate format of a report, they also include all the report data, and consequently consume a higher percentage of disk space than other tables in the database. The ChunkData table in the ReportServerTempDB database contains the session cache and the cached instances, which also store reports in an intermediate format with data, so it too requires a large amount of disk space relative to other tables.

Check the ChunkData table size

1 Open Enterprise Manager.

2 Expand the (local) server (or the instance to which you installed Reporting Services and the practice files), expand the Databases folder, and then click ReportServer.

3 On the View menu, click Taskpad if it's not already selected.

4 Click the Table Info tab in Taskpad.

Your screen looks similar to this:

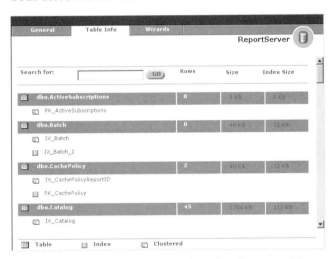

5 Scroll through the list to find the ChunkData table.

As you add snapshots and report history, this table will continue to grow much faster than the other tables in this database. You can use Taskpad to monitor its size. If it starts getting too large (which really depends on your specific environment), you might want to work with users to determine which snapshots or how much report history is really needed.

Evaluating Disk Space Requirements

Because so many variables contribute to disk space consumption, there's no specific formula that you can use to estimate disk space. However, the following list provides some general areas that you can review when evaluating the impact of implementation decisions on server disk space:

- Total number of reports
- Total number of snapshots
- Total number of snapshots saved in report history
- Total size of intermediate reports (which include report data) in snapshots and report history
- Total number of cached instances resulting from different combinations of report parameters
- Total number of users affecting session cache
- Session cache timeout length

Implementing a Backup and Restore Strategy

You can take advantage of the backup and restore utilities provided with SQL Server as part of your disaster recovery plan. Backing up your ReportServer database, as well as the master and msdb databases, on a regular basis is critical because together these databases contain everything that Reporting Services needs to function. (The master database contains user accounts, and msdb contains the scheduled jobs.) However, you really only need the ability to back up the ReportServerTempDB database one time so that you have something to restore in the event of disaster. As users browse reports, data will cache as needed—either as a session cache or as a cached instance.

If you need to restore the ReportServer database, you will also need to restore the key that is used to store the encrypted data in that database. For example, if you migrate the ReportServer database to a new SQL Server instance, you will also need to migrate the encryption key. As you learned earlier in this chapter, Reporting Services uses encryption for several purposes—storing the connection string and credentials used to connect to the Reporting Services databases, storing the credentials to use for running unattended reports, and storing credentials for selected data sources. To encrypt and decrypt this data, Reporting Services uses a public key and a symmetric key that are created at installation. Migrating the ReportServer database "breaks" the symmetric key such that Reporting Services is no longer able to decrypt the connection strings or credentials. As a result, an unauthorized migration of the database is foiled and the security of your Reporting Services implementation is protected.

▶ **Important**   Moving the ReportServer database is not the only event that modifies the symmetric key. The symmetric key is also affected by renaming the server or changing the service account that runs the ReportServer Windows service.

To help you manage changes to the server infrastructure that have an impact on the symmetric key, Reporting Services includes the rskeymgmt utility. This utility allows you to back up this key. After an event occurs that invalidates the symmetric key, you can use the rskeymgmt utility to restore the original version of the symmetric key.

Use the following syntax on the Report Server to back up the encryption key:

```
rskeymgmt -e -f [drive:][folder\]filename -p password
```

The *–e* argument instructs the utility to extract the encryption key to the file identified with the *–f* argument. The *–p* is a password that is used to scramble the symmetric key and is required if you later need to restore it. After you store the symmetric key in an external file, you can move it to a secure location. To restore the symmetric key, use the following syntax:

```
rskeymgmt -a -f [drive:][folder\]filename -p password
```

After restoring the key, you must restart Microsoft Internet Information Services (IIS) for the change to take effect.

▶ **Important**   When using the rskeymgmt utility, you need to have local system administrator privileges on the server. This utility must be run locally on the server.

If for some reason you don't have access to the backup of the encryption key (or forget the password), and the ReportServer database becomes disabled because of a problem with the symmetric key, you can also use the rskeymgmt utility to delete the encrypted data in the ReportServer database. In this case, just use rskeymgmt -d and then restart IIS. Then you can use the rsconfig utility to specify the connection information to be encrypted. You can then use the rskeymgmt utility to create a new backup of the encryption key. (You can learn more about the rskeymgmt utility in Reporting Services Books Online.)

If you delete the encrypted data in the ReportServer database and had previously configured credentials for unattended report processing, you will need to run the rsconfig utility again to add these credentials back to the Report Server configuration file (as explained earlier in this chapter). For each report and shared data source that uses stored credentials, you will need to update the credentials individually because this data is wiped out when you use the *–d* argument with the rskeymgmt utility. You will also need to open and save each subscription because they also are affected by the deletion of encrypted credentials. This is a lot of work to do if you have a lot of items using stored credentials or subscriptions, so take care to backup the symmetric key!

In this procedure, you will use the rskeymgmt utility to back up the symmetric key.

Back up the symmetric key

1 On the Start menu, click Run, type **cmd**, and then click OK to open a command prompt window.

2 Run the rskeymgmt utility by typing the following: **rskeymgmt –e –f c:\rs2000sbs\Workspace\RSkey –p** *YourPassword* (replacing *Your-Password* with a password of your choosing).

▶ **Important** This password is used to encrypt the key in the extracted file. You will need this password if you need to reapply the key to a Reporting Services instance.

3 Type **Y** to confirm that you want to extract the key and then press ENTER.

When the file is created, the screen looks like this:

Now you can move the RSKey file to a secure location in your environment.

Chapter 10 Quick Reference

To	Do this
Edit a configuration file	After reviewing valid values for modifiable configuration settings in Reporting Services Books Online, open the applicable configuration file with any XML editor and edit the file. You can edit the following files: ■ RSReportServer.config ■ RSWebApplication.config ■ ReportingServicesService.exe.config ■ RSReportDesigner.config
Change connection information for the Report Server database	Use the rsconfig utility at the command line using the following syntax: `rsconfig -c -m computername -s SQLServername -d ReportServerDatabaseName -a windows|sql -u [domain\]username -p password`

To	Do this
Encrypt credentials for unattended reports	Use the rsconfig utility at the command line using the following syntax: `rsconfig -e -u [domain\]username -p password`
Change tracing levels on the Report Server	Edit the ReportingServicesService.exe.config file using any XML editor, and change the value for the configuration setting *DefaultTraceSwitch*. Valid integer values are 0 to disable tracing or 1 through 4 to enable tracing with successively greater detail as the value increases.
Create an execution logging database	Create an execution logging database in Enterprise Manager, and then run the createtables.sql script.
Load the execution logging database with current data	Ensure the RSExecutionLog_Update.ini file correctly names the servers and database names for the ReportServer and the execution logging database. The first time the RSExecutionLog_Update DTS package is used, update the DTS package so that the global variable sConfigINI references the path and filename of the RSExecutionLog_Update.ini file, and save the DTS package. Execute the package and schedule for periodic execution to keep the execution logging database relatively current.
Analyze data in the execution logging database	Use the Report Designer in Visual Studio to create your own reports or deploy the sample reports in the ExecutionLog solution in the C:\rs2000sbsdw\chap10\ExecutionLog folder.
Apply a timeout to a source query	In Visual Studio, click the Data tab of a report, click the dataset containing the source query in the Dataset list box, and then click the Edit Selected Dataset button. Enter the timeout value in seconds in the Timeout box.
Apply a timeout to report execution	For a global timeout, click the Site Settings link in Report Manager. Select Limit Report Execution To The Following Number Of Seconds and enter a timeout value in seconds. *or* For a report timeout, open the report, click the Properties tab, and then click the Execution link. Select the Limit Report Execution To The Following Number Of Seconds and enter a timeout value in seconds.
Cancel a job	In Report Manager, click the Site Settings link, and then click the Manage Jobs link. Select the job's check box, and then click the Cancel button.
Disable a shared data source	In Report Manager, open the shared data source, and then clear the Enable This Data Source check box.

To	Do this
Monitor the ChunkData table size	In Enterprise Manager, expand the server, expand the Databases folder, and then click ReportServer (or Report-ServerTempDB). On the View menu, click Taskpad if it's not already selected, and then click the Table Info tab in Taskpad. Search for ChunkData or scroll to the table.
Back up the encryption key	Use the rskeymgmt utility at the command line using the following syntax:

```
rskeymgmt -e -f [drive:][folder\]filename
-p password
```

Delivering Reports

Chapter

11

Accessing Reports

In this chapter, you will learn how to:

■ Use Report Manager's navigation features to locate and view reports.

■ Add content to the My Reports folder.

■ Save a report.

■ Print a report.

You learned a great deal about the first two stages of the reporting life cycle in Part 2, "Authoring Reports," and Part 3, "Managing the Report Server." The third and final stage of the reporting life cycle includes the access and delivery of reports, covered in the three chapters of Part 4. You learn how features of Report Manager help you view and save reports, how report design affects report rendering, and how subscriptions to deliver reports are created and managed. In Part 5, "Programming Reporting Services"—a bonus section included on the companion CD—you explore ways to build custom scripts and applications to automate each stage of the reporting life cycle.

This chapter begins by teaching you how to retrieve reports from the Report Server. You learn the available options for locating reports on the server, exploring the contents of a report online, and for changing the size of the report in your browser. The latter half of this chapter shows you how to preserve the report and its data on the Report Server, on your computer as a local file, or as a printed report.

Finding and Viewing Reports

Using Report Manager to open and view a report has already been introduced in earlier chapters of this book, but there are a few more activities to learn that are related to finding and viewing reports. As you already know, you can use folder links to reach a report when you know the location. When you're not sure where a report is found, you can search all or part of the Report Server to find it.

After you open a report, the report remains available "as is" in your browser so that you can return later to the same view of the report for as long as your browser session is active, even if the report definition or the underlying data changes. However, the HTML Viewer in which Report Manager displays your report provides you with the option of reloading the report to get the most current report definition and to update the data. This option to refresh a report is one of several features available in the HTML Viewer that you can use while working with your report online.

How to View Reports Using Report Manager

To view a report using Report Manager, you simply click the report link on a folder's Contents page. The trick is knowing which folder contains the report that you're looking for. You can use Report Manager's folder links to move deeper into a folder hierarchy, or use navigation links to move in the opposite direction until you find the desired report. When you have a lot of folders to traverse using this method, finding a report can become a tedious process. You can eliminate this hassle by using Report Manager's search feature. You don't even need to know the report's complete name to search for it—just enter a string of characters to find reports that contain that same string in either the report name or its description.

If you return to a report that you viewed earlier in the same browser session, you will be viewing the version of the report retrieved from the session cache. The report is retained in the session cache for the duration of the browser session. If you suspect that a report definition or the source data has changed during your current session, you can force Report Manager to reload the report definition from the Report Server and to execute the report query. To do this, you use the Refresh button on the Report toolbar in the HTML Viewer. The Report toolbar contains several other features that allow you to interact more effectively with a report. For example, you can resize the report to better fit your browser window, or you can search the contents of a report for a specific string (which is different from the search feature in Report Manager described earlier). Finally, if you want easy access to a report that uses default parameter values that are different from those defined by the Content Manager, you can— if you have the right permissions and the feature is enabled—create a personal linked report to store in your private workspace, the My Reports folder.

Navigating the Folder Hierarchy

You can review the contents of the Report Server by browsing the folder hierarchy. Folders can be created by the report author if the report is deployed by using the Report Designer (as you learned in Chapter 8, "Managing Content"); by a

Content Manager if reports and resources need to be relocated after deployment (as you also learned in Chapter 8); or by a script or application (as you will learn in Chapter 15, "Programming Report Server Management," which can be found on the companion CD) for automated content management. The folder hierarchy works much like the arrangement of folders that you use to navigate the Microsoft Windows file system, in which folders can contain items or other folders that also contain items or additional folders. However, in Report Manager, the hierarchy is not represented as a tree view but rather as separate pages. You can see only those folders and items for which you have the appropriate permissions (as explained in Chapter 9, "Managing Security").

To open a folder, you click the folder link in the Contents page. The path to the current folder is displayed at the end of a series of navigation links in the top left corner of the browser window, beginning with the Home folder and continuing with each nested folder. You can quickly jump to a higher-level folder using these links.

In this procedure, you will explore the Adventure Works Chapter 11 folder hierarchy in Report Manager.

Use navigation links

1   Run publishChap11.cmd in the C:\rs2000sbs\chap11 folder to create the folders, and publish the reports that you need to follow the procedures in this chapter.

2   Open Report Manager in Internet Explorer at *http://localhost/Reports*.

3   Click the Adventure Works Chapter 11 folder link to display its contents, as shown here:

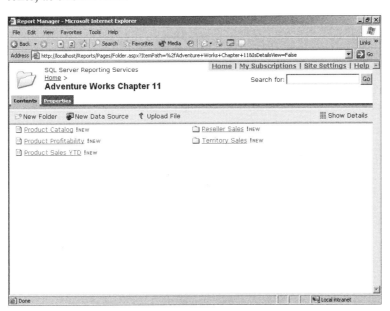

This folder contains three reports and two folder links. Notice the link for the Home folder in the top left corner of the window. Whenever you browse folders and open items, the folder links always appear in this location to identify your current location in the folder hierarchy and to help you return quickly to a folder at a higher level.

The Home link in the top right corner of the browser window also takes you to the Home folder, and is always available whether you are browsing the folder hierarchy or managing server settings, which are accessed independently of the folder hierarchy.

4   Click the Reseller Sales folder link, and then click the Reseller Sales report link.

The navigation links at the top of the screen look like this:

Home > Adventure Works Chapter 11 > Reseller Sales

The complete series of links shows the path to the current report, beginning from the Home page. Rather than use the Back button in your browser, you can quickly jump to another folder in this path by using the navigation link.

5   Click the Adventure Works Chapter 11 navigation link.

With one click, you have moved to a folder two levels above the report you were viewing.

6   Leave the Report Manager open for the next procedure.

Refreshing Reports

You can also use the Back button to return to folders or reports that you have previously opened. Whereas the Contents page of a folder will display new contents that were added since you previously viewed the page (such as new reports or new execution times for schedule reports), an on-demand report will not reflect any changes made to the report after you initially opened it—as long as you're still using the same browser session.

As you learned in Chapter 10, "Managing Server Components," the Report-ServerTempDB stores the session cache version of the report to speed up delivery of the same report during a single browser session. If you suspect that the report definition or source data has changed during your session, you can use the Refresh Report button to force a cached report to be reloaded from the Report-Server database and a new query to be executed against the source database.

In this procedure, you will use the Refresh Report button to load a revised report definition into the session cache.

Replace the session cache

1 Run updateResellerSales.cmd in the C:\rs2000sbs\chap11 folder to publish a revised version of the Reseller Sales report.

This batch command file will publish a revised report definition of the Reseller Sales report and overwrite the existing report definition.

2 In Report Manager, use the Back button to return to the Reseller Sales Report.

A portion of the report is shown here:

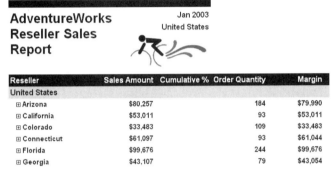

AdventureWorks Reseller Sales Report		Jan 2003 United States		
Reseller	**Sales Amount**	**Cumulative %**	**Order Quantity**	**Margin**
United States				
⊞ Arizona	$80,257		184	$79,990
⊞ California	$53,011		93	$53,011
⊞ Colorado	$33,483		109	$33,483
⊞ Connecticut	$61,097		93	$61,044
⊞ Florida	$99,676		244	$99,676
⊞ Georgia	$43,107		79	$43,054

Even though a new version of the Reseller Sales report has been stored on the Report Server, the version of the report in the session cache is displayed. Notice in this version of the report that the group header row, which currently displays United States, includes no other data.

3 Click the Refresh Report button in the Report Manager toolbar.

▶ **Note** If you use the browser's Refresh button, or if you press CTRL+F5, the report is reloaded from the cache without the report definition.

The top of the report looks like this:

AdventureWorks Reseller Sales Report		Jan 2003 United States		
Reseller	**Sales Amount**	**Cumulative %**	**Order Quantity**	**Margin**
United States	$1,183,477		2,204	$1,175,303
⊞ Arizona	$80,257		184	$79,990
⊞ California	$53,011		93	$53,011
⊞ Colorado	$33,483		109	$33,483
⊞ Connecticut	$61,097		93	$61,044
⊞ Florida	$99,676		244	$99,676
⊞ Georgia	$43,107		79	$43,054

The report is reloaded from the Report Server and the query is executed again. In this case, the source data hasn't changed, but the report definition has been updated to include subtotals in the group header row to the right of United States.

Searching for Reports

If you're not sure where to begin looking for a report, you can use the Search feature in Report Manager to find a report by name or by description. In fact, you can also use this feature to search for folders, shared data sources, and resources. However, you can't search for a specific snapshot in report history or a subscription, nor can you search for schedules or role assignments.

To search, you type in a search string using all or part of the folder or item name (or its description) in the Search For box in the top right corner of Report Manager. Reporting Services will begin the search in the current folder and will continue through all the nested folders below the current location. Report Manager won't search a folder or return an item for which you don't have permissions.

In this procedure, you will search for reports that include Product Sales in the report name or description.

Search for reports using a partial name

1 Click the Home link to return to the Home page.

By searching from the Home page, all folders to which you have permission will be searched.

2 Type **product sales** in the Search For box, as shown here:

 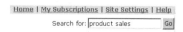

3 Click the Go button.

The Search page looks similar to this:

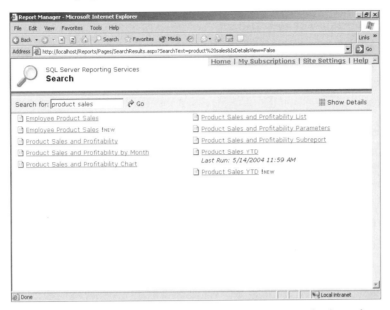

Depending on the reports you have on your server, the list of reports might be different from those shown in the illustration.

4 Click the Show Details button.

Your screen looks like this:

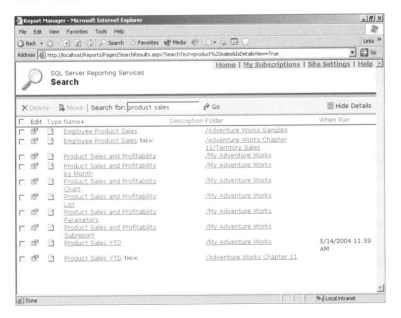

Now you can see not only the reports that met the search criteria, but also in which folder each report is stored. If the report is a snapshot, you will also see the last execution date in the When Run column. You can click on a folder link to navigate to the Contents page of that folder, or you can click on a report link to view the report.

5   Click the Employee Product Sales report link (in the Adventure Works Chapter 11/Territory Sales folder) to view the report, and then leave this report open for the next procedure.

Using the HTML Viewer

The HTML Viewer is supplied by Reporting Services to view reports online in HTML format. Above the report are a parameters section (if report parameters are used and the prompt is enabled) and a Report toolbar. The Report toolbar has useful features that allow you to explore your report more easily as well as change your viewing options.

In the parameters section of the HTML Viewer, you change the value either by selecting a value from the parameter list box or by entering a new value. The report will render with the new value only after you click the View Report button. (Whether the report requeries the data source before rendering depends on how each parameter is configured, as discussed in Chapter 7, "Building Advanced Reports.")

Beneath the parameters section in the HTML Viewer is the Report toolbar, which looks like this:

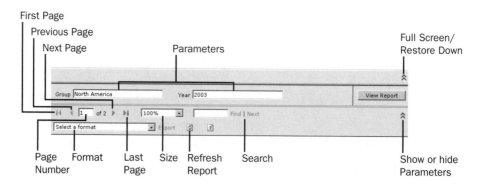

The following table describes how to use the features of the Report toolbar.

To	Do this
Jump to the beginning or end of a report	Use the First Page or Last Page button.
Scroll to the previous or next page	Use the Previous Page or Next Page button.
Jump to a specific page	Type a page number in the Page Number box, and then press ENTER.
Change the size of the report page	Click a percentage in the Size list box. You can also click Page Width if you want the report resized to fit the horizontal width of your browser, or click Whole Page if you want the report resized to fit vertically within your browser.
Search for the first occurrence of text on any page of a report	Type the search string in the search box, and then click the Find link. This link is available only when you enter a search string.
Search for the next occurrence of text within a report	Click the Next link. Like the Find link, this link is not available until you enter a search string and click the Find link once.
View the report in a different format	Click the desired format in the Format list box, and then click the Export link.
Reload the report from the ReportServer database	Click the Refresh button.
View the HTML Viewer documentation	Click the Help button.
Toggle the display of the report parameters	Click the Show or Hide Parameters button.
Toggle the display mode of the report	Click the Full Screen button to view the report in the full-screen mode and click the Restore Down button to return to the default display mode.

In this procedure, you will explore some of the features of the Report toolbar.

Accessing Reports

11

Use the Report toolbar

1   With the Employee Product Sales report open in the Report Manager, click the Full Screen button on the Report toolbar.

The screen looks like this:

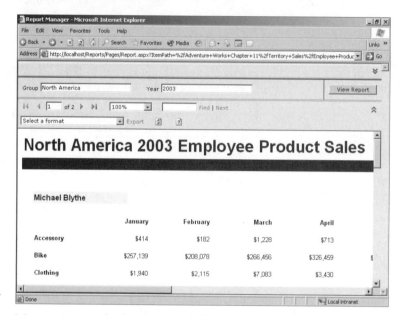

More space in the browser is dedicated to the report, but it still doesn't quite fit the screen.

2   Click the Show or Hide Parameters button.

Even more space is allocated to the report. You can also adjust the size of the report to view more data at once in the browser.

3   Click 75% in the Size list box.

Now you can see more months of the year in the browser. The exact number that you see will depend on your screen resolution.

4   Click the Next Page button to view the second page of the report.

5 Click the Restore Down button to restore the report to its original screen size, shown here:

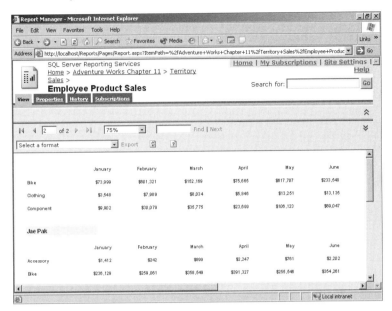

6 Keep the report open for the next procedure.

Using My Reports

If the My Reports feature is enabled on the Report Server, the My Reports folder appears on the Home page. With this feature enabled, each user has his or her own My Reports folder as a personal workspace to which no one else has access, except for report administrators. As you learned in Chapter 9, there is a default role definition for My Reports, which a report administrator can use to limit the tasks that users can perform in this workspace. If you have permissions to create a linked report from an existing report, you can create a personal linked report to access in your My Reports folder, and then you can set your own default parameter values.

You can also upload a report definition or resource file for storage in My Reports or, if you're a report author, you can create and publish a report to My Reports using Report Designer—assuming, of course, that you have the appropriate permissions. If you publish a report from Report Designer, set the project deployment folder to Users Folders/*computername username*/My Reports.

In this procedure, you will create a personal linked report from the Employee Product Sales report.

Create a personal linked report

1   If My Reports is not already enabled, click the Site Settings link in Report Manager, click Enable My Reports, and then click the Apply button.

2   If you accessed the Site Settings using the same browser session that you used in the previous procedure, click the Back button twice to return to the Employee Product Sales report.

3   Click the Properties tab, and then, if the General Properties page is not currently displayed, click the General link.

4   Click the Create Linked Report button.

5   Type a name for the report: **My Employee Product Sales.**

Your screen looks like this:

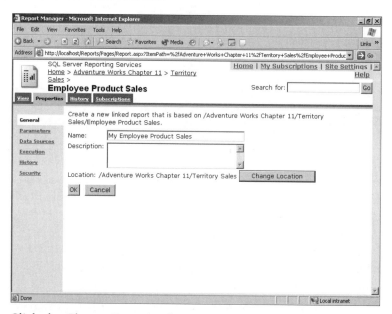

6   Click the Change Location button.

The screen looks similar to this:

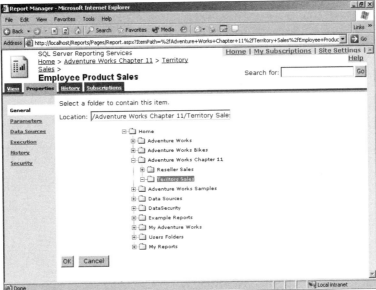

If you did not complete all the procedures in the preceding chapters, you will see fewer folders in the location tree.

7 Click My Reports.

Notice the full folder path that appears in the Location box after you click My Reports: /Users Folders/*computername username*/My Reports.

8 Click the OK button to confirm the My Reports location, and then click the OK button again to create the personal linked report.

The screen looks similar to this:

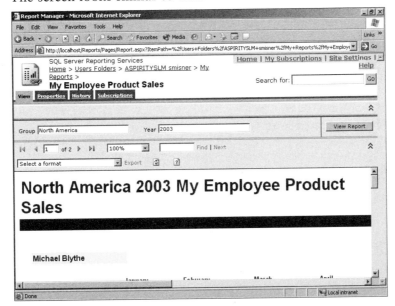

Notice the navigation links in the top left corner of the browser window that now indicate your current location in the My Reports folder. (Your links will display a different computer name and user name.)

9 Click the Properties tab, and then click the Parameters link.

10 Change the Default Value for the Group parameter to **Europe**.

The Parameters Properties page looks like this:

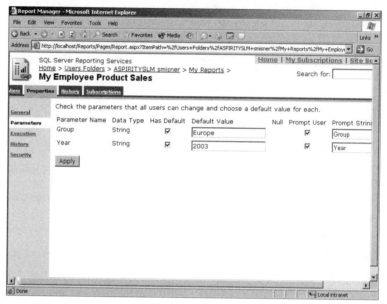

11 Click the Apply button.

12 Click the Home link.

Notice the folder on the Home page: My Reports. This is a new folder if you enabled My Reports in this procedure, but it might not be labeled as new. If you're a report administrator, you will also see a folder entitled Users Folders, in which you will be able to open each user's My Reports folder to review content placed there.

13 Click the My Reports folder link, and then click the My Employee Product Sales report link.

The top of the report looks like this:

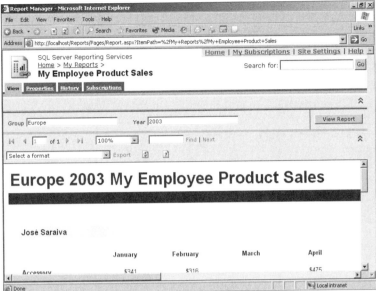

The advantage of creating a personal linked report is the ability to set the default values of each parameter that presents the data the way you want to see it when you open the report. If the base report gets deleted, however, your personal linked report will no longer operate. You will then need to manually delete the report from the My Reports folder.

Saving Reports for Future Reference

Whether a report runs on demand or on a scheduled basis, the information in the report is generally dynamic. That is, when the source data is refreshed periodically, the report eventually reflects changes in the data. If you want to have a permanent record of the data at a certain point in time, you will need to save the report. To store the report and its data on the Report Server, you can create a report snapshot. You also have the option to store the report as a file on your computer or on a network share. Alternatively, you can create a printed copy of the report for your personal use or for distribution across the organization.

How to Make a Copy of a Report

Basically, there are two ways to make a permanent copy of a report. One way is to keep the report copy as a snapshot in report history, which requires you to have access to the Report Server whenever you want to view this copy of the report. Another way is to export the report to another format, which can then be printed or saved to a local file. If you export the report to a file, you can view the file even when you can't connect to the Report Server. Of course, if you save the file to a network share, you need to be able to navigate the network's file system to open the report. Further, your computer must have the appropriate software installed before you can view the file. For example, if you export a report as a Microsoft Excel file, you must have Excel XP or later loaded on your computer before you can view the file contents.

Creating a Report History Snapshot

In Chapter 8, you learned how a report administrator can enable a report's history properties so that snapshots can be saved for reference at some point in the future. Commonly, a schedule is used to put a snapshot into report history on a regular basis. For example, you might have a schedule to place a snapshot of financial statements into report history following each month's end. However, there may be occasions when users might want to manually add a snapshot to report history as well. Just as with scheduled snapshots, the report must be configured to use a data source with stored credentials before anyone can add a snapshot to report history manually.

In this procedure, you will use the New Snapshot button to add a snapshot to the report history of the Employee Product Sales report.

Create a manual snapshot for report history

1   In Report Manager, click the Home link, click the Adventure Works Chapter 11 folder link, click the Territory Sales folder link, and then click the Employee Product Sales report.

2   Click the Properties tab, and then click the Data Sources link.

3   Click Credentials Stored Securely In The Report Server, and then type user name **ReportExecution** and password **ReportExecution**.

  You can create a snapshot only when the data source uses stored credentials.

4   Click the Apply button.

5   Click the History tab, and then click the New Snapshot button.

The screen looks similar to this:

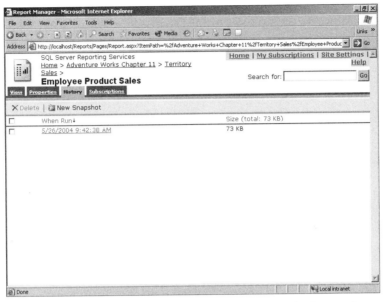

The snapshot will remain in report history until the limit of snapshots defined globally or specifically for this report is exceeded. If no limit is defined, the snapshot will remain in report history until it's manually deleted using the Delete button on this page.

6   Click the snapshot link.

A new browser window is opened with a snapshot that looks similar to this:

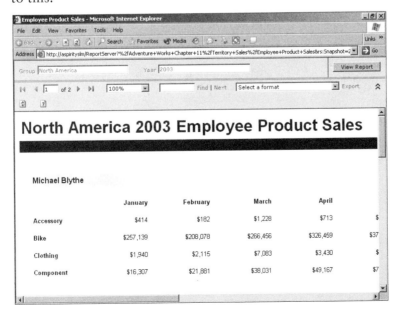

As with a snapshot that replaces an on-demand report, you
cannot change the report parameter values in a snapshot placed in
report history. The snapshot is created using the default parameter
values.

7   Close the snapshot's browser window.

Saving Reports to Local Files

You can save a report to a local file and thereby create the equivalent of a
snapshot. As a local file, you can access the report anytime without connecting
to the Report Server. To create a local file, you use the Export feature in the
HTML Viewer. The best formats to use for saving a report as a local file are
Excel, Web archive, Acrobat (PDF), and TIFF. You'll explore these and other
rendering formats in greater detail in Chapter 12, "Rendering Reports."

The export format that you choose determines which features of the online
report can be reproduced in the selected rendering. For example, a document
map is a feature that enhances navigation in a very large report that you view
using the HTML Viewer. The document map can also be rendered in a PDF
file to facilitate navigation when viewing the report with Acrobat Reader. You
will learn more about the effect of rendering on specific report features in
Chapter 12.

In this procedure, you will save the Product Catalog report as a
PDF file.

Save a report as a PDF file

1   In Report Manager, click the Adventure Works Chapter 11 navigation link, and then click the Product Catalog report.

Your screen looks like this:

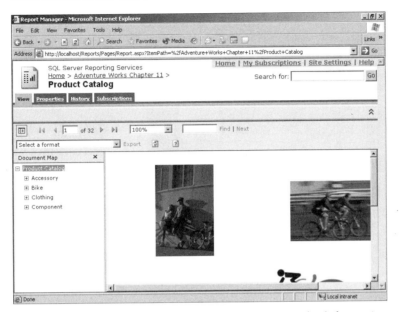

Notice the Document Map pane that appears on the left portion of the page. The Document Map is a feature added during the report authoring stage and is used to jump to a corresponding location in the report. You'll learn more about creating a Document Map in Chapter 12.

2 Click the plus sign to the left of Bike to expand the Document Map, expand Road Bike, and then click Road 150.

The information in the Product Catalog related to the Road 150 bike is displayed. A document map is very useful for navigating a large report like the Product Catalog.

3 Click Acrobat (PDF) File in the Export list box, and then click the Export link.

You have the option to view the exported file now or to save the report to the file system for viewing later. To view a file that is exported to another format, you must have the appropriate application installed on your computer. In this case, you must have Acrobat Reader.

4 Click the Open button to download the file and launch Acrobat Reader as the file viewer.

5   Click the Bookmarks tab.

The screen looks similar to this:

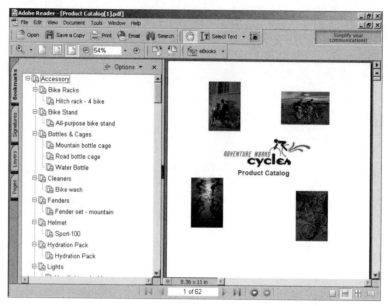

The document map is converted to bookmarks in the PDF file.

6   Click the minus sign to the left of Accessory to collapse the category, and then click Road-150.

The screen looks similar to this:

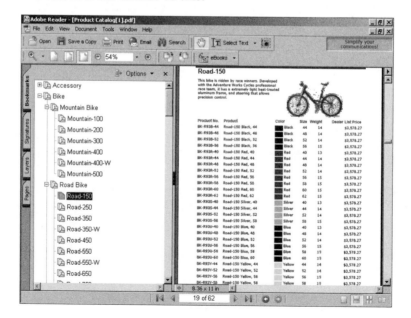

▶ **Note**   The bicycle image in the PDF file is fuzzy at the current resolution. When viewed at 100 percent, however, the image is quite clear.

Now you have a file that you can share with others who don't have access to the Report Server. As an added bonus, the PDF file contains the navigation functionality that was built into the original report to facilitate finding items of interest in a large report.

7   Close the PDF file.

Printing Reports

Because the Report Manager uses its own viewer to render a report online, the browser's print feature will not properly reproduce a print version of the report. Instead, you need to export the report to a format that is better suited for printing, such as Web archive, Acrobat (PDF), or TIFF. When you open the exported report in the appropriate viewer, you can use the viewer's print capabilities to send the report to a printer.

▶ **Tip**   You can develop a custom extension to enable users to send a report to a printer. (Custom extensions are explained in Chapter 16, "Building Custom Reporting Tool," which can be found on the companion CD.) Take a look at the PrinterDeliverySample, a custom delivery extension, that ships with Reporting. Services for a simple approach. You can find this sample in the Program Files\Microsoft SQL Server\MSSQL\Reporting Services\Samples folder.

In this procedure, you will use the print preview in your browser to view the Sales Summary report that has been exported to a Web archive format.

Preview the print version of a report

1   In Report Manager, click the Adventure Works Chapter 11 navigation link, click the Territory Sales folder link, and then click the Sales Summary report.

2   Click Web Archive in the Export list box, and then click the Export link.

3   Click the Open button to download and view the MHTML document on your computer.

The screen looks similar to this:

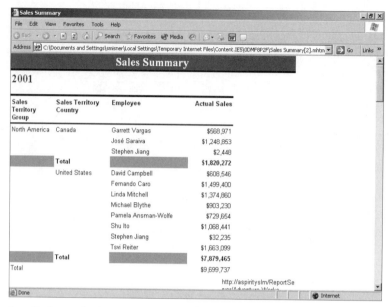

Scroll through the report to verify that all four pages of the report display as one page in the MHTML document. The report is now rendered independently of the HTML Viewer, which means you can save the report as it is or use your browser's print feature to produce a hard copy of the report.

4   On the File menu, click Print Preview.

The screen looks similar to this:

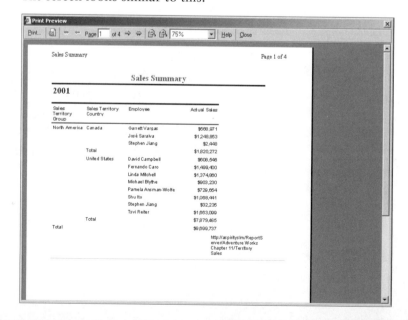

Notice that, even though the MHTML document displayed in the browser is displayed as a single page, the page breaks that are part of the report definition are retained in the print version of this document.

5   Click the Close button, and then close all browser windows.

Chapter 11 Quick Reference

To	Do this
Navigate a folder hierarchy	In Report Manager, use the folder links in the Contents page to move to successively lower levels of the hierarchy, and use the navigation links at the top of the page to move to higher levels of the hierarchy.
Replace the session cache with the current report definition and/or current data	In Report Manager, open a report that was opened earlier in the same browser session, and then click the Refresh button in the Report toolbar (not the browser toolbar).
Search for folders or items	In the Search For box in the top right corner of Report Manager, type the full or partial report name or description, and then click the Go button.
Create a personal linked report	With My Reports enabled in Site Settings, open the General Properties page of a report, and click the Create Linked Report button. Assign the report to the My Reports location. Use the Parameters Properties page of the linked report to change the default values as desired.
Add a manual snapshot to report history	Ensure the report uses a data source with stored credentials, and then click the History tab of the report and click the New Snapshot button.
Save a report as a local file	With the report open in Report Manager, click a format in the Export list box and then click the Export link. Click the Save button, select a download location for the file, and type a name.
Print a report	With the report open in Report Manager, click a format in the Export list box and then click the Export link. Click the Open button, and then use the viewer's print feature to select a printer and change print options.

Rendering Reports

In this chapter, you will learn how to:

- Export a report as a Web document with a PivotTable for online analysis.
- Render a report as a Web document for sharing.
- Convert a report to a page-oriented format for document storage or printing.
- Save a report as a Microsoft Excel workbook for offline analysis.
- Create a structured file for data exchange from a report.

In the previous chapter, you learned how to use the features of Report Manager to locate and view reports. You were also introduced to the Export feature to render reports so that you could save or print a report. In this chapter, you take a closer look at the rendering options. You compare and contrast the rendering formats by exporting reports that contain specific design features. This evaluation of the differences between rendering formats will help you improve the design of your reports by enabling you to make informed choices about available options.

Comparing Rendering Formats

Rendering is the process of converting the report definition and the report data into a specific output format. Report Manager renders reports as HTML documents by default, and provides seven alternative rendering formats from which you can choose. Each of these formats will be reviewed in this chapter. You can also add a custom rendering extension to expand the list of available formats in Report Manager, or you can build a custom application to programmatically render reports as desired, which you will learn about in Chapter 16, "Building Custom Reporting Tools." (Chapter 16 can be found on the companion CD.) Because rendering is implemented as an extension, it's possible that other rendering extensions might be added in the future (either by Microsoft or by third-party vendors) or that the behavior of existing extensions will change (with service packs).

Some rendering formats are best for viewing reports online and might include interactive features, such as HTML and HTML with Office Web Components. Other rendering formats, such as Acrobat PDF files or TIFF files, are ideal for distributing large, page-oriented reports that can be sent to a printer or viewed using an appropriate client application. Reporting Services also supplies formats that are useful for sharing the data in a report. One way to share data is to export a report to an Excel format so that users can perform more sophisticated interactive analysis of the data. You can also share data using CSV or XML formats. For example, you might need to supply invoicing data to customers in a structured format that their internal applications can use as input.

Although all the rendering formats support any of the data regions that you can use in a report definition, you will find that some data regions are more compatible with certain formats than with others. The compatibility between data regions and rendering formats will be discussed in more detail later in this chapter. You will also find that some design features are not supported by all formats. The following table shows the design features that each rendering format can use:

Design feature	HTML with Office Web Components	Web Archive	Acrobat (PDF)	TIFF	Excel	CSV	XML
Fonts	◐	○	○	○	○		
Padding		○	○	○	○		
Colors	◐	○	○	○	○		
Borders		○	○	○	○		
Line	○	○	○	○	○		
Image	○	○	○	○	○		
Background image		○	○	○			
Nested items	◐	○	○	○	○	○	○
Page header/ page footer	○	○	○	○	○		
Page breaks	○		○	○	○		

Design feature	HTML with Office Web Components	Web Archive	Acrobat (PDF)	TIFF	Excel	CSV	XML
Hyperlink	◑	○			○		
Bookmark		○			○		
Drillthrough		○			○		
Document map			○		○		
Dynamic visibility	○						

Legend:

○ is a partially supported feature.

◑ is a fully supported feature.

Rendering for Online Viewing

In a typical implementation of Reporting Services, users view reports online using Report Manager. A report is rendered as HTML 4.0 if the browser that is used to open Report Manager is either Microsoft Internet Explorer versions 5.5 or 6 or Netscape Navigator version 7. Otherwise, the report is rendered as HTML 3.2. Reporting Services can also render reports online to another Web document format, either as HTML with Office Web Components or as Multi-purpose Internet Mail Extension HTML (MHTML). For greater online interactivity, such as the ability to sort or filter data, you can export your report as HTML with Office Web Components. If you have a multi-page report that you want to embed in an e-mail message, you can export your report as MHTML.

How to Work with Web Documents

After opening a report in Report Manager, you can choose an export format that transforms the report into another type of Web document. To use the interactive features that are supported by Office Web Components, you can export a document to the format titled HTML with Office Web Components. This feature is interactive only when you export a matrix report because it uses the PivotTable component, which is similar to the PivotTable functionality available in Excel. The source data for the PivotTable is the data in your report, which requires you to have connectivity to the Report Server when working with this format.

Alternatively, you can export a report to another MHTML Web document format, called Web Archive, in the Report Manager interface. The primary benefit of this format is the consolidation of a report with multiple pages into a single page, enabling you to easily share the report information in an e-mail message. You can also use this format to facilitate printing a report from your browser (because you can't print a report directly from Report Manager, as you learned in the preceding chapter).

Rendering as HTML with Office Web Components

The HTML format of a report that you view in Report Manager supports many interactive features. Parameters, dynamic visibility, and actions all provide ways for users to explore data while online, but these features must be explicitly designed into the report in advance. A more versatile interactive format, HTML with Office Web Components, leverages the PivotTable component in an online environment to provide features that are commonly used for data analysis. For example, using this format, you can sort and filter data, add your own calculations, and export the PivotTable to Excel. However, only the matrix data region is rendered as a PivotTable component. All other data regions are rendered as static text or images. If a matrix is nested inside a list, the repeating matrices in the HTML report are rendered as repeating PivotTable components in the exported format.

▶ **Note**   You must have Office Web Components version 10 or later installed on the client computer to export to the HTML with Office Web Components format.

The HTML with Office Web Components version of your report is intended to be used online while you remain connected to the Report Server. If you want to work with the PivotTable when you're disconnected from the Report Server, you can use the Export To Microsoft Excel button on the PivotTable toolbar to create a local copy of the PivotTable. The data in this PivotTable is, in effect, a snapshot, and will not update with current data. You can then use the Offline storage option in Excel to create a local cube from this data.

In this procedure, you will export the Product Sales and Profitability by Month report as HTML with Office Web Components.

Export a matrix as HTML with Office Web Components

1   Start Microsoft Visual Studio, and open the Rendering solution in the C:\rs2000sbs\chap12 folder.

2 Right-click the solution in Solution Explorer, and then click Deploy Solution. Leave Visual Studio open for use in another procedure later in this chapter.

3 Start Report Manager by navigating to *http://localhost/Reports* in Microsoft Internet Explorer.

4 Click the Rendering folder link, and then click the Product Sales and Profitability by Month report link to view the matrix report, as shown here:

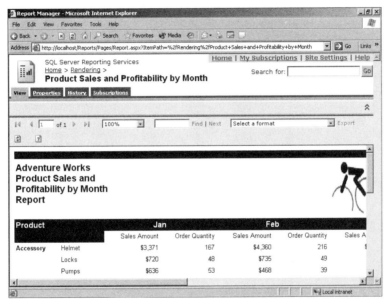

Notice the various design features in this report. At the top, a line is displayed as a border above a textbox (that contains the report name) and an image. The matrix contains months in columns and product categories and subcategories in rows. Subtotals by month, subcategory, and category are also included in the matrix. Notice that the formatting of the column headers and the total line is different from the formatting of the matrix rows. Category names are displayed in boldface, whereas subcategory names are not. A textbox in the page footer is displayed below the matrix.

5 Click HTML With Office Web Components in the Export list box, and then click the Export link on the Report toolbar.

A new browser window opens, which looks like this:

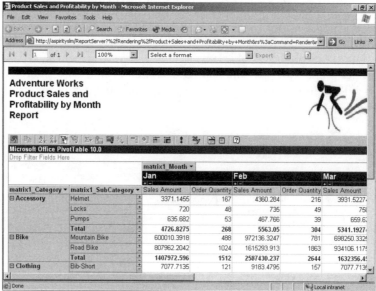

Notice here that the Report toolbar is rendered in the format of the report. The report items above the matrix and the textbox in the page footer below the matrix appear just as they did in the HTML version of the report. The matrix itself is now rendered as a PivotTable component. The background of the category and subcategory names is now gray, but the category names are still displayed in bold-face. The month names in the column header and the row grand totals are displayed using the same formatting as originally designed in the matrix.

6   Right-click any row in the matrix1_SubCategory column, point to Show Only The Top, and then click 5.

The PivotTable changes to look like this:

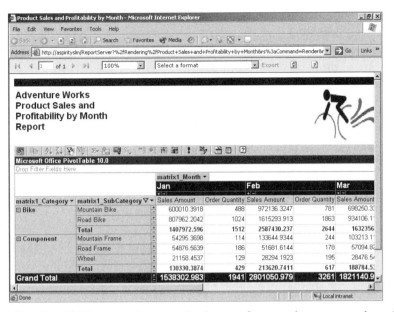

The PivotTable now shows only the top five products, even though the original report did not have this functionality.

▶ **Note**   A full explanation of PivotTable features is beyond the scope of this book. You can learn more about the PivotTable component by clicking the Help button on the PivotTable toolbar.

7   Close the browser window with the PivotTable.

Rendering as MHTML

If you want to save or share a report as a Web page, you can use the MHTML format to combine all report items into a single file, even if the report uses a subreport or other external resources, such as images stored separately on the Report Server. The MHTML format can also be used with any data region. This format is best used to combine multiple pages in a report. You can then easily e-mail the MHTML document to share with others.

You can also use this format to print a report from your browser. Even though the MHTML document displays all pages together as a single page, the printed version of the MHTML document will use the page breaks as designed in the report definition. A procedure to demonstrate printing an MHTML document was included in Chapter 11, "Accessing Reports."

12

Rendering Reports

The MHTML document does not have any interactive features. When you export a report to this format, the current view of the report is rendered. This means that if your report uses dynamic visibility, the items that are visible when you export the report will also be visible in the MHTML version of the report.

In this procedure, you will export the Product Sales and Profitability Subreport, which includes a subreport with dynamic visibility, as a single-page MHTML document.

Export a multiple page report as a Web Archive

1   In Report Manager, click the Rendering link in the top left corner of the page, and then click the Product Sales and Profitability Subreport report link.

     This report is designed with dynamic visibility. You can expand a product to view detail information (in the form of a subreport, in this case) about that product.

2   Click the Next Page button on the Report toolbar, and then expand Cable Lock to view the subreport. Click 75% in the Size list box to view the report, as shown here:

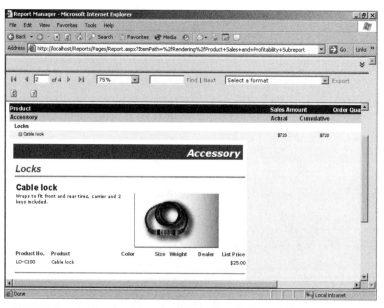

3   Click Web Archive in the Export list box, click the Export link on the Report toolbar, and then click the Open button in the File Download dialog box.

4   Scroll down through the page to find the break between the first page and the second page of the report, as shown here:

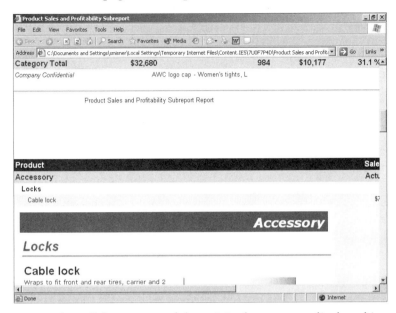

Notice that all four pages of the original report are displayed in a single page in this browser window. The page footer of the first page is immediately followed by the page header of the second page. The subreport is displayed only on the second page below the Cable Lock product.

▶   **Tip**   The MHTML format is great for creating a single Web page from a report, especially a report with multiple pages. However, as you can see from this example, it might not be the best format for a report designed with dynamic visibility, unless you're interested only in highlighting specific details in the report. Expanding each item in the report before you export is not very practical.

5   Close the browser window.

Rendering for Document Management

One benefit of Reporting Services is its role as a central location for the online storage and retrieval of information—which can be incorporated into a comprehensive corporate document management strategy. Two common formats used for document management are Acrobat PDF files and TIFF files. Reporting Services can render any report into these page-oriented formats.

How to Work with Page-Oriented File Types

When you need to provide information to people who don't have access to the reporting platform, you can retrieve a report from Reporting Services and export it as a page-oriented file. The page-oriented formats supported by Reporting Services are TIFF and PDF files. You can export a report as a TIFF file for document archival or for integration with other applications. The TIFF file is intended to be used independently of the reporting platform, so you don't need to be connected to the Report Server to view the file.

Similarly, you might want to use PDF documents offline. For example, you can create a PDF document for a product catalog that sales representatives can keep on their laptops or send to their clients as an e-mail attachment. When authoring a report that is likely to be exported as a PDF document, you can include a document map to serve as an interactive table of contents that allows the user to easily jump to another section of the document.

Rendering as a TIFF File

Reporting Services includes a rendering extension that allows you to generate a TIFF file from a report if needed. All data regions are properly rendered using this format, but only visible items will be displayed if dynamic visibility has been added to the report. Since a TIFF file is a page-oriented format, you will want to carefully check the design of reports during the authoring stage for correct print layout. For example, you'll want to make sure that you have properly set the page size properties *Width* and *Height*, as well as the margin properties *Left*, *Right*, *Top*, and *Bottom*. These properties belong to Report, which you can access in the report item list box in the Properties window or by clicking outside the design grid in the Document window. Also, during the design process, preview the report frequently and use the Print Preview button to see how the report lays out on a printed page. The TIFF format does not support the use of a document map because TIFF files are primarily used for document storage, printing, or faxing.

In this procedure, you will correct the layout of Product Sales and Profitability Chart for printing and export the report as a TIFF file.

Export a report as a TIFF file

1   In Report Manager, click the Rendering link, and then click the Product Sales and Profitability Chart report link. You might need to scroll down the page to see the top of the matrix.

Your screen looks similar to this:

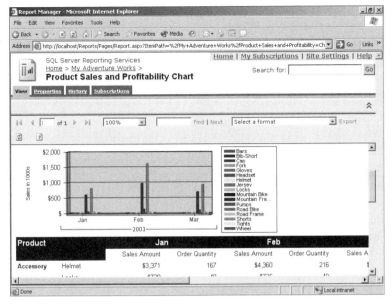

This report includes both a chart and a matrix. When rendered as HTML, the size of the Web page expands horizontally and vertically to accommodate the contents. However, the chart and the matrix won't fit a printed page if the report is designed incorrectly.

2   Click TIFF File in the Export list box, click the Export link, and then click the Open button in the File Download dialog box.

Your default viewer for TIFF files might be different, but the resulting image looks like this:

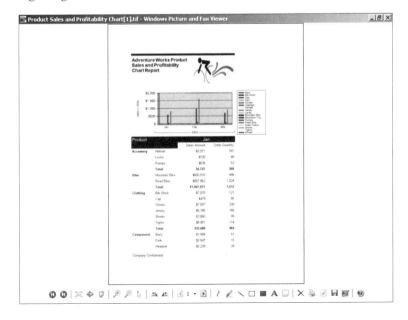

Notice that the report layout is a Portrait orientation. Although the chart fits well on the page, the matrix is cut off and is spread out across the next three pages. The orientation of this report should be changed to fit on a printed page properly.

3   Close the TIFF viewer.

4   Using Visual Studio, open the Product Sales and Profitability Chart report in the Rendering solution.

5   In the Properties window, the current item should be Report. If it's not, click Report in the report item list box to access the Report's properties.

6   Change the *Width* property to **14in** and the *Height* property to **11in**. Your screen should look similar to this:

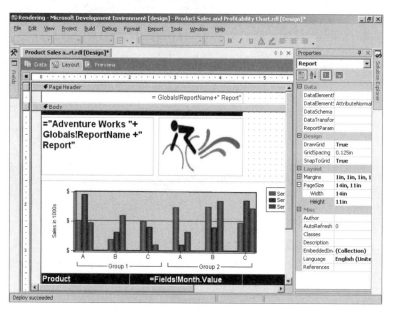

7   Click the Preview tab, and then click the Print Preview button. Your screen should look similar to this:

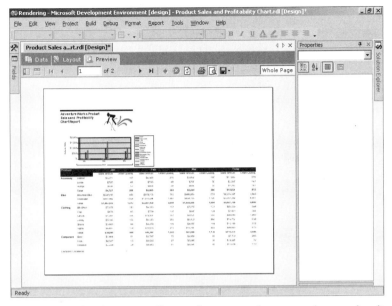

The matrix fits horizontally on the page when you change the dimensions of the page to force a Landscape orientation.

8   Click the Next Page button.

Because the full matrix doesn't fit on the page vertically, a second page is created. Notice that the column headers appear at the top of the matrix on this page.

9   Save, and then deploy the report.

10   In Report Manager, with the Product Sales and Profitability Chart open, click the Refresh Report button on the Report toolbar to load the updated report definition.

11   Click TIFF File in the Export list box, click the Export link, and then click the Open button in the File Download dialog box.

The image looks like this:

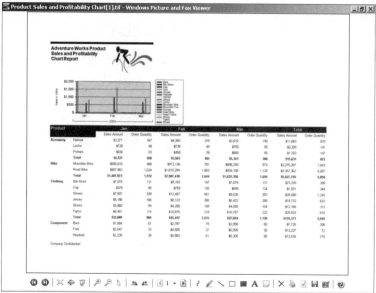

The TIFF format now displays the complete width of the matrix, just like the print preview you saw in Visual Studio. The second page with the remaining rows of the matrix is part of the same file, which you can view by clicking the Next Page (Page Down) button at the bottom of the viewer.

12   Close the TIFF viewer.

Rendering as a PDF File

A PDF file created by exporting a report from Reporting Services is much like an MHTML document in that what you see in the HTML version is what you get in the exported file. Consequently, the PDF file is not the best format for reports with interactive features like dynamic visibility. However, it's a very good format for large reports that might take some time to render online, for printing reports, and for sharing documents outside of the Reporting Services environment. Because this format renders what you see in the original report, any data region in a report renders properly in the PDF file. Because the PDF document is a page-oriented format, you must take care in the design of the report to ensure that the report items, when rendered, fit within the defined physical size of the page.

A particularly useful feature in a PDF file is the document map. It renders with the PDF file to help users find specific information within a large report. (You have to wait until all pages of an HTML report finish rendering in the background before the document map is available online, but once a PDF file is created, there's no waiting!) A document map is added in the authoring stage by assigning a label to a group (in a table, matrix, or list).

In this procedure, you will add another group to the document map for the Product Catalog. In a later procedure, you will export the Product Catalog as a PDF file.

Add groups to a document map

1 In Report Manager, click the Rendering link, and then click the Product Catalog report link.

Your screen looks like this:

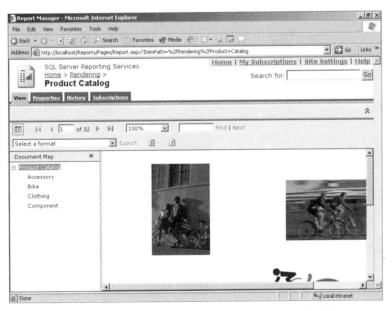

When a report is designed with a document map, the document map automatically appears as a frame in the page to the left of the report.

▶ **Note** Even though the document map appears automatically, it doesn't necessarily appear immediately in all reports. You will see the first page of an HTML document before all pages in the report have been rendered. Reporting Services can't generate the document map until all rendering is complete.

2   Click Clothing in the Document Map pane.

The report now displays the first product subcategory in this section of the report, Bib-Short. You can continue browsing through the Clothing category by scrolling through this page or by clicking the Next Page button a few times. However, having a more detailed document map would be nicer.

3   Leave the report open in Report Manager, because you will return to this report later in this procedure.

4   Using Visual Studio, open the Product Catalog report in the Rendering solution.

5   Scroll the report until you see the textboxes that contain field expressions, as shown here:

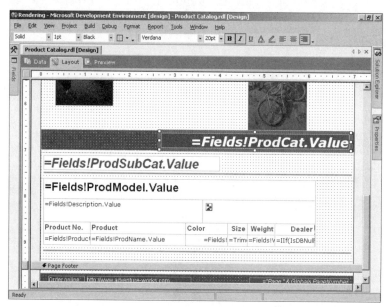

This report is constructed as a collection of nested lists. The outermost list repeats Category information, which includes the expression =Fields!ProdCat.Value. You can't click the design grid to access this list's properties because the grid is fully covered by other report items. Instead, you need to use the Properties window to change the list properties.

6   In the Properties window, click CategoryList in the report items list box, and then click the *Grouping* property's Ellipsis button.

The Details Grouping dialog box is displayed:

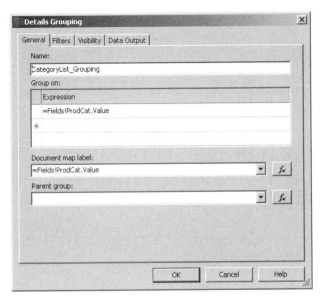

Notice that =Fields!ProdCat.Value appears in the Document Map
Label list box. This value is used to configure the current document
map. In this case, a new group is created in the list for each product
category (ProdCat) value. The label that corresponds to the position
of a particular group will be the same value. So, for example, the
Bike group in the report will be labeled as Bike in the document map.

7 Click the Cancel button.

8 In the Properties window, click SubCategoryList in the report items
list box, and then click the *Grouping* property's Ellipsis button.

9 Click =Fields!ProdSubCat.Value in the Document Map Label list
box.

Since SubCategoryList is nested within CategoryList, the label for
this group will appear as a node of the category group to which it
belongs. In other words, you will expand a category in the document
map to view the available subcategories for that category.

10 Click the OK button.

11 In the Properties window, click ModelList in the report items list
box, and then click the *Grouping* property's Ellipsis button.

12 Click =Fields!ProdModel.Value in the Document Map Label list
box.

By adding a document map label to this list group, you are adding
yet another level to the document map. Specifically, a subcategory
will expand to reveal its associated models.

13   Click the OK button, and then save the report.

14   In Solution Explorer, right-click ProductCatalog.rdl, and click Deploy. Keep the solution open in Visual Studio for use in another procedure later in this chapter.

In this procedure, you will export the Product Catalog as a PDF file.

Export a report as a PDF file

1   In Report Manager, with the Product Catalog open, click the Refresh Report button on the Report toolbar to load the updated report definition.

Notice that the Document Map now has plus signs to indicate each category that can be expanded.

2   Click Acrobat (PDF) File in the Export list box, click the Export link, and then click the Open button in the File Download dialog box.

Because this is a bigger report than you have previously viewed, the export process might take a little longer.

3   Click the Bookmarks tab to display the document map.

4   In the Document Map, collapse Accessory and Bike to view the Clothing category. Beneath the Jersey subcategory, click Long-Sleeve Logo Jersey to navigate to that product model in the Product Catalog.

Your screen looks similar to this:

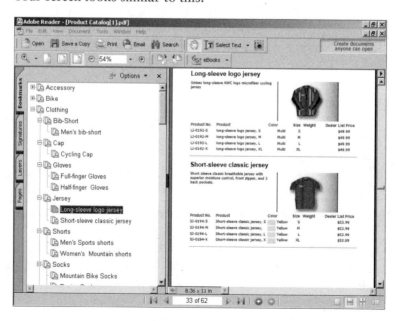

You can click any level of the document map—category, subcategory, or model—to jump to the section of the report that marks the beginning of the selected group.

5   Close Acrobat Reader.

Rendering for Data Exchange

Besides viewing reports online or creating printable documents from reports, you will likely need to use information contained in reports in other ways. It's a very common requirement of reporting systems to export data to Excel so that users can perform more complex analysis or even integrate data from other sources. For example, if you keep forecast data in an Excel spreadsheet, you could export sales data from Reporting Services to Excel and then add a formula to compute the ratio of actual performance to forecasted performance.

It's also becoming more common for businesses to exchange information electronically. A retailer can submit an order electronically, and a supplier can return an electronic invoice. This information is typically exchanged in a structured format, such as in a delimited file or an XML file. You can use Reporting Services to convert a report to a CSV or an XML file for data exchange.

How to Share Data

As you learned earlier in this chapter, you can use a report's interactive features in the default HTML format, and you can also take advantage of PivotTable interactivity by exporting a report to HTML with Office Web Components. However, these formats still have a limited scope of interactive features, and you must connect to the Report Server to use the report data. You can export a report to Excel to use the full range of its features to explore and manipulate a local copy of the data. Some interactive features that are designed into the report, such as actions, are also rendered in the Excel version of the report.

To share data with other applications or external information consumers, you can export a report to a CSV file. This file is intended for use as input into a process or application, and is not intended for a user to read. Rows and columns (delimited with a comma by default) are created for the lowest level of detail in the report, regardless of data region. Essentially, the CSV file is a flattened rowset of the report data.

Another way to share data is to export a report to an XML file. As with the CSV file, the XML file is not intended to be read by a user, but instead is meant to be used by another application. The file contains XML elements and attributes that define the structure of the data and also supply the data. However, none of the formatting from the source report is preserved in the XML file. In this case, the XML contains raw data that retains its original structure rather than being flattened, as occurs when data is exported to a CSV file.

Rendering as an Excel File

Excel is a popular application for analyzing data. By exporting data to an Excel file, you have access to the report data even when you're disconnected from the Report Server. You can also add your own formulas or incorporate data from other sources into your Excel workbook.

Even though all the data regions that can be in a report are also supported in Excel, the Excel format is best used with a table or a matrix. A chart can be rendered in Excel, but it is rendered as a picture and not as an Excel chart that you can modify. A list will be rendered with repeating groups, as it is in an HTML report, but the items contained in the list will be rendered in positions that correspond to their relative positions in the original report, and this might conflict with the position of items that aren't contained in the list. A subreport is not recommended for export to Excel.

The Excel version keeps most of the features and formatting of the original report, including pagination, actions, and a document map. However, if a report has been designed using dynamic visibility, all items hidden in the original report will be visible in the Excel version of the report.

Microsoft Visual Basic .NET formulas are converted to an Excel formula if Excel has an equivalent. The formulas that get translated are those that use report item expressions, not field expressions. Otherwise, the result of the expression is stored in a cell as a constant value. For example, if a textbox contains an expression like =Sum(Fields!UnitPrice.Value * Fields!Order-Qty.Value), there is no equivalent in Excel. When a report containing this expression is rendered to Excel, the calculation is performed and the resulting value, rather than the formula, is stored in the Excel cell.

In this procedure, you will export the Order Details report, which has interactive features such as dynamic visibility and drillthrough, as an Excel file.

Export an interactive table to Excel

1   In Report Manager, click the Rendering link, and then click the Order Details report link.

Your screen looks similar to this:

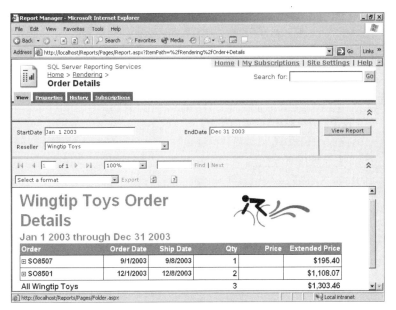

This report includes a table in which dynamic visibility is used to hide the detail rows and a subtotal row when the report is opened. Notice that on the row that contains the order header information (order number and dates), the quantity and extended price are also displayed.

2   Click the plus sign to the left of the order number SO8501 to display the detail rows, shown here:

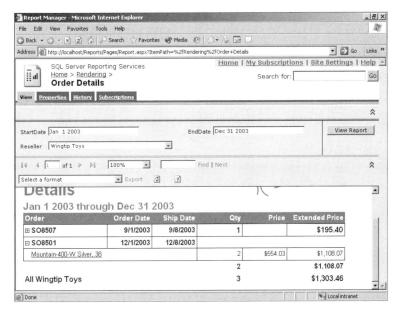

Now the quantity and extended price in the order header row are hidden. The product row and the order subtotal row are displayed below the order header row.

3 Click the plus sign to the left of order SO8501 to toggle the hidden state of rows.

Now the order header information is again displayed with the quantity and extended price, and the rows below the order header information are hidden.

4 Click Excel in the Export list box, click the Export link, and then click the Open button in the File Download dialog box to view the Excel report, as shown here:

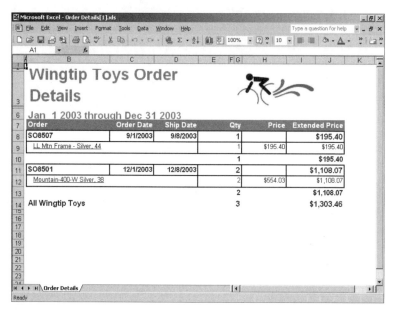

▶ **Tip**   If you save the Excel report directly to disk at this point, you must use Excel XP or later to open the file. By using the Open button, you can use the Save As Workbook feature to share the file with users who have an earlier version of Excel.

Here all detail rows that were hidden in the HTML version of the report are automatically expanded and the data in these rows is displayed. The quantity and extended price in the order header are also displayed. You can see that dynamic visibility is not rendered in the Excel report, but all the data is included in the report.

▶ **Note**   This result of handling dynamic visibility when rendering to Excel is unlike rendering to MHTML or the page-oriented formats, PDF or TIFF. In those formats, only the currently visible rows are rendered. By contrast, all rows—whether visible or not—are rendered in the Excel format.

5   Click the LL Mtn Frame – Silver, 44 link in cell B9.

Your screen looks like this:

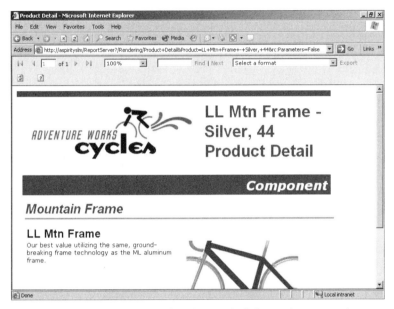

The link in the report is defined as a drillthrough action that opens the HTML version of the drillthrough report in a browser window. Notice that the URL in Internet Explorer's Address box references the Report Server virtual directory rather than the Reports directory that you have seen with other reports that you access using Report Manager. You'll learn more about accessing reports directly with URLs in Chapter 16.

▶ **Note**   The bookmark and hyperlink actions are also supported in Excel. You can work with the Excel file while disconnected from the network, but you must have connectivity when using the hyperlink action (to access the URL defined for the hyperlink) and when using the drillthrough action (to access the Report Server hosting the drillthrough report).

6   Close the browser window with the drillthrough report, and close Excel.

Rendering a Report as a CSV File

If you need to provide information in document form for a person to read and you also need to provide a structured file for input into an application, you can use one report in Reporting Services to support both requirements. When you export a report to a CSV file, the data is flattened (or denormalized) so that each row in the file represents the lowest level of detail in the report, with higher level information incorporated into the row. For example, a textbox that contains the report title will be rendered as a column in the CSV file, so each row will contain the report title even though it appears in the HTML report only once.

The format of the CSV file is predefined as comma-delimited fields with records delimited by a carriage return and line feed. If a delimiter appears in a text string, a double-quote is used as a text qualifier to surround the string. The header row of the file contains the names of the report items that correspond to each column. The CSV format just described is used by Report Manager by default. Through programmatic rendering (which is discussed in Chapter 16 on the companion CD), you can define different delimiters, specify a different text qualifier, omit the header row, supply a different file extension, or change the default encoding from Unicode.

In this procedure, you will export the Order Details report as a CSV file.

Export a table as a CSV file

1 In Report Manager, with the Order Details report open, click CSV (Comma Delimited) in the Export list box, click the Export link, and then click the Save button in the File Download dialog box.

   If you click the Open button, the file will be viewed in Excel, which can be difficult to read.

2 Save the file as Order Details.csv in the C:\rs2000sbs\Workspace folder.

3 Close the browser window that opened as part of the file download process.

4 Using Microsoft Notepad, open the Order Details.csv file.

   The file looks like this if word wrap is turned on:

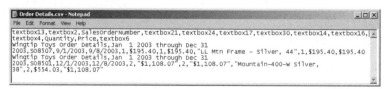

Notice that the header row contains names of the report items. In this report, the report item names were assigned by default. Normally, this doesn't matter, because the user doesn't see the report item name elsewhere. In a CSV file, however, it's difficult to know exactly what you're looking at without referring back to the report definition.

▶ **Tip** If you know that a report will be used for export as a CSV file, you should rename the report items in the authoring stage so that the output is more understandable when exported.

In this example, there are only two rows because the table in this report includes only two detail rows, which represent the lowest level of detail in this report. The first two columns of each row are the report title and the date range, which appear above the table in the HTML rendering.

The next five columns in each row represent, respectively, the order number, order date, ship date, quantity, and extended price. These latter two columns are the textboxes that are hidden when the detail rows are visible. Just like Excel rendering, the CSV rendering ignores dynamic visibility and puts all data into the target file. These columns are followed by the data in the subtotal row—again, quantity and extended price. Then the final four columns represent the data elements found in the detail row. Notice the text qualifier when a comma is embedded in a string.

5 Close Notepad.

Rendering a Report as an XML File

You can also create a structured file using an XML format. The hierarchical structure of the data is tagged in the file, unlike the CSV file, which flattened the data to its lowest level. Obviously, the application that will eventually translate this file will need to understand the meaning of this structure. Because report item names are used to distinguish XML elements in the document, you'll need to consider carefully your naming conventions in the report design.

In this procedure, you will export the Order Details report as an XML file.

Export a table as an XML file

1   In Report Manager with the Order Details report open, click XML File With Report Data in the Export list box, click the Export link, and then click the Open button in the File Download dialog box. The XML document is displayed in a browser window like this:

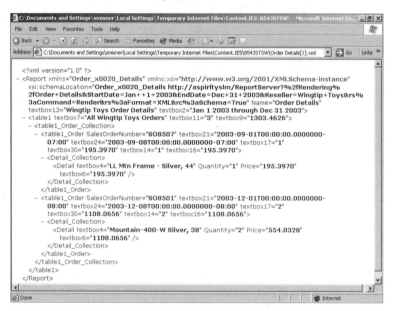

Notice that the outermost element that contains data is the *table1* element. Nested within this element are the elements that define the grouping in the table, *table1_Order*, which are themselves organized into an element called *table1_Order_Collection*, which was created by the XML rendering process. Each *table1_Order* element has a set of attributes that correspond to the report items that make up the order header in the table. Detail rows are also organized into a collection, with attributes to contain the values in each detail row.

Notice also that the subtotal information that has dynamic visibility in the HTML rendering is included twice as attributes of the *table1_Order* element. The first instance corresponds to the values that are displayed in the order header row, and the second instance corresponds to the values that are displayed with the detail rows. Because the rows in which these values appear belong to the *table1_Order* group in the table, they both become attributes of the *table1_Order* element in the XML file.

2   Close all browser windows.

Chapter 12 Quick Reference

To	Do this
Render a matrix as a PivotTable	On the Report toolbar in Report Manager, click HTML With Office Web Components in the Export list box, and then click the Export link. The report must contain a matrix I order to render as a PivotTable.
Render a multiple page report as a single page	On the Report toolbar in Report Manager, click Web Archive in the Export list box, and then click the Export link.
Add a document map to a report	Open the report using Visual Studio. In the Properties window, click the report item that contains the grouping to be added to the document map, and then click the *Grouping* property's Ellipsis button. Click the applicable expression in the Document Map Label list box, such as =Fields!ProdCat.Value.
Render a report to a page-oriented format	On the Report toolbar in Report Manager, click either Acrobat (PDF) File or TIFF File in the Export list box, and then click the Export link.
Render a report for offline analysis	On the Report toolbar in Report Manager, click Excel in the Export list box, and then click the Export link.
Render a report as a structured data file for data exchange	On the Report toolbar in Report Manager, click either CSV (Comma Delimited) File or XML File With Report Data in the Export list box, and then click the Export link.

Chapter 13

Managing Subscriptions

In this chapter, you will learn how to:

- Create a standard subscription to e-mail a report.

- Add a standard subscription to place a report on a file share.

- Define a data-driven subscription to retrieve recipients and subscription options from a relational table.

- Monitor the status of a subscription.

- Delete an inactive subscription.

In the previous two chapters, you learned about accessing reports online and about how reports can be rendered into different formats. You can also use Reporting Services to deliver reports directly to users in any rendering format (except HTML with Microsoft Office Web Components). In this chapter, you learn how to use subscriptions as an alternative method to execute and deliver reports to users. You also learn how to monitor and manage subscriptions.

Creating a Standard Subscription

Subscriptions allow users to take full advantage of the "push" paradigm supported by Reporting Services. In other words, users can decide what information they want sent to them automatically and are not limited to "pulling" information from the reporting platform. A subscription can be defined to deliver a specific report to an e-mail account or to a network file share on a scheduled basis. You can also install a custom or third-pary delivery extension if you have other delivery requirements. For example, you might want to try out the sample delivery extension to send a report to a printer that is described in Reporting Services Books Online.

By default, the Browser role includes the task assignment "Manage individual subscriptions" that allows a user to add, change, or delete his or her own subscriptions, whereas the Content Manager role is assigned the task "Manage all subscriptions" that controls all subscriptions defined on the Report Server. Users can create a subscription for any report to which they have access, but only if the report uses stored credentials (because a subscription executes a report in unattended mode).

Delivery of a subscription can be triggered either by a defined schedule or by the update of a snapshot (which can be updated manually or according to a schedule). When the triggering event occurs, the Report Server reads the delivery information from the subscription, which it passes to the delivery extension. The delivery extension is responsible for rendering and delivering the report as defined in the subscription. If an error occurs during delivery, the problem is logged in the ReportServerService_*<timestamp>*.log file.

Disabling Subscriptions

You can prevent users from using subscriptions by removing the "Manage individual subscriptions" task assignment. Users will no longer be able to access the Subscription page of a report when using Report Manager, but any active subscriptions will continue to execute.

Rather than completely disabling subscriptions, you might prefer to prevent the use of a specific delivery extension. If you remove a delivery extension from the RSWebApplication.config configuration file, this extension is no longer available as a report delivery option in Report Manager. You can also remove the delivery extension from the RSReportServer.config file, but any subscriptions that were using that delivery extension will become inactive. Inactive subscriptions, because they don't do anything, don't cause any problems on the Report Server, but it's considered good practice to delete the inactive subscriptions that result from the removal of a delivery extension. (Handling inactive subscriptions is discussed later in this chapter.)

How to Create a Standard Subscription

Whether you are a user or an administrator of Reporting Services, you can create a standard subscription for a specific report by selecting a delivery method and delivery options. The delivery method that you select determines which delivery options you must supply. For example, if you choose e-mail delivery, you must enter at least one e-mail address. In addition, you can decide whether the report should be sent as a link or as an attachment, or even whether the report should be sent at all. If you choose not to send the report or a link to the report, the user simply receives a notification message that the report is ready. If you use file share delivery, you must specify a share location and a filename. Regardless of the delivery method, you can select a rendering format for the report.

After providing the delivery information, you must define the conditions that will trigger execution of the subscription. You can specify a one-time or recurring schedule, which can be a shared schedule or a subscription-specific schedule. If the report executes as a snapshot, you can trigger delivery of the subscription when the report snapshot is updated instead of using a schedule.

For a report that has report parameters, you can select the values to be used when the report executes. You can type a parameter value in a textbox, or choose a value from a list box, depending on how the parameter was designed. Reporting Services doesn't validate parameter values when you create a subscription, so take care when entering a value into a textbox. An error will not be apparent until the delivery of the report is triggered. At that time, an error message will be displayed on the Subscriptions page and an entry will be added in the ReportServerService trace log file.

Delivering a Report by E-Mail

Use e-mail delivery when you want to mail a rendered report. If you use the Web Archive rendering option, the report is embedded in the e-mail message. If you do not use this option, the report is sent as an attachment. Alternatively, you can define the subscription to send a link to a report on the Report Server, or even to send just a notification message that a report is ready for viewing on the server.

To use e-mail delivery, you must have a local or remote Simple Mail Transfer Protocol (SMTP) server available on the same network as your Report Server. During installation of Reporting Services, you can specify an SMTP server address and an e-mail address that appears as the sender of the message. You can change these values, as well as configure other e-mail delivery settings, by editing the RSReportServer.config file. For example, you can restrict the delivery of reports to specific domains by adding the DSN name or the IP address to *PermittedHosts*. You can find a complete list of available settings and valid values in Reporting Services Books Online.

In this procedure, you will create a subscription for the Employee Product Sales report that embeds the report in an e-mail message and sends the report.

Create a standard e-mail subscription

1   Run PublishChap13.cmd in the C:\rs2000sbs\chap13 folder to publish the reports that you need so that you can follow the procedures in this chapter.

▶ **Important**   To complete the procedures related to e-mail delivery in this chapter, you must have your Microsoft Internet Information Services (IIS) server configured to use SMTP with a local domain alias of adventure-works.com, or substitute your own e-mail address in place of the supplied e-mail addresses. For specific instructions, refer to the "Introduction" to this book.

2   Open Report Manager in Microsoft Internet Explorer at *http://localhost/Reports*.

If Report Manager is already open, you will need to use Internet Explorer's Refresh button to view the published reports.

3   Click the Delivery folder link.

4   Click the Show Details button, and then click the Properties icon in the Edit column to the left of the Employee Product Sales report, as shown here:

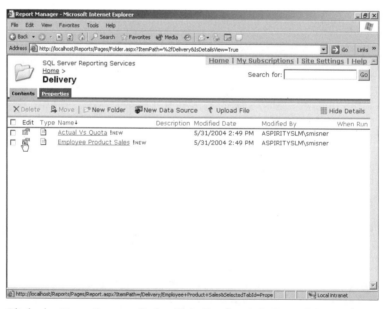

5   Click the Data Sources link, click Credentials Stored Securely In The Report Server, type **ReportExecution** as the user name and **ReportExecution** as the password, and then click the Apply button.

You will not be able to add a subscription to a report unless it uses stored credentials.

6 Click the Subscriptions tab.

Your screen looks like this:

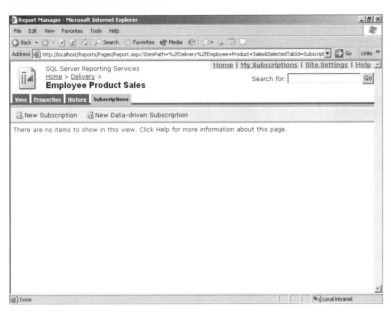

7 Click the New Subscription button.

The Subscription definition page is displayed:

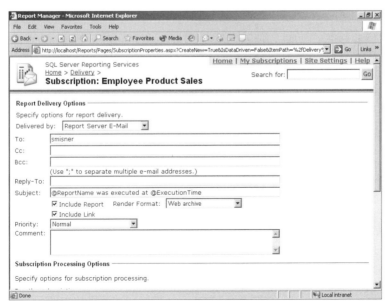

The default delivery method is Report Server E-Mail. In the To text-box, the current user name is automatically added as the default recipient. (You can override this behavior by editing the RSReport-Server.config configuration file so that the To field is not populated automatically.) Notice also the default Subject textbox: @Report-Name Was Executed At @ExecutionTime. The current report name and the execution name are inserted when the e-mail message is pre-pared for delivery. These two names match Global properties in Report Designer, but you cannot use any of the other global proper-ties in the Subject line.

8 Replace the value in the To textbox with **PacificDirector@adventure-works.com**.

As with a regular e-mail message, you can send a subscription to multi-ple users by separating the e-mail addresses with a semicolon (;), or you can send the report to copied recipients and blind-copied recipi-ents. Optionally, you can include a Reply-To e-mail address.

9 Click the Render Format list box to review the available options, but keep the default value of Web Archive.

Notice that the only rendering option missing from this list is HTML with Office Web Components. As you learned in Chapter 12, "Ren-dering Reports," this rendering format is useful only when the user is online and connected to the Report Server, so it doesn't work in an e-mail message.

10 Clear the Include Link check box.

The Report Delivery Options portion of the page looks like this:

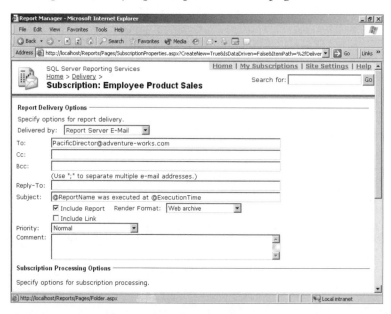

In this case, only an embedded report will be sent in the e-mail message. If also you clear the Include Report check box, only a notification message will be sent.

11 Click the Select Schedule button.

12 Click Once to specify the frequency of the report.

In this procedure, you will run the subscription one time to generate output. Normally, you would specify a periodic frequency for a subscription schedule. This schedule that you create will apply to the current subscription only.

13 Type a start time that is 3 minutes ahead of the current time, and click the correct AM or PM option.

Your screen looks similar to this (with a different time specified):

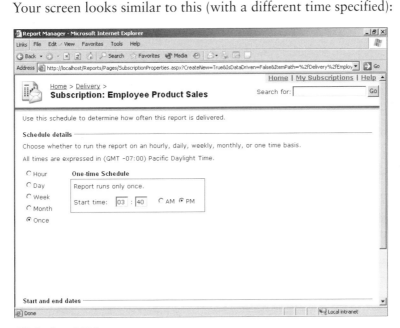

14 Click the OK button.

15 Replace the *Group* parameter value with **Pacific**.

16 Select the Use Default check box for the *Year* parameter.

▶ **Note**   If you were to select a report snapshot for the subscription, you wouldn't be able to edit parameter values used as query parameters. The values in the rendered report for the subscription will match those of the snapshot. However, if the report parameter is used as a filter, you can modify it in a subscription.

The bottom of the Subscription page looks like this:

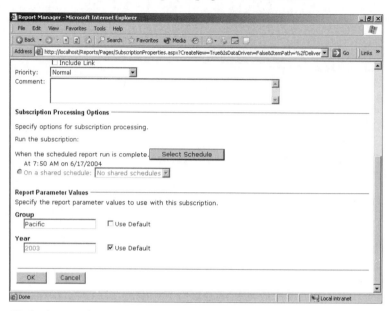

17 Click the OK button.

The Subscriptions page for the Employee Product Sales report looks like this:

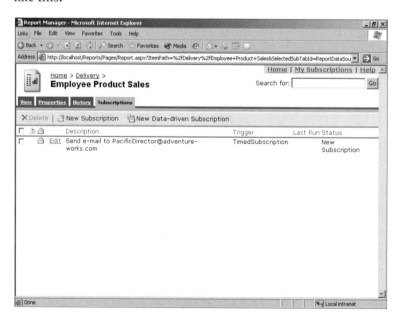

▶ **Important**   The SQL Server Agent must be running to create a subscription. If it's not running, you will receive an error when you click the OK button to create the subscription.

18 After waiting 3 minutes, click the Refresh button on the Internet Explorer toolbar.

The Subscriptions page for the Employee Product Sales report looks similar to this:

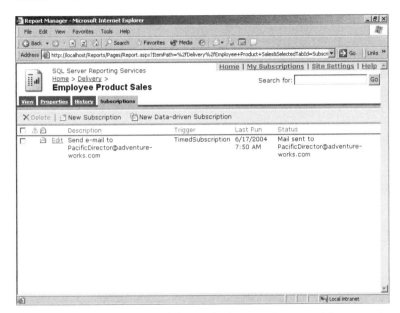

When the subscription is delivered, the Last Run and Status columns are updated.

19 If you're using a local SMTP Server, open Microsoft Windows Explorer, navigate to the C:\Inetpub\mailroot\Drop folder, and double-click the e-mail file (with extension .eml) located there. Otherwise, if you're using a local POP3 Server, navigate to C:\Inetpub\mailroot\Mailbox\adventure-works.com \P3_PacificDirector.mbx and open the message file in that folder.

Your screen looks similar to this:

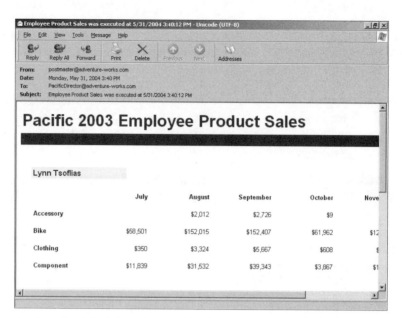

At the scheduled time, Reporting Services executed the report, which it embedded as MHTML into the body of an e-mail message. Notice that the subject line is updated with the report name and execution time. The From e-mail address is defined in the Report Server configuration file.

Delivering a Report to a File Share

Instead of e-mailing a report to recipients, you can use file share delivery to put a copy of a report on a file share in a designated location. You can use any rendering format except HTML with Office Web Components. With file share delivery, you can choose to overwrite an existing file or have Reporting Services generate incremental filenames to track versions of the same report. You must supply credentials with write permission on the file share.

In this procedure, you will create a subscription for the Actual Vs Quota report, which renders the report as a Microsoft Excel file and places it on a file share.

Create a standard file share subscription

1   Open Windows Explorer, right-click on the C:\rs2000sbs\Workspace folder, and then click Sharing And Security.

2   On the Sharing page of the Workspace Properties dialog box, click Share This Folder, and then click the Permissions button.

> ▶ **Note**   The specifics for establishing a file share might vary if you're using a different operating system. The instructions in this procedure are written with the assumption that you are using an edition of Microsoft Windows Server 2003 or Windows XP with simplified file sharing disabled.

3   On the Share Permission page of the Permissions For Workspace dialog box, click the Add button and type **ReportServer2000** in the Enter The Object Names To Select box. Click the Check Names button to validate the account, and then click the OK button.

> ▶ **Note**   ReportServer2000 is the Windows account added in Chapter 2, "Installing Reporting Services," to run the ReportServer service. You can use another user account in its place if you prefer.

4   Select Change in the Allow column of the Permissions dialog, and then click the OK button twice to close all dialog boxes.

5   In Report Manager, click the Delivery link.

6   Click the Properties icon in the Edit column to the left of the Actual Vs Quota.

7   Click the Data Sources link, click Credentials Stored Securely In The Report Server, type **ReportExecution** as the user name and **ReportExecution** as the password, and then click the Apply button.

8   Click the Subscriptions tab, and then click the New Subscription button.

9   In the Delivered By list box, click Report Server File Share.

A new Subscription definition page is displayed:

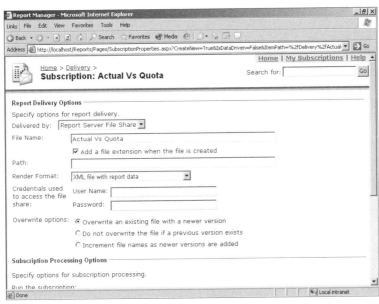

10   In the Path textbox, type *****computername***\\Workspace**.

▶   **Important**   Replace *computername* with the name of your local computer. Do not use localhost. If you do, Reporting Services will not be able to access the correct file share. Whenever specifying a file share path on a remote computer, you must use the UNC naming convention instead of a mapped network drive.

11   Click Excel in the Render Format list box.

Notice that the only rendering option missing from this list is HTML with Office Web Components. This format doesn't work properly when stored on a file share.

12   Type **ReportServer2000** as the User Name, but leave the password blank for now.

13   Click Increment File Names As Newer Versions Are Added.

Your screen looks like this:

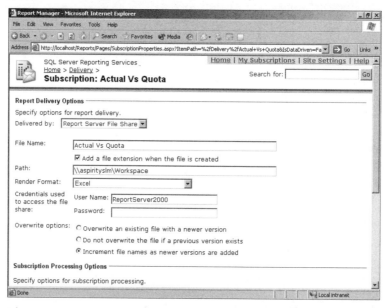

This overwrite option configures Reporting Services to append a number to the filename that increments by one each time this subscripton is executed if there is an existing file of the same name already on the file share. With this option, the existing file is not overwritten, and a separate file—distinguished by a number added to the filename—is placed on the file share.

14   Click the Select Schedule button.

15 Click Once to specify the frequency of the report.

In this procedure, you will run the subscription just once to generate output.

16 Type a start time that is 3 minutes ahead of the current time, and click the correct AM or PM option.

17 Click the OK button.

18 Type the password for the ReportServer2000 account.

▶ **Note**   Like stored credentials used with a data source, the password entered for subscriptions is also encrypted and stored in the ReportServer database.

If you had entered the password right after you entered the user name, the password would have been cleared because you left the page to make changes to the subscription schedule page. Anytime you return to a page that has credentials, even if you've entered the full credentials earlier, you are always required to enter the password.

19 Select the Use Default check boxes for both the *Group* and *Calendar-Year* parameters.

The bottom of the page looks like this:

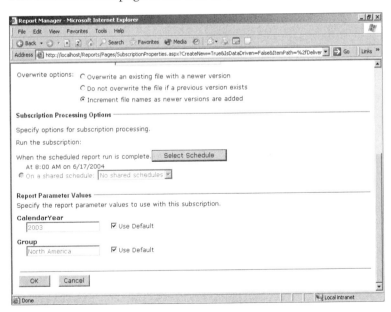

20 Click the OK button.

The Subscriptions page for the Actual Vs Quota report looks like this:

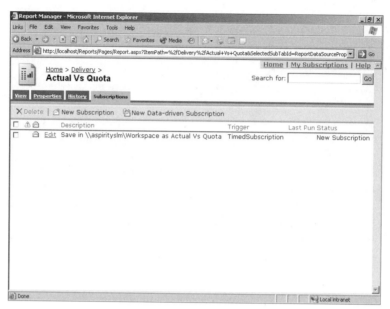

21 After waiting 3 minutes, click the Refresh button on the Internet Explorer toolbar.

The Subscriptions page for the Actual Vs Quota report looks similar to this:

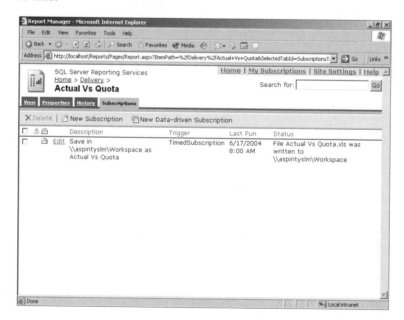

When the subscription is delivered, the Last Run and Status columns are updated.

22 In Windows Explorer, open the C:\rs2000sbs\Workspace folder.

The Actual Vs Quota.xls file is in the Workspace folder. Even though you set the Overwrite Option to increment the number added to the filename, the first instance of the file is assigned the same name as the report. The filename is incremented only when a file of the same name already exists.

23 Double-click the Actual Vs Quota.xls file to open the file in Excel.

Your screen looks like this:

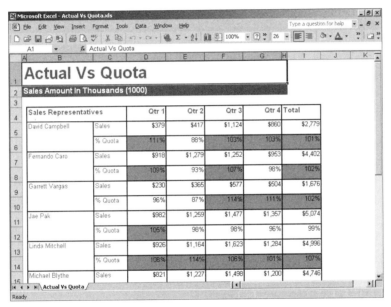

24 Close both Excel and Windows Explorer, but keep the Actual Vs Quota subscription properties page open in Report Manager.

Creating a Data-Driven Subscription

Using a data-driven subscription, Reporting Services can execute a report one time, render it in several different formats, and then send the results to many destinations. Destinations can be e-mail recipients or file shares. With a data-driven subscription, you can e-mail a report to a list of users that can change dynamically over time, and you can customize the rendered format of the report for each recipient. You can even customize parameter values by recipient as well as configure delivery options, such as including a report in an e-mail message or sending a link to the report. You need to create a relational table to manage these settings, and then create a data-driven subscription that queries this table when the report is rendered.

How to Create a Data-Driven Subscription

Before you create a data-driven subscription, you must create a subscription delivery table that will contain the destination details as well as the delivery settings. This table can simply contain a single column to store a destination, or it can contain a column for every report delivery option. When you create the data-driven subscription, you specify a query to the subscription delivery table and then map the columns of the query results to the delivery options.

In addition to using this table to store delivery options, you can assign parameter values by destination. Your table should include a column for each parameter that you want to customize in the report. You then map the column to the parameter when creating the data-driven subscription.

Creating a Subscription Delivery Table

A subscription delivery table allows you to manage a list of destinations with delivery options, rendering preferences, and parameter values. Reporting Services does not provide an interface for you to build and maintain this table, but you can use your favorite SQL Server tool to set up the table and load it with data. At a minimum, you need to define a column for the subscription destination if all you want to do is manage a list of recipients. The main advantage of this table, however, is the ability to configure many options to customize the subscription for each recipient.

In this procedure, you will review the contents of the SubscriptionGroupDirector table in the rs2000sbsDW database.

Browse the contents of a subscription delivery table

1   Open Enterprise Manager, expand the default instance (or the instance to which you installed Reporting Services and the practice files), expand the Databases folder, expand the rs2000sbsDW database, and then click Tables.

2   Right-click SubscriptionGroupDirector, point to Open Table, and then click Return All Rows.

The table looks like this:

Notice that the records in this table define subscription options for each Sales Director. You will use this table to apply these options to a data-driven subscription that customizes the delivery of reports to each territory group director. Two of the directors will have the report included in the e-mail message, while one will have a link to the report. Each director will receive a different rendered format, and each will see different data in the report because a different parameter is used to filter the data for each director.

▶ **Note**   The structure of this table is provided as an example. You can create a more complex table if you need to manage additional subscription options.

3   Close Enterprise Manager.

Creating a Data-Driven Subscription

After you create a subscription delivery table and populate it with data, you are ready to create a data-driven subscription. Rather than set the delivery options directly, as you did with the e-mail delivery, you will define a query that returns rows from the subscription delivery table. You then assign columns of the table to corresponding delivery settings and, optionally, to parameter values. A report is created for each row that is in the table, and delivered according to the settings specific to each row.

In this procedure, you will create a new data-driven subscription to send the Actual Vs Quota report by using the information in the subscription delivery table.

Create a data-driven subscription

1   In Report Manager, on the Actual Vs Quota subscription properties page, click the New Data-Driven Subscription button on the toolbar.

2   Type a description: **Actual Vs Quota Subscription**.

3   Click Report Server E-Mail in the Specify How Recipients Are Notified list box.

4   Keep the default data source option, Specify For This Subscription Only.

Your screen looks like this:

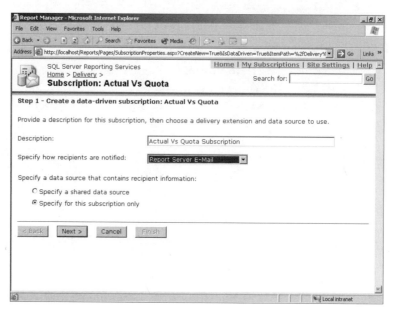

5   Click the Next button.

6   Type this connection string: **data source=localhost; initial catalog=rs2000sbsDW.**

7   Type **ReportExecution** as the user name and **ReportExecution** as the password.

Your screen looks like this:

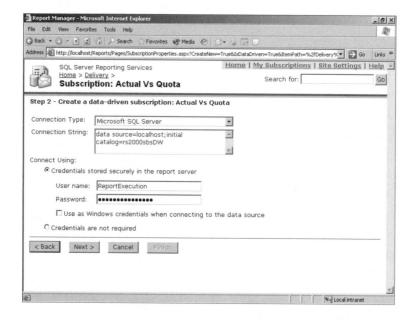

▶ **Note**   The connection string and credentials used here are used to connect to the subscription information table and are not used by Reporting Services to execute the report. For report execution, the data source defined for the report is still used.

8   Click the Next button.

9   In the textbox, type **select * from SubscriptionGroupDirector**.

▶ **Note**   This example retrieves all rows from the SubscriptionGroupDirector table. You can, of course, write a query to filter the table to return only certain rows according to specific criteria.

10   Click the Validate button.

The lower part of your screen looks like this:

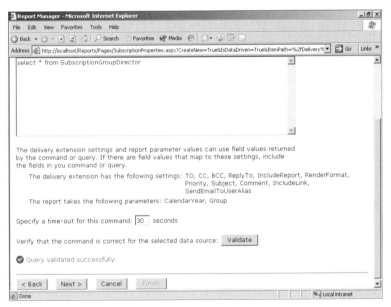

The result of the validation appears as a message at the bottom of the same page. If the validation is unsuccessful, you will not be able to proceed until the query validates, even if you choose not to use the Validate button. For the query to validate successfully, the data source must be correctly defined and the credentials must be successfully authenticated.

Notice also that you can change the query timeout for this query to retrieve the recipient and subscription options from the subscription delivery table.

11 Click the Next button.

12 Configure the delivery extension settings according to the following table:

Delivery setting	Option	Value
To	Get the value from the database	To
Reply-To	Specify a static value	Sales@adventure-works.com
Include Report	Get the value from the database	IncludeReport
Render Format	Get the value from the database	RenderFormat
Include Link	Get the value from the database	IncludeLink

As you can see, each delivery setting can be configured using a column from a subscription delivery table, or by supplying a static value or no value for some settings.

13 Click the Next button.

14 Select the Use Default check box for the *CalendarYear* parameter.

15 For the *Group* parameter, click Get The Value From The Database, and then click *GroupParameter* in the corresponding list box. Your screen looks like this:

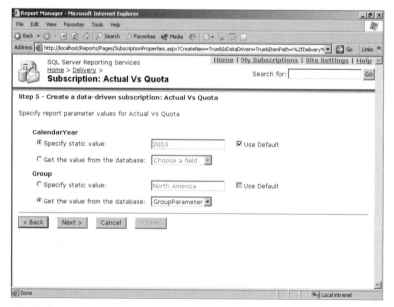

16 Click the Next button.

17 Click On A Schedule Created For This Subscription, and then click the Next button.

18 Click Once to specify the frequency of the report.
You will run the subscription just one time to generate output.

19 Type a start time that is 3 minutes ahead of the current time, and click the correct AM or PM option.

20 Click the Finish button.
The Subscriptions properties page looks like this:

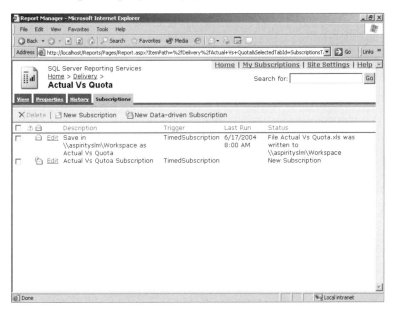

21 After waiting 3 minutes, refresh the Subscriptions page for the Actual Vs Quota report, which looks similar to this:

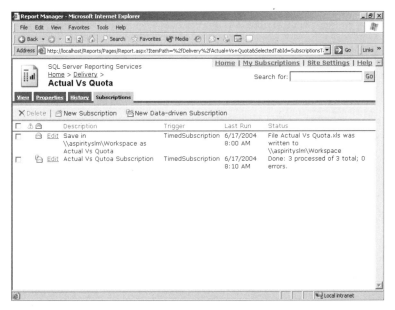

When the subscription is delivered, the Last Run and Status columns are updated. The number of deliveries and the number of errors (if any) are displayed in the Status column.

22 If you're using a local SMTP Server, open Windows Explorer, navigate to the C:\Inetpub\mailroot\Drop folder, and double-click the e-mail file (with extension .eml) located there. Otherwise, if you're using a local POP3 Server, navigate to the C:\Inetpub\mailroot\Mailbox\adventure-works.com folder.

23 If you're using SMTP, check the time stamp of the new e-mail files, and then double-click the first e-mail file that was generated at the time that the data-driven subscription executed. If using POP3, open the P3_PacificDirector.mbx.

Your screen looks similar this:

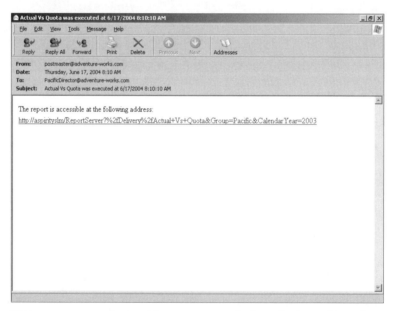

This message to the PacificDirector includes a link to the report. In this case, the report executes on demand. If more sales had been added to the database after the subscription processing completed, the report could contain data different from that of a report that might have been rendered with the same parameter values and delivered in an e-mail message. You should factor in this possibility when deciding when to schedule subscriptions and which delivery options to use.

24 In Windows Explorer, double-click the second e-mail file that was generated for the data-driven subscription if using the local SMTP server, or open the P3_NADirector.mbx mailbox to retrieve the message there.

Your screen looks similar this:

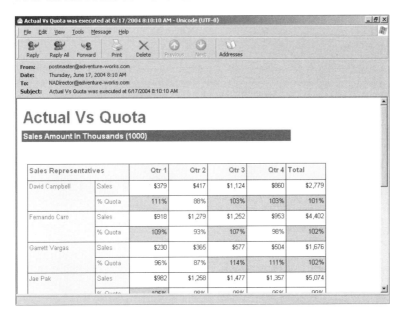

This message to the NADirector has an embedded report. The data in this report is current as of the subscription execution time. The parameter value supplied in the subscription filters the data in this report so that only North America sales data is sent to the NADirector.

25 In Windows Explorer, double-click the third e-mail file that was generated for the data-driven subscription if using the local SMTP server or open the e-mail message in the P3_EuropeDirector.mbx folder.

Your screen looks similar this:

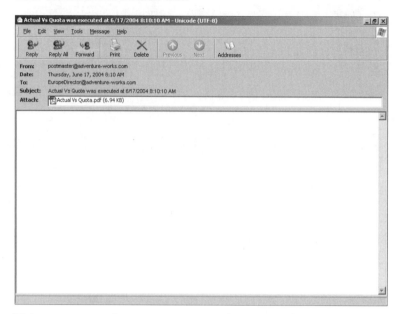

This message to the EuropeDirector has a PDF file attachment.

26 Double-click the Actual Vs Quota.pdf file to view the file.

As with the embedded report, the data in this report is current as of the subscription execution time. Only European sales are shown in this report.

27 Close the e-mail messages and close Windows Explorer.

Managing Subscriptions

The Subscriptions page of a report shows you information about the existing subscriptions and the status of each subscription when it last executed. If a subscription has been created, but not yet executed, the status will be "New Subscription." If you are assigned the "Manage individual subscriptions" task, you can see only your own subscriptions on this page, but if you are assigned the "Manage all subscriptions" task, you can see all subscriptions associated with a report.

Another way to monitor the status of all of your own subscriptions is to use the My Subscriptions page. This page consolidates your subscriptions for all reports on the Report Server. You can also check the log files in the file system to troubleshoot problems with subscriptions. You'll find that certain types of problems can render a subscription inactive. If you're unable to correct the condition that caused a problem, you can delete an inactive subscription.

How to Manage Subscriptions

You can review all your subscriptions on the My Subscriptions page. This page also allows you to edit or delete a subscription. However, you can't use this page to create a new subscription. When a subscription executes, Reporting Services logs the status of each subscription on the My Subscriptions page as well as the Subscriptions page of the report.

When something goes wrong with a subscription, the status column on the My Subscriptions page or the report's Subscriptions page will indicate that a problem was encountered. In such a case, you need to dig deeper to find the root cause of the problem. Each time that a subscription executes, Reporting Services adds an entry to the trace log file. Check the ReportServerService trace log file when you're troubleshooting a problem with a subscription, because the log entry includes more detailed information about the problem encountered.

Using the My Subscriptions Page

The My Subscriptions page is the best way to check the status of your subscriptions because they're all organized into a single page. The link to the My Subscriptions page is available at all times at the top of any Report Manager page. The subscriptions on this page are only those subscriptions that you create. If your role on the Report Server grants you permission to manage all subscriptions, you must open a specific report and navigate to its Subscriptions page to see the subscriptions created by other users.

The status information for a successful subscription execution depends on the type of subscription. The status of a successful e-mail delivery will show that mail was sent to the recipients. If the Report Server could not connect to the mail server, the status will reflect this failure. Similarly, the status information of a successful file share delivery will note that the file was written to the named location. However, if the file could not be written to the target location, then the status will record the failure.

In the case of a data-driven subscription, the status will include the number of records for which notifications were delivered and the number of errors that were generated. The number of notifications should match the total number of records returned by the query to the subscription delivery table. If the number of errors is greater than zero, you will need to review the trace log to discover what caused the subscription to fail.

In this procedure, you will review the My Subscriptions page and edit an existing subscription.

Review the My Subscriptions page

1   In Report Manager, click the My Subscriptions link in the top right corner of the browser window.

Your screen looks similar to this:

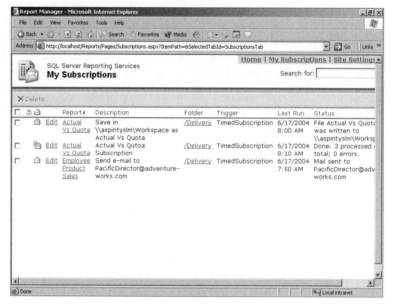

2   Click the Last Run column to change the sort order of the subscriptions.

The first time you click a column to change the sort order, the subscriptions sort in ascending order. Click the column again to reverse the sort order. Right now, only a few subscriptions appear on this page, so the sorting feature is not particularly helpful. However, as you add more subscriptions, you'll find the ability to sort a long list of subscriptions useful. You can sort the subscriptions using any column on this page. You can also use this page to open a report to which a subscription is attached or even the folder in which the report is stored.

3   Click the Edit link to the left of the file share delivery subscription for the Actual Vs Quota report.

Now you will edit the subscription to execute it one more time. Before it actually executes, you'll change the credentials assigned to the data source to force an error.

4 Click the Select Schedule button.

5 Change the Start Time of the report to 5 minutes from now, and then click the OK button.

6 Type **NADirector** as both the user name and password, and then click the OK button.

7 Click the Actual Vs Quota report link for the same subscription, click the Properties tab, and then click the Data Sources link.

8 Change the Connect Using option to The Credentials Supplied By The User Running The Report and then click the Apply button.

Because a subscription must use stored credentials to execute, choosing this connection option will cause the subscription to fail.

9 After waiting 5 minutes, click the My Subscriptions link.

Your screen looks similar to this:

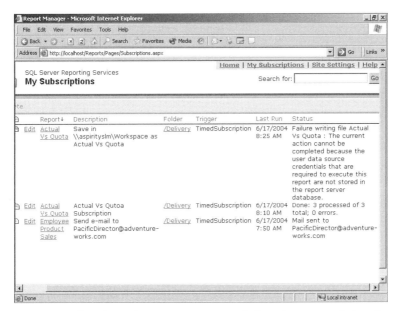

The status for the subscription notes a failure because of the change in the report's use of credentials.

Troubleshooting Subscriptions

If you have permissions to access the trace log files, you can review the ReportServerService_<*timestamp*>.log file to get more information related to subscription processing and deliveries. For example, if a data-driven subscription is done processing but includes errors, you can use the log file to investigate the underlying errors. The subscription might have processed just fine, but the delivery extension might not have been able to connect to the mail server to forward the messages. If, for some reason, the mail server might not be available when the Report Server tries to connect, you can configure a certain number of retry attempts. By default, this value is set to three. You can edit the RSReportServer.config file to raise or lower this setting as appropriate for your environment.

Many other situations can cause a subscription to fail. Usually the status message or the trace log will indicate what is causing the problem, but in some cases you'll need to peform basic troubleshooting. Here are some options to consider:

■ On the Report Server, make sure the delivery extension has not been removed or disabled. (Always back up the configuration file before making changes!)

■ Check that the ReportServer and the SQLServerAgent services are both running.

■ Make sure the destination server is running—either the e-mail server or the target computer with a file share, depending on the delivery extension used.

■ If using file share delivery, confirm that the file share is configured for write access, that the subscription is using the proper credentials, and that the disk is not full.

Sometimes the problem can be caused by the report itself. If a subscription uses a snapshot, which itself is based on a schedule, confirm that the snapshot schedule is still active. Changing credentials for the data source to anything other than stored credentials will also cause a subscription to fail. Any modifications to the report definition, such as a parameter name or data type, can also invalidate a subscription. Finally, if the report is too big for the recipient's mailbox, the report will be undeliverable.

Deleting Subscriptions

When a subscription can't be processed, it becomes inactive. You will need to resolve the problem that caused subscription processing to fail. You can also delete a subscription when it becomes inactive or when you no longer need it.

You can delete one or more subscriptions on a report's Subscriptions page or on the My Subscriptions page. To delete a subscription, select the subscription's check box and then click the Delete button. The Delete button is not activated until you select at least one subscription.

In this procedure, you will delete a subscription.

Delete an inactive subscription

1   On the My Subscriptions page, select the file share delivery subscription for the Actual Vs Quota report.

Your screen looks like this:

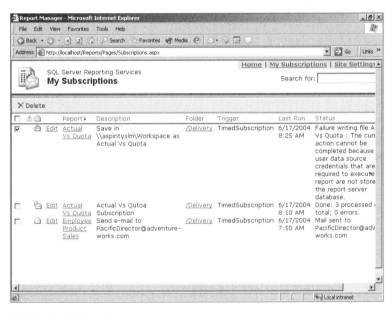

2   Click the Delete button.
3   Click the OK button to confirm the deletion.

Chapter 13 Quick Reference

To	Do this
Reconfigure or disable delivery extensions	Edit the delivery extension configuration settings in the RSWebApplication.config file to affect interaction between Report Manager and delivery extensions. *or* Configure new values for the delivery extension, such as the number of retry attempts, in the RSReportServer.config file, or remove all delivery extension values to disable.
Create an e-mail subscription	In Report Manager, open the Subscriptions page of a report, and then click the New Subscription button. Use the default delivery method, Report Server E-Mail, and type one or more recipient e-mail addresses. Specify a rendering format for the report to be sent, and choose whether to include the report in the message or a link to the report on the Report Server. Assign a schedule to the report or base the subscription on the update of a report snapshot. If the report has parameters, select the default parameter value or provide a value for this subscription.
Create a file share subscription	In Report Manager, open the Subscriptions page of a report, and then click the New Subscription button. Change the delivery method to Report Server File Share, and enter a file share on the network using a UNC format. Enter credentials for an account with permissions to write to the file share. Specify a rendering format for the report to be placed on the file share and select overwrite options. Assign a schedule to the report or base the subscription on the update of a report snapshot. If the report has parameters, select the default parameter value or provide a value for this subscription.
Create a data-driven subscription	Create and populate a subscription delivery table to contain destination information and subscription options by destination. In Report Manager, open the Subscriptions page of a report, and then click the New Data-Driven Subscription button. Choose a delivery method and a data source that will be used to connect to the subscription delivery table. Enter a query to retrieve values from the subscription delivery table, and map these values to delivery settings and parameter values for the subscription. Assign a schedule to the report, or base the subscription on the update of a report snapshot.
Monitor subscriptions	In Report Manager, view the status of a subscription as of its last execution using the report-specific Subscriptions page or the global My Subscriptions page.
View trace logs for subscription processing and delivery information	Review the log entries in the ReportServerService_*<timestamp>*.log file.
Delete a subscription	In Report Manager, open the report-specific Subscriptions page or the global My Subscriptions page, select one or more subscriptions, and then click the Delete button.

Index

N

O

P

About the Author

Hitachi Consulting is Hitachi, Ltd.'s global business and IT consulting company. We serve Fortune 2000 companies across many industries throughout the United States. We work with you to understand your needs and to enable and implement key business strategies. We deliver practical solutions to generate demand, ensure supply, and help you manage your enterprise effectively. Hitachi Consulting was first to market in the authoring of Reporting Services courseware, and continues to lead the market in Reporting Services implementations, specializing in custom reporting solutions and conversions. Our commitment to delivering measurable results is unparalleled, as is our dedication to transferring knowledge. Let us inspire your next success!

Stacia Misner is a manager for Hitachi Consulting's National Business Intelligence practice. Her career spans 20 years as an information technology professional, educator, and consultant. She has specialized in the development of business intelligence solutions and delivery of training on business intelligence technologies over the past five years. Ms. Misner has delivered reporting solutions in a variety of industries, including retail, financial services, automotive, and telecommunications. Ms. Misner is the co-author of *Business Intelligence: Making Better Decisions Faster* (Microsoft Press, 2002) and is a co-author of Hitachi Consulting's FastTrack to Reporting Services course.

The manuscript for this book was prepared and submitted to Microsoft Press in electronic form. Pages were composed by Microsoft Press using Adobe FrameMaker+SGML for Windows, with text in Sabon and display type in ITC Franklin Gothic. Composed pages were delivered to the printer as electronic pre-press files.

Interior Graphic Designer:	James D. Kramer
Principal Compositor:	Dan Latimer
Interior Graphic Artist:	Joel Panchot
Principal Copy Editor	Vicky Thulman
Indexer:	Ginny Bess

Best practices *straight from the experts*

Code Complete, Second Edition
ISBN 0-7356-1967-0   Suggested Retail Price: $49.99 U.S., $72.99 Canada

Discover timeless techniques and strategies. Widely considered one of the best practical guides to programming, Steve McConnell's original CODE COMPLETE has been helping developers write better software for more than a decade. Now this classic book has been fully updated and revised with leading-edge practices—and hundreds of new code samples—illustrating the art and science of software construction. Capturing the body of knowledge available from research, academia, and everyday commercial practice, McConnell synthesizes the most effective techniques and must-know principles into clear, pragmatic guidance. No matter what your experience level, development environment, or project size, this book will inform and stimulate your thinking—and help you build the highest quality code.

Software Requirements, Second Edition
ISBN 0-7356-1879-8   Suggested Retail Price: $39.99 U.S., $57.99 Canada

Proven practices for requirements engineering—plus more examples, new topics, and sample requirements documents. Discover effective techniques for managing the requirements engineering process all the way through the development cycle. SOFTWARE REQUIREMENTS, Second Edition, features new case examples, anecdotes culled from the author's extensive consulting career, and specific *Next Steps* for putting the book's process-improvement principles into practice. Engineering authority Karl Wiegers amplifies the best practices presented in his original award-winning text—now a mainstay for anyone participating in the software development process.

Writing Secure Code, Second Edition
ISBN 0-7356-1722-8   Suggested Retail Price: $49.99 U.S., $72.99 Canada

Keep hackers at bay with proven techniques from the security experts—now updated with lessons from the Microsoft® security pushes. Learn how to keep the bad guys at bay with the techniques in this entertaining, eye-opening book—now updated with the latest security threats plus lessons learned from the recent security pushes at Microsoft. Easily digested chapters explain proven security principles, strategies, and coding techniques to give you the peace of mind that comes from knowing you've done everything possible to make your code more resistant to attack. Sample code provided to demonstrate the specifics of secure development.

To learn more about Microsoft Press® products for professional Developers, please visit:

microsoft.com/mspress

What do you think of this book?
We want to hear from you!

is interested in hearing your feedback about this publication so that we can continually improve our books and learning resources for you.

To participate in our survey, please visit:

www.microsoft.com/learning/booksurvey

And enter this book's ISBN, 0-7356-2106-3. As a thank-you to survey participants in the United States and Canada, each month we'll randomly select five respondents to win one of five $100 gift certificates from a leading online merchant.* At the conclusion of the survey, you can enter the drawing by providing your e-mail address, which will be used for prize notification *only*.

Thanks in advance for your input. Your opinion counts!

Sincerely,

Microsoft® Learning

Learn More. Go Further.

To see special offers on Microsoft Learning products for developers, IT professionals, and home and office users, visit: *www.microsoft.com/learning/booksurvey*

System Requirements

To install Microsoft SQL Server Reporting Services, your computer will need to meet the following minimum system requirements.

- Processor: Intel Pentium II or compatible 500-MHz or higher processor.
- Operating system: Microsoft Windows 2000, Windows XP Professional, or Windows Server 2003 with the latest service pack applied.
- Database: Microsoft SQL Server 2000, Standard or Enterprise Edition, with SP3a applied using Windows or Mixed Mode authentication.
- Memory: 256 MB of RAM; 512 MB or more is recommended. (Additional memory may be required based on your operating system requirements.)
- Hard disk:
  - 50 MB for Report Server
  - 100 MB for Microsoft .NET Framework 1.1
  - 30 MB for Report Designer
  - 145 MB for Reporting Services samples and Books Online
- CD: CD-ROM drive.
- Monitor: VGA or higher resolution monitor.
- Input device: Microsoft Mouse or compatible device .

To use the samples provided on the companion CD and perform the exercises in the book, your computer configuration will need to include the following additional requirements:

- Microsoft Internet Explorer 6.0 or later (*http://www.microsoft.com /windows/ie/evaluation/sysreqs/default.mspx*).
- Microsoft Internet Information Services (IIS) 5.0 or later.
- Microsoft Visual Studio .NET 2003, any edition (*http: //msdn.microsoft.com/vstudio/productinfo/sysreqs/default.aspx*).
- 140 MB (minimum) disk space where you install the sample files.

The step-by-step exercises in this book and the accompanying sample files were tested using Windows XP Professional, Visual Studio .NET 2003 Enterprise Architect, and Reporting Services Developer Edition. If you're using another version of the operating system or a different edition of either application, you might notice some slight differences.